PRO/CON VOLUME 2

GOVERNMENT

Published 2002 by Grolier Educational
Sherman Turnpike
Danbury, Connecticut 06816

© 2002 Brown Partworks Limited

Library of Congress Cataloging-in-Publication Data

Pro/con
   p. cm
Includes bibliographical references and index.
Contents: v. 1. The individual and society – v. 2. Government – v. 3. Economics – v.
4. Environment – v. 5. Science – v. 6. Media.
   ISBN 0-7172-5638-3 (set : alk. paper) – ISBN 0-7172-5639-1 (vol. 1 : alk. paper) –
ISBN 0-7172-5640-5 (vol. 2 : alk. paper) – ISBN 0-7172-5641-3 (vol. 3 : alk. paper) –
ISBN 0-7172-5642-1 (vol. 4 : alk. paper) – ISBN 0-7172-5643-X (vol. 5 : alk. paper) –
ISBN 0-7172-5644-8 (vol. 6 : alk. paper)
   1. Social problems. I. Grolier Educational (Firm)

HN17.5 P756 2002
361.1–dc21

                                                                           2001053234

Printed and bound in Singapore

SET ISBN 0-7172-5638-3
VOLUME ISBN 0-7172-5640-5

For Brown Partworks Limited
Project Editors: Aruna Vasudevan, Fiona Plowman
Editor: Sally McFall
Consultant Editor: Ronald Lee, Visiting Assistant Professor and
Fellow at Kenyon College, Gambier, Ohio
Designer: Sarah Williams
Picture Researcher: Clare Newman
Set Index: Kay Ollerenshaw

Managing Editor: Tim Cooke
Design Manager: Lynne Ross
Production Manager: Matt Weyland

GENERAL PREFACE

Decisions

Life is full of choices and decisions. Some are more important than others. Some affect only your daily life—the route you take to school, for example, or what you prefer to eat for supper—while others are more abstract and concern questions of right and wrong rather than practicality. That does not mean that your choice of presidential candidate or your views on abortion are necessarily more important than your answers to purely personal questions. But it is likely that those wider questions are more complex and subtle and that you therefore will need to know more information about the subject before you can try to answer them. They are also likely to be questions about which you might have to justify your views to other people. In order to do that you need to be able to make informed decisions, be able to analyze every fact at your disposal, and evaluate them in an unbiased manner.

What is *Pro/Con*?

Pro/Con is a collection of debates that presents conflicting views on some of the more complex and general issues facing Americans today. By bringing together extracts from a wide range of sources—mainstream newspapers and magazines, books, famous speeches, legal judgments, religious tracts, government surveys—the set reflects current informed attitudes toward dilemmas that range from the best way to feed the world's growing population to gay rights, and from the connection between political freedom and capitalism to the fate of Napster.

The people whose arguments make up the set are all acknowledged experts in their fields, and that makes the vast differences in their points of view even more remarkable. The arguments are presented in the form of debates for and against various propositions, such as "Does Global Warming Threaten Humankind?" or "Should the Media Be Subject to Censorship?" This question format reflects the way in which ideas often occur in daily life: in the classroom, on TV shows, in business meetings, or even in state or federal politics.

The contents

The subjects of the six volumes of the set—*Individual and Society, Government, Economics, Environment, Science*, and *Media*—are issues on which it is preferable that people's opinions are based on information rather than simply on personal bias.

Special boxes throughout *Pro/Con* comment on the debates as you are reading them, pointing out facts or analyzing arguments to help you think about what is being said.

Introductions and summaries also provide background information that might help you reach your own conclusions. There are also comments and tips about how to structure an argument that you can apply on an every day basis to any debate or conversation, learning how to present your point of view as effectively and persuasively as possible.

VOLUME PREFACE
Government

"I have come to the conclusion that politics are too serious a matter to be left to the politicians."
—Charles de Gaulle, French statesman

Dissatisfaction

At a time of widespread dissatisfaction with "politics as usual" Americans have grown increasingly detached from politics and the political process. Evidence of this is that fewer and fewer Americans, especially younger people, follow current events by reading a newspaper on a daily basis or even bothering to vote on election day. But the United States is a democracy, and democracy is a form of self-government: the rule of the people. A well-functioning democracy requires an informed and engaged citizenry that has the qualities necessary for self-government.

Choices

James Madison, who is generally regarded as the father of the U.S. Constitution, said:

As there is a degree of depravity in mankind which requires a certain degree of circumspection and distrust, so there are other qualities in human nature, which justify a certain portion of esteem and confidence. Republican government presupposes the existence of these qualities in a higher degree than any other form.

Among those qualities is the ability to form intelligent opinions and make intelligent choices about important matters of public concern. Political education is therefore critical in democracy understood as self-government. This volume in the *Pro/Con* series is intended to help you make informed opinions by introducing some of the most important and enduring controversies concerning U.S. government.

Critical thinking

The ability to think critically about political issues is more than just an area to be taught or learned, but also a skill that needs to be nurtured and developed through practice. Of course, it is important to have a good understanding of how the American political system works and was designed to work—and this book will help you achieve that end. But it is also vital to have the skill of forming one's own opinions by carefully weighing the merits of opposing arguments.

Indeed, U.S. politics is characterized by disagreement about principles of justice, especially the meaning of— and the relation between—the principles of freedom and equality. As a consequence, it cannot be studied in the same way that one studies, for example, math or science.

The best introduction to American government is to jump right into the controversies and debates that animate American politics and make it such a challenging but also exciting object of study, and this volume helps you do so by presenting new and classic readings.

HOW TO USE THIS BOOK

Each volume of *Pro/Con* is divided into sections, each of which has an introduction that examines its theme. Within each section are a series of debates that present arguments for and against a proposition, such as whether or not the death penalty should be abolished. An introduction to each debate puts it into its wider context, and a summary and key map (see below) highlight the main points of the debate clearly and concisely. Each debate has marginal boxes that focus on particular points, give tips on how to present an

argument, or help question the writer's case. The summaries to the debates have supplementary material to help you do further research.

Boxes and other materials provide additional background information. There are also special materials on how to improve your debating and report-writing skills. At the end of each book is a glossary that provides brief explanations of key words in the volume. The index covers all six books, so it will help you trace topics throughout the set.

background information
Frequent text boxes provide background information on important concepts and key individuals or events.

summary boxes
Summary boxes are useful reminders of both sides of the argument.

further information
Further Reading lists for each debate direct you to related books, articles, and websites so you can do your own research.

other articles in the *Pro/Con* series,
See Also boxes list related debates throughout the *Pro/Con* series.

marginal boxes
Margin boxes highlight key points in the argument, give extra information, or help you question the author's meaning.

key map
Key maps provide a graphic representation of the central points of the debate.

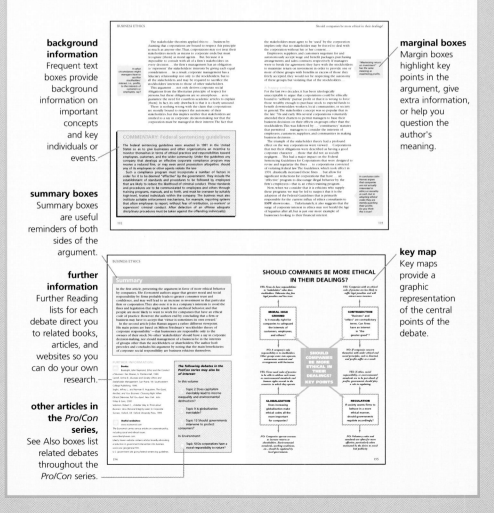

CONTENTS

PART 1
DEMOCRACY

When democracy emerged over 2,000 years ago, it was a tiny island in a sea of nondemocracies, confined to certain Greek polities (political organizations). For most of its history it remained rare, short-lived, and despised by most thinking people. Yet today it is probably the least controversial topic covered in this volume—few people, after all, are openly against it.

The modern movement toward democracy began in 17th-century England, won major victories in the American and French revolutions of the late 18th century, and spread across the world in the 19th and 20th centuries. By 1999, according to Freedom House, 120 of the 192 governments in the world were democratically elected. In the words of Nobel Prize winner Amartya Sen, democracy is now "established as the 'normal' form of government to which any nation is entitled—whether in Europe, America, Asia, or Africa."

Democracy is most widely accepted in the United States, which prides itself on being the world's oldest democracy. Yet in listening to discussions about democracy in contemporary America, one will notice that Americans disagree about the most elementary things. For example, a common complaint about democratic politicians is that they cannot decide anything without taking a poll to see what the voters think. In other words, democratic politicians are too slavishly devoted to the will of the people. Yet another common complaint is that democratic politicians do not care what the people think and, when making decisions, consider what is best for themselves or for their wealthy supporters and friends. That is, democratic politicians are not devoted enough to the people's will. These contradictory gripes are not necessarily voiced by two different sets of people, but seem to reflect the mood of the electorate at different times, as if Americans are unable to answer the question: Is the United States too democratic or not democratic enough?

Representation in democracy

Unlike the ancient Greeks, modern Americans do not assemble to make even the most important political decisions; they elect representatives to make the decisions for them. The 18th-century philosophers Jean-Jacques Rousseau and Baron de Montesquieu argued as to whether direct rule of the people was better than representative democracy. Rousseau raised the disturbing accusation that people are not really free if they decide only who will make decisions for them. His warning is still relevant today, when so many feel they have no real influence over their government, and that elected officials who make the decisions on which lives and livelihoods depend—whether to declare war or not, whether to offer health insurance to all citizens or not—are out of touch with and unresponsive to their constituents. New technologies like the Internet help remove practical obstacles to large-scale citizen assemblies, at least in part; consequently, the American people may be able to take a more direct hand in governing themselves.

Capitalism in democracy

Capitalism—in which individuals and corporations, rather than the state, direct economic activity—allows some people to become very rich and others to become very poor. Such inequality, in Robert Lekachman's view, mocks the basic democratic principle of one man, one vote, since wealthy individuals and

---

"Democracy gives every man the right to be his own oppressor."
—JAMES RUSSELL LOWELL, U.S. POET, ESSAYIST, AND DIPLOMAT

Yet Montesquieu's argument that the people are incompetent to manage public business directly casts doubt on the desirability of such assemblies.

Representation is only one institution that frustrates majority rule. Robert A. Dahl argues that such constitutional devices as the separation of powers and checks and balances, which make relations between the executive, legislative, and judicial branches of government so complex, and federalism, which divides power between federal and state governments, are impediments to democracy. Dahl believes that the American Founders deliberately framed a Constitution that would frustrate the majority and protect advantaged minorities. A modern Rousseauian, he claims that Americans who think they are living in a democracy are mistaken—the United States is not truly democratic. James W. Ceaser responds to Dahl, saying that the Founders designed the political system, with its inherent antimajoritarian devices, with other advantages in mind. While admitting that the system is not without its flaws, he suggests that it is preferable to the system Dahl proposes.

corporations can "purchase" votes by making campaign contributions and hiring lobbyists and lawyers to influence public officials and secure advantages for themselves. He prefers government intervention in the economy to narrow the gap between rich and poor. But Milton Friedman thinks that a government with both economic and political power would ruin democracy, since it could easily tyrannize those it was elected to serve.

Equality in democracy

John Baker believes democracy must offer economic as well as political and social equality. As long as some people are poor or degraded, the United States will not be democratic enough. William A. Henry thinks that the United States has become too democratic and that Americans, in their blind pursuit of equality, have abandoned the idea of excellence and now regard judging people and their deeds as a dangerous vice. The debate between Baker and Henry takes up a question every one of the controversies in this section has some bearing on: For what principle or set of principles does democracy stand?

Topic 1

IS DIRECT RULE BY THE PEOPLE BETTER THAN REPRESENTATIVE DEMOCRACY?

YES
"ON DEPUTIES OR REPRESENTATIVES"
FROM *ROUSSEAU'S POLITICAL WRITINGS*
JEAN-JACQUES ROUSSEAU

NO
"OF THE REPUBLICAN GOVERNMENT AND THE LAWS IN RELATION TO DEMOCRACY"
FROM *THE SPIRIT OF THE LAWS*
CHARLES DE SECONDAT DE MONTESQUIEU

INTRODUCTION

In the 1960s a group of young activists calling themselves Students for a Democratic Society (SDS) called on American citizens to do more than just vote for one politician or another to represent them in government. They argued that people should actively participate in decisions about matters of public concern. In opposing representative democracy in the name of participatory democracy, SDS in effect called for a return to the original meaning of democracy: direct democracy.

When certain Greek states first instituted democracy more than 2,000 years ago, it was a form of government in which all citizens were entitled and encouraged to participate directly in public deliberation and lawmaking. The Greek conception of democracy referred to direct rule by the people.

In the modern world direct democracy has by and large been rejected in favor of representative democracy, a form of government that involves the election by the people of representatives with the authority to enact laws. The United States is, like most other Western countries, a representative democracy. In 1787 Alexander Hamilton, one of the Framers, wrote an article in support of the newly proposed American Constitution. He presented modern representative democracy as a significant improvement on ancient direct democracy.

He wrote: "It is impossible to read the history of the petty republics of Greece and Italy without feeling sensations of horror and disgust at the distractions with which they were continually agitated, and at the rapid succession of revolutions by which they were kept perpetually vibrating between the extremes of tyranny and anarchy." Fortunately for mankind, Hamilton argued, great improvements in the "science of politics" had remedied the defects and excesses of democracy. Among the principles of government "which were either not known at all, or imperfectly known to the ancients," Hamilton said, was representation.

Representative democracy, its supporters argue, is an improvement on direct democracy because representatives do not merely do the bidding of the people, but deliberate and judge wisely on behalf of the people. As Hamilton's colleague James Madison argued in his own essay on the American Constitution, the effect of representation could be "to refine and enlarge the public views, by passing them through the medium of a chosen body of citizens, whose wisdom may best discern the true interest of their country, and whose patriotism and love of justice will be least likely to sacrifice it to temporary or partial considerations," with the result that "the public voice, pronounced by the representatives of the people, will be more consonant to the public good than if pronounced by the people themselves."

Not everyone agreed. Jean-Jacques Rousseau, an 18th-century French political philosopher, lamented the passing of direct democracy in the modern world. His argument that representative democracy is a bad form of governance rested essentially on a twofold criticism of representation: that it undermines both virtue and freedom. If virtue means good citizenship, then representation undermines virtue by enabling citizens to shirk their responsibility as good citizens to help manage the community's affairs. "In a well-run republic," Rousseau wrote, "everyone rushes to the assemblies; under a bad government no one likes to take a single step to get there, because no one takes any interest in what is being done in them." Moreover, in Rousseau's view, representation undermines freedom. Once citizens have elected representatives to legislate for the common good (or what Rousseau referred to as the general will), they are no longer ruling themselves. As Rousseau put it most boldly, "the moment a people gives itself representatives, it is no longer free."

> *"The biggest argument against democracy is a five-minute discussion with the average voter."*
> —SIR WINSTON CHURCHILL, ENGLISH STATESMAN

Montesquieu was Rousseau's contemporary and a fellow Frenchman. He was a philosophical authority for men like Hamilton and Madison who established the U.S. system of representative government.

Montesquieu argued that democratic government does not require that the people govern directly, only that they participate in the selection of those who do govern. In fact, Montesquieu argued that it is better for the people to delegate authority to representatives and other public officials ("ministers" or "magistrates") who are more capable than the people themselves of managing the public business. While Rousseau asserted that democratic government demanded direct rule by the people, Montesquieu worried it would result in bad government.

ON DEPUTIES OR REPRESENTATIVES
Jean-Jacques Rousseau

YES

See pages 200–201, The Case of President Clinton.

As soon as public service ceases to be the principle concern of the citizens, and they prefer to serve with their purses rather than their persons, the state is already nearing its ruin. Is it necessary to march into battle? They pay troops and stay at home. Is it necessary to go to the council? They appoint deputies and stay at home. Thanks to laziness and money, they finally have soldiers to enslave the homeland and representatives to sell it.

Problems

It is a worry brought on by commerce and the arts, the avid pursuit of profits, softness, and the love of comfort that replaces personal services with money. The citizen gives up part of his profits to increase them at his convenience. Give only money and soon you have chains. The word *finance* is a term for slaves; it is unknown in the ancient city state.

In a truly free state, the citizens do everything with their own hands, and nothing with money. Far from paying to be exempted from their own duties, they would pay to fulfill them personally. Far be it from them to accept commonplace ideas; I believe forced labor is less contrary to liberty than taxes.

The better constituted the state, the more public concerns prevail over private ones in the minds of the citizens. There are even many fewer private concerns, because the sum of common happiness furnishes a more considerable portion of each individual's happiness, and there remains less for the individual to seek through his own private efforts.

Rousseau did a lot of work on the relationship between society and its governors, which he called the social contract. You can read his conclusions at www.grtbooks.com on the Internet.

In a well-run republic, everyone rushes to the assemblies; under a bad government no one likes to take a single step to get there, because no one takes any interest in what is being done in them, because everyone sees that the general will cannot prevail, and, finally, because domestic cares are all consuming. Good laws lead to the making of better ones; bad laws bring about worse ones. The state must be counted as lost, as soon as someone says, with regard to the affairs of the state, "What do I care?"

The waning of patriotism, the pursuit of private interests, the vastness of states, conquests, and the abuse of government have suggested the use of deputies or representatives of the people in the nation's assemblies. These are what certain countries dare to call the third estate. Thus, the particular interests of two orders occupy first and second place, and the public interest only the third.

Sovereignty

Sovereignty cannot be represented for the same reason that it cannot be alienated; it consists essentially in the general will, and a will cannot be represented: it is either the same will or it is different; there is no middle ground. Deputies of the people, therefore, are not, nor can they be, its representatives, they are merely its agents; they can decide nothing definitively. Any law the people has not ratified in person is invalid; it is not a law. The English people thinks it is a free people; it is greatly mistaken; it is free only during the election of the members of parliament; as soon as they are elected, it is enslaved, it is nothing. The way in which the English people uses the brief moments of its liberty truly makes it deserve to lose that liberty.

English elections were notorious for corruption. Only the wealthier citizens could vote.

Representatives

The idea of representatives is modern: it comes to us from feudal government, from that iniquitous and absurd type of government which degrades the human race and dishonors the name of man. In ancient republics and even in monarchies, the people never had representatives; the word itself was unknown. It is quite remarkable that in Rome where the tribunes were so sacred, no one ever even imagined that they could usurp the functions of the people, and that in the midst of such a great multitude, they never attempted to pass a single plebiscite on their own authority. The difficulties sometimes caused by the crowd should be judged, nevertheless, by what happened in the time of the Gracchi, when part of the citizens cast their votes from the rooftops.

By "feudal government" Rousseau means a system in which the governors are considered superior to their subjects.

A "plebiscite" is a vote by which the people of an entire country or district express an opinion for or against a proposal, especially on a choice of government ruler.

Where right and liberty mean everything, disadvantages mean nothing. This wise people always kept everything in proper proportions: the Roman people allowed its lictors to do what its tribunes would not have dared to do; it had no fear that its lictors would try to represent it.

To explain, nevertheless, how the tribunes sometimes represented the Roman people, it is enough to understand how the government represents the sovereign. Since the law is merely the declaration of the general will, it is clear that the people cannot be represented in the exercise of

Rousseau refers to a period when peasants flocked to ancient Rome to elect a popular tribune or representative. A "lictor" was an officer of the Roman state.

COMMENTARY: Jean-Jacques Rousseau

Political philosopher, author, and educator Jean-Jacques Rousseau (1712–1778) was born in Geneva, Switzerland. His mother died soon after his birth, and his father fled abroad to avoid imprisonment. Having received no formal education he ran away from home and, in 1728 and spent the next few years traveling from country to country until he finally settled in Paris. Once there, he was able to make a living as a scribe of words and music. He also began to correspond with the French philosophers and writers Voltaire and Diderot and to contribute many articles to their *Encyclopédie*.

Writing

In his early writing Rousseau argued that the human being is essentially a good and "noble savage" when in the "state of nature"—the natural state in which humankind existed before civilization and society corrupted it. Rousseau viewed society as "corrupt" and "artificial." Probably his most influential work is the 1762 book *Du contrat social* (*The Social Contract*). In contrast to his earlier work, Rousseau argued that good men are the result of society's presence. The "social contract" he proposes is an agreement among humankind in which each individual surrenders his rights to the collective, which represents the common good, and which sets the conditions for membership in society. His text espoused the famous slogan "Liberty, Equality, Fraternity," which became the catchline of the French Revolution and later the American Revolution.

French political philosopher, educationalist, and author Jean-Jacques Rousseau.

One of the main tenets of Rousseau's philosophy is that morality and politics should not be separated, and that if the state behaves incorrectly, it ceases to have genuine authority over the individual. He also believed that the state is created to preserve freedom. Rousseau also wrote on education, and his ideas have influenced modern educational theory. Rousseau eventually went insane. He died in 1778.

legislative power, but it can and should be in that of executive power, which is merely force applied to law. This shows that if the matter were examined closely, it would be found that very few nations have laws. Be that as it may, it is certain that the tribunes, having no share in executive power, could never represent the Roman people by the rights their offices conferred upon them, but only by usurping those of the senate.

Among the Greeks, whatever the people had to do, it did by itself; it was constantly assembled in the public square. The Greeks inhabited a region with a mild climate; they were not greedy; slaves did their work; their greatest concern was their liberty. No longer having the same advantages, how can you preserve the same rights? Your harsher climates increase your needs; six months of the year, the public square is unbearable, your muted tongues cannot make themselves understood in the open air, you set more value on your earnings than on your liberty, and you fear slavery much less than poverty.

Rousseau argues that in modern society people are too busy or too lazy to become involved in direct rule. Do you think his argument is still true?

Liberty v. servitude

What! Is liberty maintained only with the support of servitude? Perhaps so. The two extremes meet. Everything that is not found in nature has its drawbacks, and civil society more than all the rest. There are unfortunate situations in which the liberty of one man can be preserved only at the expense of another man's, and in which the citizen can be perfectly free only if the slave is completely enslaved. Such was the situation in Sparta. As for you, modern peoples, you have no slaves, but you are slaves; you pay for their liberty with your own. You boast of your preference in vain; I find more cowardice than humanity in it.

Sparta was a city-state in ancient Greece, famed for its warlike character and efficient bureaucracy.

I do not mean by all this that it is necessary to have slaves, nor that the right of slavery is legitimate, since I have proved the contrary. I am merely stating the reasons why modern peoples who believe themselves free have representatives, and why ancient peoples have none. Be that as it may, the moment a people gives itself representatives, it is no longer free; it no longer exists.

OF THE REPUBLICAN GOVERNMENT AND THE LAWS IN RELATION TO DEMOCRACY
Charles de Secondat de Montesquieu

Look up these three terms. Are Montesquieu's definitions still correct?

NO

X There are three species of government: republican, monarchical, and despotic.

The nature of three different governments

In order to discover their nature, it is sufficient to recollect the common notion, which supposes three definitions, or rather three facts: that a republican government is that in which the body, or only a part of the people, is possessed of the supreme power; monarchy, that in which a single person governs by fixed and established laws; a despotic government, that in which a single person directs everything by his own will and caprice. This is what I call the nature of each government.

Republican government, and the laws in relation to democracy

When the body of the people is possessed of the supreme power, it is called a democracy. When the supreme power is lodged in the hands of a part of the people, it is then an aristocracy.

"Suffrage" means the right to vote, a vote, or political support.

In a democracy the people are in some respects the sovereign, and in others the subject. There can be no exercise of sovereignty but by their suffrages, which are their own will; now, the sovereign's will is the sovereign himself. The laws, therefore, which establish the right of suffrage are fundamental to this government. And indeed it is as important to regulate in a republic, in what manner, by whom, to whom, and concerning what suffrages are to be given, as it is in a monarchy to know who is the prince, and after what manner he ought to govern.

The basis of Montesquieu's argument is that the public must entrust social management to the people they elect.

The people, in whom the supreme power resides, ought to have the management of everything within their reach: that which exceeds their abilities must be conducted by their ministers. But they cannot properly be said to have their ministers, without the power of nominating them: it is, therefore, a fundamental maxim in this government, that the people should choose their ministers—their magistrates.

They have occasion, as well as monarchs, and even more so, to be directed by a council or senate. But to have a proper confidence in these, they should have the choosing of the members; whether the election be made by themselves, as at Athens, or by some magistrate deputed for that purpose, as on certain occasions was customary at Rome.

The people are extremely well qualified for choosing those whom they are to intrust with part of their authority. They have only to be determined by things to which they cannot be strangers, and by facts that are obvious to sense. They can tell when a person has fought many battles, and been crowned with success; they are, therefore, capable of electing a general. They can tell when a judge is assiduous in his office, gives general satisfaction, and has never been charged with bribery: this is sufficient for choosing a praetor [an ancient Roman magistrate dealing mostly with judicial functions]. They are struck with the magnificence or riches of a fellow-citizen; no more is requisite for electing an edile [a type of magistrate in ancient Rome]. These are facts of which they can have better information in a public forum than a monarch in his palace. But are they capable of conducting an intricate affair, of seizing and improving the opportunity and critical moment of action? No; this surpasses their abilities.

The author argues that choosing representatives is easier for ordinary people than for government.

The ability of the citizens

As most citizens have sufficient ability to choose, though unqualified to be chosen, so the people, though capable of calling others to an account for their administration, are incapable of conducting the administration themselves.

The public business must be carried on with a certain motion, neither too quick nor too slow. But the motion of the people is always either too remiss or too violent. Sometimes with a hundred thousand arms they overturn all before them; and sometimes with a hundred thousand feet they creep like insects.

Montesquieu's use of poetic imagery rather than political debate was typical of the 18th century. What do you think he means here?

As the division of those who have a right of suffrage is a fundamental law in republics, so the manner of giving this suffrage is another fundamental.

The suffrage by lot is natural to democracy; as that by choice is to aristocracy.

The suffrage by lot is a method of electing that offends no one, but animates each citizen with the pleasing hope of serving his country.

Yet as this method is in itself defective, it has been the endeavor of the most eminent legislators to regulate and [also to] amend it.

Montesquieu admits that voting by lot could be improved.

Charles de Secondat de Montesquieu (1689–1755), French philosopher and jurist.

COMMENTARY:
Charles de Secondat de Montesquieu

Charles de Secondat de Montesquieu was born in 1689 in Bordeaux, France. He was a counselor and then president of the *parlement* in Bordeaux. In 1721 he achieved literary success with the publication of *Lettres persanes* (*Persian Letters*), which was basically a satire on French society, politics, religion, and culture. Montesquieu's best known work is probably *De l'esprit des lois* (*The Spirit of the Laws*), published in 1748. According to Montesquieu, there were three main types of government—a republic, a monarchy, and a despotism. He believed that a government elected by the people was the best form of government and that the right balance of power was necessary in order to maintain a democracy. Montesquieu thought that it was important to create separate branches of government with different but equal powers. In this way it was impossible for one branch of government to limit the power of the other two or to threaten the rights of the people. Montesquieu's ideas formed the basis of the Constitution of the United States of America.

Solon and suffrage

Solon made a law at Athens that military employments should be conferred by choice; but that senators and judges should be elected by lot. The same legislator ordained that civil magistracies, attended with great expense, should be given by choice, and the others by lot.

In order, however, to amend the suffrage by lot, he made a rule that none but those who presented themselves should be elected; that the person elected should be examined by judges, and that everyone should have a right to accuse him if he were unworthy of the office; this participated at the same time of the suffrage by lot and of that by choice. When the time of their magistracy had expired, they were obliged to submit to another judgment in regard to their conduct. Persons utterly unqualified must have been extremely backward in giving in their names to be drawn by lot.

Solon (640 or 638–559 B.C.) was an important Athenian lawgiver who reformed the Constitution of Athens and laid down the foundations of Athenian democracy.

The people and power

It is likewise a fundamental law in democracies, that the people should have the sole power to enact laws. And yet there are a thousand occasions on which it is necessary the senate should have the power of decreeing; nay, it is frequently proper to make some trial of a law before it is established. The constitutions of Rome and Athens were excellent—the decrees of the senate had the force of laws for the space of a year, but did not become perpetual till they were ratified by the consent of the people.

Montesquieu argues that the public should be able to confirm laws after they have been created.

Summary

This dispute between Jean-Jacques Rousseau and Charles de Secondat de Montesquieu constitutes a classic philosophical debate about whether direct rule by the people is better than representative democracy. Rousseau argues strongly that it is; Montesquieu argues just as strongly that it is not. According to Rousseau, representation facilitates a disengagement from public life that is harmful to citizen virtue. Moreover, electing representatives to make important decisions on which our lives and livelihoods depend means that we are not truly free because we are not ruling ourselves. Rousseau's criticisms of representative democracy can help us appreciate the enduring appeal of direct democracy. Montesquieu, on the other hand, puts forward arguments in favor of representative democracy. He suggests that most people do not have, at least to a sufficient degree, those qualities such as ability, interest, energy, patience, and knowledge that are necessary to be good legislators. Although the people are not well qualified to rule directly, they are well qualified for choosing those who should govern.

FURTHER INFORMATION:

Books:

Montesquieu, Charles de Secondat de, *The Spirit of the Laws*, Vol. I, Book II (translated by Thomas Nugent). New York: Hafner Publishing Co., 1949.

Ritter, Alan and Conaway, Julia (editors), *Rousseau's Political Writing*. New York: W.W. Norton & Company, Inc., 1988.

Useful websites:

www.democrats.org
Democratic National Committee site.
www.economist.com
Site of *The Economist* magazine and associated publications. Easy-to-understand articles on current issues.
www.grtbooks.com
Includes online texts of celebrated writers, including Montesquieu, John Milton, and Sir Isaac Newton.
www. libraryspot.com
A useful general reference site for biographies, quick reference, and quotations.
www.realdemocracy.com
Supports direct democracy.
www.rnc.org
Republican National Committee site.

www.wabash.edu/Rousseau/
Website of Rousseau association, includes links to works online.
www.whitehouse.gov
White House official site.

The following debates in the Pro/Con series may also be of interest:

In this volume:

Part 1: Democracy, pages 8-9

Topic 2 Are all human beings created equal?

Research Skills, pages 58-59

The Case of President Clinton, pages 200-201

IS DIRECT RULE BY THE PEOPLE BETTER THAN REPRESENTATIVE DEMOCRACY?

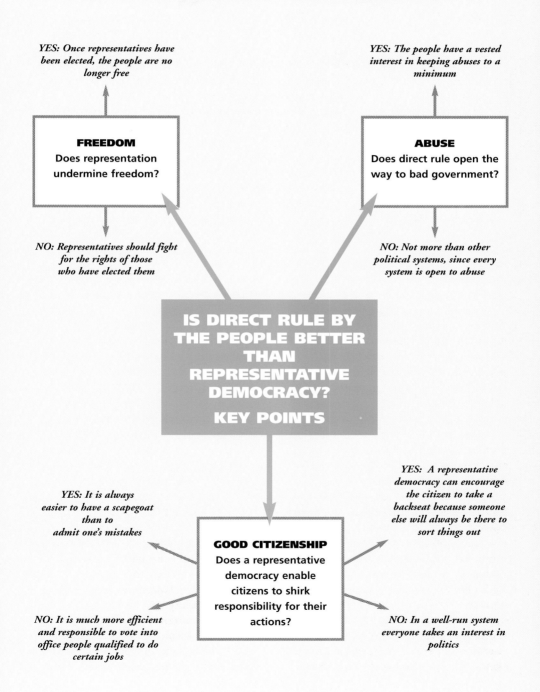

YES: Once representatives have been elected, the people are no longer free

FREEDOM
Does representation undermine freedom?

NO: Representatives should fight for the rights of those who have elected them

YES: The people have a vested interest in keeping abuses to a minimum

ABUSE
Does direct rule open the way to bad government?

NO: Not more than other political systems, since every system is open to abuse

IS DIRECT RULE BY THE PEOPLE BETTER THAN REPRESENTATIVE DEMOCRACY?
KEY POINTS

YES: It is always easier to have a scapegoat than to admit one's mistakes

YES: A representative democracy can encourage the citizen to take a backseat because someone else will always be there to sort things out

GOOD CITIZENSHIP
Does a representative democracy enable citizens to shirk responsibility for their actions?

NO: It is much more efficient and responsible to vote into office people qualified to do certain jobs

NO: In a well-run system everyone takes an interest in politics

Topic 2
ARE ALL HUMAN BEINGS CREATED EQUAL?

YES
"IS EQUALITY POSSIBLE?"
FROM *ARGUING FOR EQUALITY*
JOHN BAKER

NO
"THE VITAL LIE" AND "NATURE AND NURTURE"
FROM *IN DEFENSE OF ELITISM*
WILLIAM A. HENRY III

INTRODUCTION

The dominating idea of the American political order, according to the early 19th-century French historian and political scientist Alexis de Tocqueville, is the idea of equality. The United States was founded on the belief that all people are created equal and have equal rights, as the document by virtue of which Americans are an independent people proclaims (see quotation right).

Americans of all political persuasions express a commitment to the principle of universal human equality as enunciated in the Declaration of Independence. And yet Americans have also disagreed sharply about what this principle of equality rightfully means, and what different meanings might imply for public policy.

During the founding period and the 19th century equality essentially meant equality of rights or equality of opportunity. This understanding of equality consists in the equal entitlement of all to their "inalienable rights"; it does not insist that human beings are equal in all respects. It excluded slaves, for example. This idea was well expressed by Abraham Lincoln in his interpretation of the Declaration of Independence in 1857: "The authors of that notable instrument ... did not intend to declare all men equal in all respects. They did not mean to say all were equal in color, size, intellect, moral developments, or social capacity. They defined with tolerable distinctness, in what respects they did consider all men created equal—equal in 'certain inalienable rights, among which are life, liberty, and the pursuit of happiness.'"

This understanding of equality assumes that individuals are not equally endowed by nature with talent and ability. As a consequence a fair competition between citizens for the goods of society will inevitably result in unequal outcomes. Such inequalities are legitimate to the extent that they reflect the natural differences in talent and ability among citizens, and do not infringe on the equal rights guaranteed all citizens. This kind of understanding of equality in terms of equality of opportunity calls for a minimal role for government to secure merely the conditions whereby natural differences in talent and ability can be allowed to express themselves.

The 20th century brought a rival notion of equality, defined in terms of equality of outcome. This understanding of equality pushes beyond mere equality of opportunity toward equality itself. It was famously expressed by

---

"We hold these truths to be self-evident: that all men are created equal; that they are endowed by their Creator with certain unalienable Rights; that among these are Life, Liberty, and the pursuit of Happiness."

DECLARATION OF INDEPENDENCE

President Lyndon B. Johnson in 1965. In the midst of civil unrest then taking place in northern ghettos, Johnson explained his concern to achieve the complete integration of blacks into mainstream America: "It is not enough to just open the gates of opportunity. All our citizens must have the ability to walk through those gates. This is the next and more profound stage of the battle for civil rights. We seek not just freedom but opportunity, not just equality as a right and a theory, but equality as a fact and as a result."

An understanding of equality in terms of equality of outcome rejects the notion that economic inequalities reflect natural differences between human beings in talent and ability. Such a notion of equality assumes that talent and ability are more evenly distributed than is ordinarily believed, but that deep structural problems in society, such as discrimination, make it difficult for some individuals to get ahead. People who favor this understanding of equality appreciate the need for a significant role for government in narrowing the gap between rich and poor. One way to reduce this gap is through compensatory or affirmative-action programs that reserve economic opportunity for those groups traditionally excluded from it.

The following two articles provide conflicting answers to the question. John Baker warns against too easily accepting the view that inequality is an inevitable fact of life. He concedes that there are natural differences between human beings, but he denies that this justifies many of the inequalities found in modern society. He is concerned about the "major, structured inequalities which frustrate needs, undermine respect, destroy community, and restrict freedom." Baker therefore calls for supporters of democracy to believe in not only political but also social and economic equality.

William A. Henry III, however, worries that people have become wedded to an understanding of equality that is dangerously utopian. In their pursuit of equality understood in terms of equality of outcome, he argues, Americans have lost sight of the fact that talent and ability are not distributed equally. As a consequence they have abandoned the idea of human excellence.

IS EQUALITY POSSIBLE?
John Baker

YES

✅ Is equality a dream?

The author begins by putting forward the opposing arguments to the question. This clearly shows the position he is arguing against.

The opponents of equality sometimes object that however much people *ought* to be equal, they aren't and never will be. Equality is just an idle dream. For if equality were possible, why are we surrounded by inequality? Why has there never been an egalitarian society? Why have egalitarian movements always failed?

In one form, the objection is perfectly sound. Nobody with any sense of reality can believe that societies can be planned to perfection, that somehow you could eradicate every social evil, inegalitarian or otherwise. This objection applies to almost any social ideal. But it's simply a misunderstanding of the point of having ideals and standards in the first place to complain that reality can never fully live up to them. There will of course always be inequalities inasmuch as social institutions will always have imperfections which some people will take advantage of. That's not a serious objection to equality at all.

Having conceded that some social inequalities are inevitable, Baker focuses on the real issue: the major inequalities that mark all societies.

The real issue concerns the big, important inequalities which are so marked in our own and every other modern society. If even they were impossible to get rid of, egalitarianism really would be in trouble.

But people aren't equal!

Look at the world around you and everywhere you see inequalities. Any two people you choose are likely to differ not just physically, but in their desires, abilities, and characters. One is ambitious, another content. One is a brilliant musician, another mediocre. One is friendly and generous, another aggressive and dishonest. People *aren't* equal—how can anyone imagine that they could be?

The author exposes a central flaw in the opposing argument: Equality does not aim to make people the same by removing their individuality.

Though this is a familiar objection with a strong air of common sense, it involves a simple mistake. Egalitarianism doesn't aim to make people equal in their personal characteristics: it isn't committed to everyone being the same. On the contrary, egalitarians argue for a society in which each person can express her or his own individuality, however unconventional. So it's actually more likely that equality will bring out differences rather than repress them. These differences—a better word for them than "inequalities"—are likely to exist in any society, but they're not on equality's hit list.

People are now unequal in many other ways. In particular, some live in luxury while others starve; some control great power and wealth while others are poor and oppressed; some enjoy honor and deference while others suffer degradation and contempt. Egalitarians do oppose these inequalities. But it's no defense of *these* inequalities to say that people aren't equal in these ways. Everyone knows that they aren't—what's not at all obvious is that they have to be.

So it's important to remember to distinguish between the inequalities egalitarianism accepts and those it rejects. That distinction matches, to a large extent, the common-sense contrast between the inequalities which seem to be part of the human condition and those which seem open to change. If you want to show that equality's impossible, you have to go beyond that common-sense distinction, and show that the inequalities of wealth, power, and status which look changeable really aren't. That requires a lot more argument than just asserting that people aren't equal. In general, it requires you to explain why such inequalities exist, and why they can't be done away with.

> Baker says it is important to distinguish between the inequalities that can be changed and those that cannot. You cannot simply argue that equality is impossible—you need to question why that is so.

Is inequality in our nature?

The most popular explanation of inequality is probably that it's part of "human nature." It's only natural that people should want to be rich and powerful and famous; given their unequal abilities, it's only natural that some should end up better off than others. According to this view, equality is only on the agenda if people can be turned from ordinary human beings into angels who no longer care about their own interests—and that, of course, is impossible.

> The author admits that inequality is part of human nature. Does this admission weaken his argument?

It's a plausible argument. Certainly, its general view of what people are like seems to be proved by everyday experience. To be sure, there are a few examples even in our own society of genuine equality—some families, some communes, some religious and political groups. But these look like the exceptions that prove the rule: that, in general, people are too selfish and too ambitious for equality.

But everyday experience can be deceptive. First of all, it may only be telling you that you can never have perfect equality. Somebody will always be able to get a little more power or wealth or prestige than somebody else; there will always be petty hierarchies, squabbles, winners, and losers. As we've seen, that's no objection at all. Egalitarians are

Baker addresses the opposing argument by pointing out that perfect equality does not concern egalitarians.

[primarily] concerned with the major, structured inequalities which frustrate needs, undermine respect, destroy community, and restrict freedom, not with getting rid of every single case of personal advantage.

Secondly, it's wrong for objectors to imagine that exceptions to inequality are also exceptions to self-interest. Even the most egalitarian kibbutz [communal agricultural enterprise] operates on the basis that everyone benefits from participating. Nobody is expected to do nothing but give. Each member benefits materially and in ways such as by having greater job satisfaction, more control over their work, and respect from others.

Baker identifies some gains to be made from equality. Can you think of others?

But the structure of the kibbutz means that you can only benefit yourself by acting in ways which benefit others, too. The same thing applies in other examples of equality, like working in a co-op, living in an egalitarian household, or belonging to a self-help group like Alcoholics Anonymous. In each case, there's a *social structure* which links helping yourself with helping others.

Nature or nurture?

The third problem with everyday experience is that it tends to make things which are in fact peculiar to our own society look as if they're just human nature. The fact is that every society shapes human beings in various ways, bringing out some feelings more strongly than others, rewarding some forms of action and punishing others. The great inequalities of our own society both determine and reinforce the forms it gives to selfishness and ambition, so that, for instance, it is considered more attractive to satisfy your ambition by making a lot of money than by being a social worker. In a different society, self-interest and ambition might have a very different appearance and might be very much less likely on their own to lead inevitably to inequality.

Do you think that society places more importance on making money than on being a good member of the community?

If equality doesn't really depend on people being angels, and if societies can shape people's natures, then maybe human nature is compatible with equality after all. But is there any evidence to believe that it is? Perhaps the best evidence comes from [research] on societies [which] live by foraging, gathering wild plant foods, and hunting animals. Unlike co-ops, communes, and kibbutzim, their life could hardly be called an experiment: it is in all probability typical of the ways in which societies [lived for many] generations. No one could consider these peoples to be exceptions to human nature, even if they're now rare. Foraging societies vary in structure, but some of them are strongly egalitarian.

Baker concludes with a surprising parallel drawn from anthropology.

COMMENTARY: Equality for all

"All human beings are born equal in dignity and rights."
—UNIVERSAL DECLARATION OF HUMAN RIGHTS

In 1948, in the aftermath of a brutal world war, the United Nations General Assembly adopted the Universal Declaration of Human Rights. The Declaration recognizes the "equal and inalienable rights of all members of the human family" to basic human rights and freedoms. The 58 member states of the United Nations and the authors of the Declaration themselves represented a diverse mixture of cultures, political systems, and ideologies, yet they shared a vision of a more equitable and fair world.

Drafting the Declaration

The Universal Declaration is a remarkable example of international cooperation and consensus. The text was drafted over a two-year period between January 1947 and December 1948, when it was adopted without dissent. Inevitably, there were many debates during the process. Some Islamic states objected to articles on the right to change religious belief, while several western countries disapproved of the inclusion of economic, social, and cultural rights. The six members of the Soviet bloc, Saudi Arabia, and the Union of South Africa abstained from the vote. An eight-member committee, chaired by Eleanor Roosevelt, widow of the former U.S. president, prepared the preliminary text. The committee agreed that the principles of non-discrimination and civil and political rights were of central importance, as well as social, cultural, and economic rights. The Declaration sets out to protect such fundamental rights as the right to life, liberty, and security of person; equality before the law; the right to a fair trial; the right to education and to own property; and freedom of opinion and expression.

Making a difference

The aim of the Universal Declaration of Human Rights was to set "a common standard of achievement for all peoples and all nations," rather than to be an enforceable legal treaty. However, two international covenants codifying the rights outlined in the Declaration were adopted and finally enforced in 1976, after decades of debate. They made many of the provisions of the Universal Declaration legally binding for the states that endorsed them. Today, it is probably the most cited human rights document in the world. It has been translated into around 250 different languages, it continues to influence legislation throughout the international community, and subsequently has an effect on the quality of people's lives. Each year the date on which the Universal Declaration was adopted, December 10, is celebrated worldwide as Human Rights Day.

IN DEFENSE OF ELITISM
William A. Henry III

NO

Who do you think the author means when he says "we"?

… We have foolishly embraced the unexamined notions that everyone is pretty much alike (and, worse, should be), that self-fulfillment is more important than objective achievement, that the common man is always right, that he needs no interpreters or intermediaries to guide his thinking, that a good and just society should be far more concerned with succoring its losers than with honoring and encouraging its winners to achieve more and thereby benefit everyone…. We have devoted our rhetoric and our resources to the concept of entitlement, the notion that citizens are not to ask what they can do for their country, but rather to demand what it can do for them. The list of what people are said to be "entitled" to has exploded exponentially as we have redefined our economy, in defiance of everyday reality, as a collective possession—a myth of communal splendor rather than simultaneous individual achievements.

Henry deliberately echoes a famous speech by former President John F. Kennedy.

Taking equality to extremes
Save perhaps in the statistics-dominated realms of sports and finance, where accomplishment remains readily quantifiable and seemingly ideologically neutral, American society has lost the confidence and common ground to believe in standards and hierarchies. We have taken the legal notion that all men are created equal to its illogical extreme, seeking not just equality of justice in the courts but equality of outcomes in almost every field of endeavor.

Indeed, we have become so wedded to this expectation that our courts may now accept inequality of outcomes as prima facie proof of willful bias. We have distorted public rhetoric to the point that no one may say what everyone knows, that the emperor has no clothes—that is, that the people offered up as the result of meritocratic searches are often the beneficiaries of quotas, political mandates, and unacknowledged double standards….

"Prima facie" means based on first impressions.

Some people are better than others
In the pursuit of egalitarianism, an ideal wrenched far beyond what the founding fathers took it to mean, we have willfully blinded ourselves to home truths those

Why does the author refer to the Founders? What can be gained by this?

solons [lawgivers] well understood, not least the simple
fact that some people are better than others—smarter, harder
working, more learned, more productive, harder to replace.
Some ideas are better than others, some values more
enduring, some works of art more universal. Some cultures,
though we dare not say it, are more accomplished than
others and more worthy of study.

Every corner of the human race may have something to
contribute. That does not mean that all contributions are
always equal. We may find romantic appeal, esthetic power,
and political insight in cultures that never achieved modern
technological sophistication. That does not mean we should
equate them with our own. It is scarcely the same thing to
put a man on the moon as to put a bone in your nose. And
even were all cultures equal, that would not mean they made
equal contributions in the shaping of the American ideal.

> *Is Henry in danger of sounding racist when he makes these judgments about other cultures?*

Why the historical record is thin

In the effort to wish it so, we have warpingly redefined
contribution and reduced its meaning. It is not necessarily
a conspiracy of silence that the historical record is so thin
in detailing women painters and writers of the early
Renaissance or black nuclear physicists and Hispanic political
leaders of the early 20th century. Sometimes the record is
thin because the accomplishments were too. I expect many
people will reflexively find these observations racist. But I am
not asserting that, say, people of African descent cannot
compete equally—only that their ancestral culture did not
give them the tools and opportunity to do so. To me the real
racism lies in the condescending assumption that we must
equate all cultures to assuage African Americans, or any other
minorities, instead of challenging them to compete with, and
equal, the best in the culture where they live now.

> *This argument reflects very traditional approaches to understanding history.*

> *The author switches from "we" to "I." Does making the argument more personal make it less controversial?*

Reinventing the past

Many groups have been held down by past circumstances but
should now be able to contribute equally. A healthy society
must be prepared to embrace all people of talent. Yet in order
to motivate them for the future, we cannot reinvent the past
to pretend that the dispossessed made glorious contributions
then, or that studying the quotidian existence of bygone
peasants will more than marginally enlighten us about the
past's richest legacy, the high-culture attainments for which
these serfs provided, at best, support staff.…

Let us assume for a moment that America one day reaches
egalitarian heaven, with absolutely equal distribution of

The author argues that hierarchies are natural because intelligence is genetic. Would it help his argument if he expanded further on this point?

wealth and social position across the board. Barring the dead hand of Marxism at the tiller, the economic stratification so deplored by the left would set in again almost immediately—because intelligence varies genetically and because intelligence by and large determines economic success. It is the nature of human society to be stratified. And it is this elitist tendency that rankles egalitarians.

Offending the egalitarians

The idea that life has winners and losers—that something inherent in individuals leads some to create and amass and others to thumb-twiddle and squander—offends egalitarians' sense of fair play. Their outlook reminds me of a nature videotape that I saw being hawked on television as I wrote this. Billed as *Great Escapes*, the tape consists entirely of animals that are normally preyed upon instead escaping from larger or fiercer predators. "If you love underdogs," the announcer intones, "then this tape is for you." The worldview of the tape conveniently omits the bloody fact that carnivorous predators must kill or starve. The way of nature is combat and conquest, not nurturing communalism.

Even in intellectual debate it is sometimes helpful to draw examples and anecdotes from daily life.

Accepting that people have varying gifts and abilities and will arrive at varying outcomes is not diminishing their humanity. It is more demeaning to engage in the egalitarian deceit of equating achievements and outright charity.

Fairness v. equality

Above all, fairness is not the same thing as equality. It is unfair to the able to deny them special programs for the gifted, to impinge on their attainments, to take a larger share of their money away in taxes simply to deprive them rather than to raise revenue. It is unfair to men and whites and children of privilege to hold their achievements suspect. It is unfair to women and blacks and the poor to create compensatory programs so pervasive that they can never know with full confidence the joy of having achieved something entirely on their own. A fair society is one in which some people fail....

This photograph shows two suffragists marching in the "Wake Up America" parade in New York in 1917. The struggle for women's suffrage—the legal right to vote in elections—became an issue in the 19th century, but women in the United States did not win equal voting rights until 1920.

Summary

John Baker and William A. Henry III present two opposing views of human nature. Baker points out the inequalities in contemporary society. "Some live in luxury," he writes, "while others starve; some control great power and wealth while others are poor and oppressed; some enjoy honor and deference while others suffer degradation and contempt." According to Baker, these inequalities, far from reflecting natural differences in ability, are the product of a society that promotes unnatural greed and ambition. In response to those who argue that inequality is a part of human nature, Baker points to tribal societies as evidence that human nature is more egalitarian than many people tend to believe. A just political order, Baker strongly implies, would be close to the egalitarian model of tribal society.

Henry fiercely opposes Baker's egalitarian ideas. He argues against his kind of egalitarianism in the name of what he calls "elitism." He does not deny that all human beings are created equal in deserving equal opportunity, but he contends that the differences among people in talent and ability make inequality of outcome inevitable. Any attempts to eliminate this inequality of outcome is therefore, in his view, waging war on human nature itself.

FURTHER INFORMATION:

Books:

Baker, John, *Arguing for Equality*. New York: Verso, 1987.

Henry III, William A., *In Defense of Elitism*. New York: Doubleday, 1994.

Verba, Sidney and Orren, Gary R., *Equality in America: The View from the Top*. Cambridge, MA: Harvard University Press, 1985.

Articles:

Diamond, Martin, "The American Idea of Equality." *The Review of Politics* 83: 3.

Useful websites:

www.equal.cre.gov.uk
Commission for Racial Equality website has information abour racial equality.

www.equalitynow.org/
An international human rights organization fighting for civil, political, economic, and social rights for women.

www.cge.org.za/
Commission on Gender Equality website.

The following debates in the series may also be of interest:

In this volume:
Topic 3 Are democracy and capitalism at odds with each other?

In *Individual and Society*:
Part I: Issues of equality and inequality

In *Economics*:
Topic 2 Does capitalism inevitably lead to income inequality and environmental destruction?

Part 2: Government and economic policy

Part 3: Trade and global economics

ARE ALL HUMAN BEINGS CREATED EQUAL?

YES: Egalitarians accept that perfect equality doesn't exist—what they object to are major inequalities of power, wealth, and status

YES: Equality is not about making everybody the same—true equality would make personal differences more apparent

GETTING RID OF INEQUALITY
Not everybody is the same. Is equality possible in our society?

DIFFERENCE VERSUS INEQUALITY
Would making all people equal affect their sense of individuality?

NO: Equality is not possible because some people are better at things than others, as the historical record proves

NO: We can never be equal because everybody is different—with varying talents and abilities to contribute

ARE ALL HUMAN BEINGS CREATED EQUAL?
KEY POINTS

YES: People are unequal in many ways—it isn't fair or just that some people live in luxury, while others starve

YES: There is anthropological evidence that in early human societies everybody could contribute and benefit to the best of their ability

YES: Human nature can be compatible with equality. People are not naturally selfish—society shapes them to be that way

JUSTICE
Is there a difference between fairness and equality?

NATURE/NURTURE
Is inequality an unchangeable part of human nature or something created by human society?

NO: Inequality is not the same as fairness—in a fair society some people will always fail

NO: It is natural for human society to be stratified—intelligence varies genetically, and that determines economic success

NO: Human beings are naturally selfish and ambitious. Society will always have underdogs.

Topic 3
ARE DEMOCRACY AND CAPITALISM AT ODDS WITH EACH OTHER?

YES
"CAPITALISM OR DEMOCRACY"
FROM *HOW CAPITALISTIC IS THE CONSTITUTION?*
ROBERT LEKACHMAN

NO
"THE RELATION BETWEEN ECONOMIC FREEDOM
AND POLITICAL FREEDOM"
FROM *CAPITALISM AND FREEDOM*
MILTON FRIEDMAN

INTRODUCTION

Democracy is a form of government based on the idea that all citizens should be treated as political equals. Capitalism, on the other hand, is an economic system that, by encouraging citizens of varied acquisitive talents to devote themselves to the pursuit and enjoyment of wealth, allows and even encourages citizens to become economically unequal.

Is there, then, a tension between democracy and capitalism? In the United States people are used to accepting the legitimacy of both concepts in society. And yet we need look no further than the day's headlines to see that the extraordinarily complicated relationship between democracy and capitalism is an enduring public issue for the United States. Indeed, it is the constant source of protracted political struggles and debates over such thorny issues as taxes, government spending, and

campaign financing, as can be seen by the debates in George W. Bush's administration over across-the-board tax cuts and campaign finance reform.

Whether or not we think that there is a tension between democracy and capitalism has important implications for our understanding of the proper relationship between government and the economy. Partisans of equality argue that the tension between the egalitarian promises of democracy and the inegalitarian outcomes of capitalism is fundamental, and they are therefore likely to favor substantial government intervention in the economy to bring about more equality. This intervention may take the form of, for example, tax laws designed to equalize incomes. Such laws, however, limit people's freedom to spend their money as they wish.

Partisans of liberty therefore hold the view that this kind of egalitarian redistribution of income is an illegal invasion of economic freedom. Since, according to this view, economic freedom is essential to democracy, government intervention in the economy to bring about more equality is undemocratic. Libertarians thus favor an economy free of all but minimal political controls. In thinking about the tension between capitalism and democracy, we are forced to ask whether we care more about the liberty that allows us to become economically unequal or the difficulties that such inequality presents for our society.

"We can have democracy in this country, or we can have great wealth concentrated in the hands of a few, but we can't have both."

—LOUIS DEMBITZ BRANDEIS, U.S. SUPREME COURT JUDGE

The following articles lay out the positions on this issue distinctly. Robert Lekachman argues that there is a basic tension between America's capitalist economic system and its democratic political setup. According to him, the marketplace and the acquisitive talents of those operating in it have led to such vast inequalities in economic power that the United States can no longer truly be considered a democracy.

America has failed to live up to the democratic principle that the government should show equal concern for the fate of all its citizens, Lekachman suggests, because wealthy individuals and corporations use their money to influence political outcomes in their favor. "If tax initiatives designed for reform routinely yield benefits to affluent stockholders and corporations," he laments, "if even in time of fiscal austerity subsidies to shipbuilders, owners of corporate jets, commercial farmers, and badly managed auto and steel companies continue to draw congressional approval … the causes are not far to seek, and astonishment is for the naive." To restore democracy in America, Lekachman looks to a revival of the political left and its commitment to a government powerful enough to reduce economic inequality in U.S. society.

The conservative American economist Milton Friedman, on the other hand, worries that so powerful a government is potentially tyrannical. According to him, concentrating both economic and political power in the hands of the government threatens not only economic freedom but also political freedom. "The fundamental threat to freedom is power to coerce," Friedman writes. "By removing the organization of economic activity from the control of political authority, the market eliminates this source of coercive power. It enables economic strength to be a check to political power rather than a reinforcement."

To prevent a dangerous concentration of political power, Friedman argues in favor of the preservation of an economic market that is subject to only limited control by the government. This is, he believes, the kind of relationship between government and the economy that would best help ensure that the United States is a nation of free and prosperous men and women.

CAPITALISM OR DEMOCRACY
Robert Lekachman

The author begins with the main premise of his argument: that there is an inherent contradiction at the heart of U.S. politics.

The Constitution and the Bill of Rights make two promises to Americans that have frequently clashed in the course of our national history. In recent years, their inherent incompatibility has become glaringly apparent. One commitment is to political equality, an implication that any individual's vote, effect upon his neighbors, and influence upon his elected representatives is approximately as important as another's. The second is an open invitation to all comers to enrich themselves by their own efforts. Political and economic markets overlap, however, and wealth translates into political influence, favorable legislation, and helpful decisions by bureaucrats. Rich people, not their poorer cousins, own newspapers, news magazines, and TV channels. The First Amendment protects a free press. To echo [the American journalist] A. J. Liebling, only the wealthy own one. In the long run, political freedom cannot survive within the unfavoring context of plutocracy.

"Plutocracy" means government by the wealthy.

Capitalism leads to greed

Why are we willing to endanger political freedom and equality for the sake of capitalism? Even capitalism's most sophisticated apologists readily concede that their preferred system lacks the glamour, awe, and mystery that customarily hedge the courts of kings and pontiffs. As [British economist] Alfred Marshall remarked in speaking of human motivation, crass pursuit of profit by sellers and of individual gratification by their customers is notoriously consistent with the strongest but not the highest of personal impulses—with avarice, not altruism.

Lekachman says that capitalism encourages greed. Do you agree?

[There is a] friction between the equality implied by constitutional guarantees and protections and the admitted, even flaunted, inequality of income and wealth generated by the normal operation of capitalist markets. To be rich is to increase the life chances of one's sons and daughters, to ensure the quality of one's legal representation in court proceedings, to guarantee oneself the choice between abortion and carriage of a pregnancy to term. Pressure from private markets mocks constitutional guarantees of equality in other ways as well, and increases the unfortunate

Lekachman is making the point that if you are rich, you enjoy benefits that place you in a fundamentally better situation than somebody who is not.

resemblance of political markets to commercial ones. Business enjoys two shots at influencing political processes toward desired outcomes. Large corporations compete ideologically in the media both on their own behalf and in support of candidates whom they favor or who oppose officials they oppose. [Also] business occupies a favorable situation as the principal provider of jobs and incomes, which gives it a practical as well as an ideological lever.

The author is arguing that business has an ideological and a practical influence on the political process.

Influencing the media

In the ideological competition, the odds are heavy against critics of business, organized labor, consumer groups, and environmentalists for reasons both self-evident and slightly less apparent. Money purchases Mobil and Exxon "informational" advertisements on editorial pages all over the country. Corporate cash sponsors Milton Friedman's television series *Free to Choose* and promotes the book based upon it. Few newspapers are independently owned; more and more are units in chains that dispense meticulously balanced samples of columnists about as far left as (but no farther than) Mary McGrory and about as far right as (but no farther than) George Will. When has a genuine radical last been interviewed on public or commercial television? It is an old story that the mass media operate so as to narrow the boundaries of political choice. So long as [TV reporters] and the network staffs behind them determine what is news and who are acceptable exponents of opinion, neither the American left nor the individualist right is likely to emerge into the public perception.

Friedman is a U.S. economist and exponent of monetarism (see page 43).

Do you agree that people with radical views find it difficult to get media exposure?

How capitalism benefits

Inequality promotes conservative causes. If tax initiatives designed for reform routinely yield benefits to affluent stockholders and corporations, if even in time of fiscal austerity subsidies to shipbuilders, owners of corporate jets, commercial farmers, and badly managed auto and steel companies continue to draw congressional approval, if public rage against Exxon and its peers translates mysteriously not into nationalization, divestiture, or stringent public regulation but into an exceedingly mild windfall profits tax, and if the principal results of tax revolts along the lines of California's Proposition 13 are benefits for businessmen, the causes are not far to seek, and astonishment is for the naive.

Particularly when unemployment is high and rising, business wields to maximum advantage its second edge over competing interests. Corporations auction themselves off to

Passed in 1978, Proposition 13 severely restricted the ability of local government to raise revenue through property taxes.

communities in need of jobs and taxes by offering to locate new plants or corporate headquarters in that fortunate municipality which designs the most lucrative package of subsidies, tax remissions, and relaxation of regulations. Open-shop states all but trumpet the docility of grateful workers eager to perform hard labor for low rewards. Chairmen of boards threaten to desert struggling communities in the Northeast and industrial Middle West unless their city councils match competing propositions.

An "open-shop state" is one in which a person does not have to belong to a labor union to perform a particular job.

Political freedom in danger

It is no exaggeration, then, to conclude that the combination of business domination of the media and corporate manipulation of public fears of losing jobs and income substantially constricts political freedom. Much of the stuff of politics concerns the design of tax, spending, and regulatory policies, over which business exerts tacit vetoes. New York City is a strong case in point. As the price of rescue from imminent bankruptcy in the spring of 1975, the metropolis's elected officials were compelled to share their authority over taxing and spending with a Financial Control Board and Municipal Assistance Corporation administered by and for the commercial and business community. The not unexpected result is that public transportation is a shamble, uncollected garbage piles up, streets are pitted with potholes, and fire companies' response time to alarms has lengthened. In an already conservative polity, the victory in 1980 of a candidate more conservative than Barry Goldwater is a testimonial to public willingness to meet the terms of organized business out of hope that benefits will sift down to average families.

Is it accurate to equate politics mainly to financial regulations?

Barry Goldwater (1909–1998) was the Republican presidential candidate in 1964. The author is referring to the election of Ronald Reagan in 1980.

In the remainder of this [20th] century, Americans are likely to face a stark choice between extending current trends toward unchecked plutocracy and encouraging the emergence of an effective democratic political left. Plutocracy is certain to swamp the legal and constitutional structures that incorporate traditional guarantees of individual liberty into our polity. Although my aspirations may smack of the fruitlessly utopian at present, I have enough confidence in both the strength of democratic tradition and the weakness of the plutocratic approach to solving our economic afflictions to expect that as current exercises in nostalgia prove disappointing, and as the inequity of current policies impresses itself even on some of their beneficiaries, American politics will awaken from its slumber and the left will rise again. Unless it does, the contest between market inequity and political equality will terminate disastrously.

COMMENTARY: Democracy and capitalism

The term democracy, from the Greek *demos*, meaning "people," and *kratos*, "rule," means literally rule by the people. Democracy originated in the city-states of ancient Greece, where the whole citizen body (excluding women and slaves) formed the legislature. Greek democracy, however, had little influence on the development of modern democratic practices.

Modern democracy

Modern ideas of democratic government were influenced by concepts of divine, natural, and customary law in medieval Europe. European rulers began to consult group interests in their realm for approval of their policies. Modern parliaments and legislative assemblies have their origins in the meeting of representatives of such group interests. The events of the Enlightenment and the American and French Revolutions also had a profound influence on the development of democracy, especially with the emergence of the concepts of natural rights and political equality. In the 19th and 20th centuries freely elected representative bodies became the main institutions of democratic governments. Ideas of democracy also came to encompass freedom of speech and the press, and the rule of law.

The roots of capitalism

Capitalism has been the dominant economic system in the western world since the end of feudalism. In a free-market or capitalist economy most of the means of production are privately owned, and income is distributed primarily through the operation of markets. While examples of capitalist institutions existed in the ancient world, the main development of capitalism took place in the 16th, 17th, and 18th centuries. The Protestant Reformation of the 16th century led to a less disapproving religious attitude toward the acquisition of wealth. Also, in Europe wages did not rise as fast as prices in this period, and capitalists benefited from the resulting inflation. From the 18th century in England capitalist development moved from commerce, or trade, to industry, or manufacture. Adam Smith's *Inquiry into the Nature and Causes of the Wealth of Nations* (1776) suggested leaving economic decisions to free-market forces, and his ideas were increasingly put into practice. Government's role in the economy is simply to ensure stable conditions for business. The operations of the market—what goods are produced, how much is produced, how much they cost—are controlled by laws of supply, demand, and competition. Smith's ideas dominated international economics until the Great Depression of the 1930s brought policies of noninterference in economic matters in most countries to an end. However, since World War II, the United States, United Kingdom, West Germany, and Japan have seen a revival of less interventionist policies.

THE RELATION BETWEEN ECONOMIC FREEDOM AND POLITICAL FREEDOM
Milton Friedman

NO

It is widely believed that politics and economics are separate and largely unconnected; that individual freedom is a political problem and material welfare an economic problem; and that any kind of political arrangements can be combined with any kind of economic arrangements. Such a view is a delusion. [It is my thesis that] there is an intimate connection between economics and politics, that only certain combinations of political and economic arrangements are possible, and that in particular, a society which is socialist cannot also be democratic, in the sense of guaranteeing individual freedom.

Clearly define the parameters of your argument at the outset. Summarizing its main points gives a structure to the rest of the argument.

Economic and political freedom

Economic arrangements play a dual role in the promotion of a free society. On the one hand, freedom in economic arrangements is itself a component of freedom broadly understood, so economic freedom is an end in itself. In the second place, economic freedom is also an indispensable means toward the achievement of political freedom.

The author believes that there is a fundamental connection between economic and political freedom.

The first of these roles of economic freedom needs special emphasis because intellectuals in particular have a strong bias against regarding this aspect of freedom as important. They tend to express contempt for what they regard as material aspects of life, and to regard their own pursuit of allegedly higher values as on a different plane of significance and as deserving of special attention. For most citizens of the country, however, if not for the intellectual, the direct importance of economic freedom is at least comparable in significance to the indirect importance of economic freedom as a means to political freedom.

Friedman claims that intellectuals think that economic freedom is not important. Do you agree? Are political and economic freedom of equal importance?

Viewed as a means to the end of political freedom, economic arrangements are important because of their effect on power. The kind of economic organization that provides economic freedom directly, namely, competitive capitalism, also promotes political freedom because it separates economic power from political power and in this way enables the one to offset the other.

The free market

Historical evidence speaks with a single voice on the relation between political freedom and a free market. I know of no example in time or place of a society that has been marked by a large measure of political freedom, and that has not also used something comparable to a free market to organize the bulk of economic activity.

A free market is an economy operating by free competition with little state or government intervention.

Because we live in a largely free society, we tend to forget how limited is the span of time and the part of the globe for which there has ever been anything like political freedom: the typical state of mankind is tyranny, servitude, and misery. The 19th and early 20th century in the western world stand out as striking exceptions to the general trend of historical development. Political freedom in this instance clearly came along with the free market and the development of capitalist institutions. So also did political freedom in the golden age of Greece and in the early days of the Roman era.

Friedman uses historical examples to suggest that political freedom did not exist before the free market.

So long as effective freedom of exchange is maintained, the central feature of the market organization of economic activity is that it prevents one person from interfering with another in respect of most of his activities. The consumer is protected from coercion by the seller because of the presence of other sellers with whom he can deal. The seller is protected from coercion by the consumer because of other consumers to whom he can sell. The employee is protected from coercion by the employer because of other employers for whom he can work, and so on. And the market does this impersonally and without centralized authority.

Indeed, a major source of objection to a free economy is precisely that it does this task so well. It gives people what they want instead of what a particular group thinks they ought to want. Underlying most arguments against the free market is a lack of belief in freedom itself.

The need for government

The existence of a free market does not of course eliminate the need for government. On the contrary, government is essential both as a forum for determining the "rules of the game" and as an umpire to interpret and enforce the rules decided on. What the market does is to reduce greatly the range of issues that must be decided through political means, and thereby to minimize the extent to which government need participate directly in the game. The characteristic feature of action through political channels is that it tends to require or enforce substantial conformity. The great advantage of the market, on the other hand, is that it permits wide diversity. It is, in political terms, a system of proportional representation. Each man can vote, as it were, for the color of tie he wants and get it; he does not have to see what color the majority wants and then, if he is in the minority, submit.

Protecting freedom

It is this feature of the market that we refer to when we say that the market provides economic freedom. But this characteristic also has implications that go far beyond the narrowly economic.

Political freedom means the absence of coercion of a man by his fellow men. The fundamental threat to freedom is power to coerce, be it in the hands of a monarch, a dictator, an oligarchy, or a momentary majority. The preservation of freedom requires the elimination of such concentration of power to the fullest possible extent and the dispersal and distribution of whatever power cannot be eliminated— a system of checks and balances.

By removing the organization of economic activity from the control of political authority, the market eliminates this source of coercive power. It enables economic strength to be a check to political power rather than a reinforcement.

Checking political power

Economic power can be widely dispersed. There is no law of conservation which forces the growth of new centers of economic strength to be at the expense of existing centers. Political power, on the other hand, is more difficult to decentralize.

There can be numerous small independent governments. But it is far more difficult to maintain numerous equipotent small centers of political power in a single large government than it is to have numerous centers of economic strength in a single large economy.

There can be many millionaires in one large economy. But can there be more than one really outstanding leader, one person on whom the energies and enthusiasms of his coun-trymen are centered? If the central government gains power, it is likely to be at the expense of local governments.

There seems to be something like a fixed total of political power to be distributed. Consequently, if economic power is joined to political power, concentration seems almost inevitable. On the other hand, if economic power is kept [separate] from political power, it can serve as a check and a counter to political power.

Friedman clearly defines his terms. But is this the only definition of political freedom?

By repeating the points of the argument, you will spell out your thesis. Friedman states again that political freedom depends on economic freedom.

Friedman concludes that a free market actually improves a democracy in some ways.

COMMENTARY: Milton Friedman (1912–)

The economist Milton Friedman was born in 1912 in Brooklyn, New York. Friedman gained his undergraduate degree at Rutgers University and his master's degree at the University of Chicago. He received his Ph.D. from Columbia University in 1946 and in the same year joined the faculty of the University of Chicago, where he began a long and eminent career in teaching and research. Friedman was presented with several awards and honorary doctorates from colleges and universities around the world. In 1976, he received his greatest honor when he was being awarded the Nobel Prize for Economics.

This photograph of Milton Friedman from 1981 shows the economist in a thoughtful mood.

Guru of monetarism

Friedman developed and popularized monetarist economics. Monetarists believe that governments can best influence economics by affecting money supply—the amount of cash in circulation—and interest rates, which dictate the cost of borrowing money. Such an approach contrasts with fiscal policy, in which governments try to influence economies through other mechanisms, such as taxation and regulation. Friedman initiated a debate on the role of money in the wake of narrow interpretations of Keynesian economic theory, which discounted the significance of money when analyzing inflation. Friedman's theories influenced the policies pursued by central banks, and his *A Monetary History of the United States, 1867–1960*, which analyzed the Great Depression (1929–1933), is thought to be his most important achievement.

Gifted economist

Although he never took a government position himself, Friedman's ideas had direct influence on government policy. He became an adviser to the Reagan administration (1981–1988), and his ideas were applied by Margaret Thatcher's Conservative government (1979–1989) in Britain. He was also a passionate believer in free enterprise and individualism, and he popularized his views through a regular *Newsweek* column. Friedman was one of the most influential economists of the 20th century. He was a prolific writer and a skilled debater who managed to communicate his ideas to ordinary people as well as the academic community.

Summary

Are democracy and capitalism at odds with each other? These articles present two very contrasting answers to this question. According to Robert Lekachman, unregulated capitalism generates a concentration of economic power that undermines democracy. The vast disparities in wealth produced by capitalism enable the rich to use their wealth and power to influence the political process in their favor. As a consequence, he argues, the United States is not in fact a democracy at all but rather a plutocracy, i.e., a government of, by, and for the wealthy. Lekachman thus favors more control by the government over the economy so that inequalities are reduced, and the democratic ideal can be realized.

While Lekachman thinks that democracy and capitalism are antagonistic, Milton Friedman understands them to be mutually supportive. According to Friedman, free-market capitalism serves as a check on the potentially tyrannical powers of government.

A government that is strong enough to reduce economic inequality, he argues, is also strong enough to reduce its citizens to the status of subjects. Limited government control over the economy, Friedman concludes, is not just an economic imperative but a political imperative as well.

FURTHER INFORMATION:

 Books:

Friedman, Milton, with the assistance of Rose D. Friedman, *Capitalism and Freedom.* Chicago: University of Chicago Press, 1982.

Goldwin, Robert A., and Schambra, William A. (editors), *How Capitalistic Is the Constitution?* Washington, D.C.: American Enterprise Institute, 1982.

Lindblom, Charles, *Politics and Markets.* New York: Basic Books, 1977.

Okun, Arthur, *Equality and Efficiency.* Washington, D.C.: The Brookings Institution, 1975.

Przeworski, Adam, *Democracy and the Market: Political and Economic Reforms in Eastern Europe and Latin America.* Cambridge, England: Cambridge University Press, 1991.

 Useful websites:

http://ncesa.org.html/livingdem.html

For "Building a Living Democracy" by Gar Alperovitz, http://web.mit.edu/newsoffice/tt/2000/oct18/economists.html

For article on teaming capitalism and democracy. capitalism.org

Promotes capitalism as an ideal social system.

The following debates in the Pro/Con series may also be of interest:

In this volume:
 Topic 4 Is the U.S. truly democratic?

Topic 11 Can the wealthy buy their way into political office?

In *Economics*:
 Part 1: Economic Systems

Part 2: Government and Economic Policy

Part 3: Trade and Global Economics

ARE DEMOCRACY AND CAPITALISM AT ODDS WITH EACH OTHER?

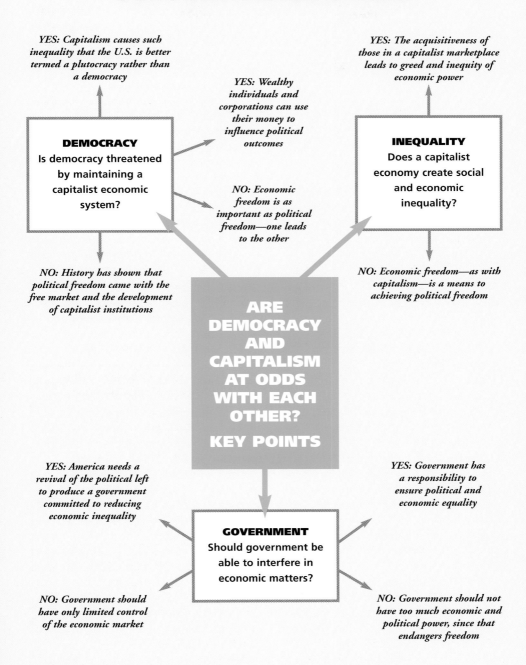

YES: Capitalism causes such inequality that the U.S. is better termed a plutocracy rather than a democracy

YES: Wealthy individuals and corporations can use their money to influence political outcomes

YES: The acquisitiveness of those in a capitalist marketplace leads to greed and inequity of economic power

DEMOCRACY
Is democracy threatened by maintaining a capitalist economic system?

NO: Economic freedom is as important as political freedom—one leads to the other

INEQUALITY
Does a capitalist economy create social and economic inequality?

NO: History has shown that political freedom came with the free market and the development of capitalist institutions

NO: Economic freedom—as with capitalism—is a means to achieving political freedom

ARE DEMOCRACY AND CAPITALISM AT ODDS WITH EACH OTHER?
KEY POINTS

YES: America needs a revival of the political left to produce a government committed to reducing economic inequality

YES: Government has a responsibility to ensure political and economic equality

GOVERNMENT
Should government be able to interfere in economic matters?

NO: Government should have only limited control of the economic market

NO: Government should not have too much economic and political power, since that endangers freedom

45

Topic 4

IS THE UNITED STATES TRULY DEMOCRATIC?

NO

"ON REMOVING CERTAIN IMPEDIMENTS TO DEMOCRACY IN THE UNITED STATES."
FROM *THE MORAL FOUNDATIONS OF THE AMERICAN REPUBLIC*
ROBERT A. DAHL

YES

"IN DEFENSE OF REPUBLICAN CONSTITUTIONALISM: A REPLY TO DAHL"
FROM *THE MORAL FOUNDATIONS OF THE AMERICAN REPUBLIC*
JAMES W. CEASER

INTRODUCTION

The dictionary defines democracy as "government by the people." It goes on to provide a fuller description: "A government in which supreme power is vested in the people and exercised by them directly or indirectly through a system of representation usually involving periodically held free elections." How democratic is the U.S. according to this definition? In the first half of the 19th century the assessment of Alexis de Tocqueville, a young French aristocrat, was positive. "If there is one country in the world where one can hope to appreciate the true value of the dogma of the sovereignty of the people," Tocqueville wrote, "that country is America."

Yet many contemporary observers of American politics disagree. They believe that government actually prevents the people from ruling. They argue that the undemocratic character of our government prevents us from curing our current political ills. As one

prominent proponent of this view has written, "We suffer, in the face of our era's manifold crises, not from too much but from too little democracy."

But did the Constitution establish a democratic government? The answer is complex. When the Framers wrote the Constitution in 1787, they did not intend to create pure democracy. They rejected direct democracy in favor of a republic. James Madison, writing to secure New York's ratification of the proposed Constitution, distinguished between democracies and republics in the following way: "In a democracy the people meet and exercise the government in person; in a republic, they assemble and administer it by their representatives and agents."

The Framers favored a republic not only because the size of the country and the distance between communities would have made direct democracy physically impossible, but also because they worried that a government in which all citizens directly participate would make possible the oppressive rule of a popular majority. The positive effect of representation, Madison argued, is "to refine and enlarge the public views, by passing them through the medium of a chosen body of citizens, whose wisdom may best discern the true interest of their country, and whose patriotism and love of justice will be least likely to sacrifice it to temporary or partial considerations." The result would be that "the public voice, pronounced by the representatives of the people, will be more consonant to the public good than if pronounced by the people themselves." According to Madison, there should be a distance between the national government and the people because direct popular government enables a majority moved by a common interest adverse to the rights of others or to the public good to have its way.

Should we then regard the Constitution's republicanism as antidemocratic? Madison insisted that the proposed American republic is "wholly popular." The electors of the national representatives are "not the rich, more than the poor; not the learned, more than the ignorant; not the haughty heirs of distinguished names, more than the humble sons of obscure and unpropitious fortune." They are rather the "great body of the people" of the U.S. What is more, the candidates are any citizens whose merits may recommend them to the esteem of their fellow citizens without any qualification of wealth, birth, religion, or profession. According to this view, then, the Constitution did establish a democratic government, if what is meant by democracy is a system of representative government based on popular consent.

The following articles engage in the debate over whether the U.S. is truly democratic. Robert Dahl argues that the American system of government is "defective by democratic criteria." He concedes that the Framers' concern to design a system of government that would protect the rights of a minority against an oppressive majority is laudable; but he argues that the system

> *"Democracy is not a fragile flower; still it needs cultivating."*
> —PRESIDENT RONALD REAGAN

they produced tilts too far in the opposite direction by making it easier for what he calls "privileged minorities" to thwart the popular will. Dahl thinks that the U.S. system of government is profoundly undemocratic, and he calls for major political reform to remove the "impediments to democracy."

James Ceaser, on the other hand, argues that Dahl's interpretation of the political system fails to acknowledge the reasons for its antimajoritarian devices. He explains how constitutional federalism, the separation of powers, and other arrangements of the system designed by the Framers formed their version of representative democracy. He also points out that majorities do not always make wise decisions.

While Ceaser concedes that there are flaws in the system, he questions whether the current system of government, with its impediments, is perhaps preferable to the system of democracy that Dahl proposes.

ON REMOVING CERTAIN IMPEDIMENTS TO DEMOCRACY IN THE UNITED STATES
Robert A. Dahl

NO

The author opens with the main premise of his argument: that the U.S. political system is undemocratic.

The political system the Framers helped bring into existence was in at least two major respects defective by democratic criteria. First in spite of the eloquent universality of the language used in the Declaration of Independence and common at the time, in actuality the Framers gave much narrower scope to the principles of consent and political equality. Without seriously qualifying, much less abandoning their universal norms, they created a government that would demand obedience to its laws from a majority of adults—women, non-whites, and some white males—who were excluded from active participation in making those laws, whether directly or through their elected representatives. The majority of adults were thus provided with as little opportunity to give their active consent to the laws which they were bound to obey as their colonial predecessors had enjoyed under laws enacted by the English Parliament.

Do you agree with Dahl that the first government could not be called a democracy because most citizens were excluded from voting?

Second, in order to achieve their goal of preserving a set of inalienable rights superior to the majority principle—a goal many of us would surely share—the Framers deliberately created a framework of government that was carefully designed to impede and even prevent the operation of majority rule. Thus when the country committed itself to their framework of government, two different arguments became confounded in the national consciousness, and they remain confounded to this day.

Although Dahl assumes widespread support for the principle that the majority is right, many people disagree. Can you suggest examples in which the most popular view is not necessarily the best?

Two arguments

There is the liberal argument that certain rights are so fundamental to the attainment of human goals, needs, interests, and fulfillment that governments must never be allowed to derogate from them. But in addition there is the American constitutional argument that the highly specific, unique set of political arrangements embodied in our constitutional and political practices is necessary to preserve these rights. While [I] accept the liberal argument, the American constitutional argument seems seriously defective. [T]he elaborate system of checks and balances, separation of powers, constitutional federalism, and other institutional arrangements influenced by these structures and the constitutional views they reflect are both adverse to the majority principle, and in that sense to democracy, and yet arbitrary and unfair in the protection they give to rights. However laudable their ends, in their means the Framers were guilty of overkill. As only one example, the presidential veto has generally been used, and quite recently for purposes no loftier than simply to prevent the adoption of policies disliked by the president and the political coalition whose interests he seeks to advance. It is not as if a president uses the veto only when a majority coalition threatens the inalienable rights of a minority. What is typically at stake is purely a disagreement about policy. Insofar as all policies have costs and gains and thus influence the distribution of advantages and disadvantages, the policies of a majority (like those of a minority) are likely to be adverse to the interests of some persons; but we can hardly say—nor can the Framers have intended to say—that every privilege that happens to exist does so by inalienable right.

Support your argument with good examples. Dahl presents the presidential veto as an example of how the Constitution works against democracy.

System handicaps the disadvantaged

Yet there is this strong bias against minorities in the political system the Framers helped to create. Because they succeeded in designing a system that makes it easier for privileged minorities to prevent changes they dislike than for majorities to bring about the changes they want, it is strongly tilted in favor of the status quo and against reform. In their effort to protect basic rights, what the Framers did in effect was to hand out extra chips in the game of politics to people who are already advantaged, while they handicapped the disadvantaged who would like to change the status quo. From a moral perspective, the consequences seem arbitrary and quite lacking in a principled justification.

Why might the Framers have devised a political system biased in favor of the status quo?

We ought to be able to design a way of preserving fundamental rights that is not so biased in favor of existing privilege and against reform. A number of other countries that place fewer barriers in the way of majority rule than exist under our political system manage to preserve at least as high a standard of political liberty, with less procedural unfairness. But to bring about such changes meets precisely the obstacle to change just mentioned, the antimajoritarian bias of the constitutional and political system.

The guiding criteria against which to measure political performance are the criteria of procedural democracy, which constitute the doctrine of procedural democracy.

Collective decision making

To become fully operative with respect to any association, the doctrine of procedural democracy presupposes a judgment that at least two conditions exist among some set of persons who constitute or intend to constitute an association. First there is a *need for collective decisions* binding on the members of the association. That is, this set of persons is confronted by a matter which they think it would be disadvantageous to leave entirely to individual action or to choices made exclusively through a market, and comparatively advantageous to make collectively and enforce on the members.

Second among the persons obligated to abide by collective decisions on this matter, there is a subset, the *demos*, whose members are *roughly equally qualified, taken all around*. That is, no member of this qualified subset, or demos, believes that any other member of the association or any subset of persons different from the demos is significantly more qualified than the demos to arrive at a correct choice with respect to matters requiring collective decisions. Under the *maximal* interpretation, the members believe that the demos includes all qualified members of the association and all members of the demos are in all relevant characteristics equally qualified with respect to matters requiring collective decisions. Under the *minimal* interpretation, no members of the association are in any relevant characteristic so clearly more qualified as to justify their making the decision for all the others on the matter at hand.

A government of any association in which these conditions are judged to exist is, on these matters, *a putatively democratic government in relation to its demos*. Thus a judgment that these conditions exist implies a rejection of claims that might be advanced on behalf of a government over the demos on these matters by a putative aristocracy, meritocracy, or governing elite.

Criteria for procedural democracy

The doctrine of procedural democracy holds that for any putatively democratic government, collective decision making by the demos should satisfy at least three criteria.

1. The criterion of *political equality*. The decision rule for determining outcomes must equally take into account the preferences of each member of the demos as to the outcome. To reject this criterion is to deny the condition of equally rough qualification taken all around. This criterion implies

---

What might be some of the pitfalls of collective decision making?

"Demos" is taken from the Greek word meaning "people." See box on Democracy and capitalism on page 39.

A "meritocracy" is a system in which the talented can move ahead according to their achievements.

that the procedures and performance of any putatively democratic government ought to be evaluated according to the extent to which the preferences of every member of the demos are given weight in collective decisions, particularly on matters members think are important to them.

2. The criterion of *effective participation*. In order for the preferences of each member of the demos to be equally taken into account, every member must have equal opportunities for expressing preferences, and decision making. This criterion implies, then, that any putatively democratic government ought to be evaluated according to the opportunities it provides for, or the costs it imposes on, expression and participation by the demos.

Do you think the U.S. electorate meets this criterion of enlightened understanding? Does everyone have the same opportunity to understand political issues?

3. The criterion of *enlightened understanding*. In order to express preferences accurately, each member of the demos ought to have adequate and equal opportunities for discovering and validating, in the time available, what his or her preferences are on the matter to be decided. This criterion thus implies that any putatively democratic government ought to be evaluated according to the opportunities it furnishes for the acquisition of knowledge of ends and means, of oneself and other selves, by the demos.

Any government that satisfies these criteria, and only such a government, is *procedurally democratic in relation to its demos.*

IN DEFENSE OF REPUBLICAN CONSTITUTIONALISM
James W. Ceaser

Dahl gives the Founders a mixed review, praising them for establishing liberty but criticizing them for not committing us to democracy. Their undemocratic legacy, according to Dahl, is found in the very form of our government, which, through such devices as federalism, separation of powers, and bicameralism, impedes simple majority rule. Dahl proposes to remove this impediment to democracy by doing away with these "antimajoritarian" devices—in short, by doing away with the Constitution—and by replacing it with a multiparty, unicameral parliamentary system. While one might argue over whether this system would work quite as democratically as Dahl supposes (real majority sentiment can sometimes get lost in the bargaining process among parliamentary parties), it seems reasonable to assume that, by his own standard of democracy, his system would be more democratic than the Constitution.

> *Bicameral means consisting of two legislative chambers, in this case the House and the Senate.*

Choosing a form of democracy

The pertinent question is whether we prefer the impediments, with the values connected to them, to Dahl's form of democracy. In this instance—and this instance alone—Dahl attempts to answer the question by presenting an account of the different values that the Framers weighed when they constructed the Constitution. What we discover is that the Founders did have a "laudable" value in mind: the protection of fundamental rights. But, Dahl goes on, we now know that the antimajoritarian elements of the Constitution were not really necessary for that purpose and the Framers "were guilty of overkill."

> *Ceaser asks a question that reaches to the center of the debate.*

The existence of these antimajoritarian devices serves—and perhaps even was partly intended to serve—the very different purpose of aiding the privileged in society: "Because they [the Founders] succeeded in designing a system that makes it easier for privileged minorities to prevent changes they dislike than for majorities to bring about the changes they want, it is strongly tilted in favor of the status quo and against reform."

What is striking about this account of the Constitution is its reduction of the possible aims of government to protecting the individual rights and promoting mass national democracy. This interpretation however fails to take into account many of the objectives of our complex governmental structure and the reasons for its antimajoritarian devices. If by *democracy* one takes Dahl's standard of a unitary national government under the rule of a unicameral parliament, there are other important objectives, besides protecting individual rights, that would explain the Founders' dislike for this form of government. Dahl seems to have shown his respect for the Framers by not exposing their other anitmajoritarian heresies. Here we shall have no such scruples.

Ceaser suggests that while pure democracy might be a fine principle, it is not necessarily the best foundation for U.S. government.

Federalism

Why, for example, does the Constitution support the antimajoritarian device of federalism? Not only to protect individual rights, the Founders tell us, but to assure a sphere of partial autonomy for governments below the national level. By including this device, the Framers were thus guilty of the antimajoritarian goal of allowing people to participate in state and local governments and of permitting local majorities to make certain decisions that differ from those of national majorities.

Can you think of issues on which local opinion in your region is different from that of the nation as a whole?

Separation of powers

Why did the Framers provide for a separation of the executive from the legislature? Again it was not only to protect individual rights but to promote the goal of a "vigorous executive" whose performance of the *essential* executive tasks would not be immediately dependent on the shifting majorities in the legislature. An independent executive, according to Alexander Hamilton, was necessary for "the protection of the community against foreign attacks … and [for] the security of liberty against the enterprises and assaults of ambition, of faction, and of anarchy."

See Does the separation of powers produce ineffective government? on pages 98–109.

Alexander Hamilton (1757–1804), one of the Framers of the Constitution.

This language may sound archaic and no longer relevant, especially in light of the widespread belief among so many political scientists about the supposed superiority of the parliamentary system. Yet parliamentary systems succeed in solving the problem of energy in the executive only where the governing party has a majority or a near majority in the parliament. Where, as Dahl prefers, there is a multiparty system, and where no party approaches a majority, we sometimes find dangerously weak governments, as in Israel and Italy [in 1986] or in France (1946-1958).

Why finally do we have bicameralism and checks and balances? Again not just to protect individual rights but to reduce the likelihood of unwise choices by democratic majorities. The Founders were not afraid to state openly that democratic majorities, pandered to by flatterers or encouraged by demagogues, could produce unstable policies or make unwise decisions. Requiring concurrence by more than one body represented an effort by the Founders to find an institutional arrangement to help cope with this problem. If this system sometimes blocks or retards policies sought by a majority that are not unwise or mistaken—as it surely has—this does not by itself discredit the arrangement, for there is almost no institutional solution that does not entail some costs in producing a benefit.

Ceaser makes his central point. The U.S. is not truly democratic because true democracy can be dangerous unless it is kept in check by the political system.

Representative democracy

The foregoing discussion presupposes an acceptance of at least the possibilities that majorities may not always know what is best and that there may be a decision making process able to improve on majority opinion. The Framers called their version of this improved system "representative" or "republican" government, distinguishing it from "democracy." Early in his article, when attacking the system of checks and balances and the presidential veto, Dahl comes close to denying the existence of any standard, except for the protection of individual rights, by which it might be claimed that majorities can err.

Yet when it comes time to sketch the character of his own regime, Dahl concedes that democracies can fail in making the correct choices if citizens do not meet the "criterion of enlightened understanding." But instead of relying like the Framers on institutions of government to help deal with this problem, Dahl puts faith in an ambitious program of adult education. He would make available "quasi-expert intermediaries spread among the whole body of citizens," who could help the less-informed citizens "to gain an adequate understanding of their own basic needs and of the policies best designed to satisfy these needs." Although this proposal to put a policy analyst in every shopping mall would resolve the employment problem for doctoral candidates in the social sciences, it remains an open question how many citizens would avail themselves of this opportunity to be patronized and how many would actually leave with their options having been made more enlightened.

Is Ceaser right to mock the suggestion that experts educate citizens about political issues? How else might they become informed?

When encountering the criticisms of someone who argues that the present-day regime in the United States is not democratic, defenders of the regime may feel tempted to deny the charge and congratulate themselves on how democratic it is. The denial is by and large in order, but the congratulations should be made with care. Despite the minor deviations noted above, the American regime today is quite democratic in its procedures. Of all the world's democracies, or at least of those of considerable size, it is, all things considered, quite possibly the most democratic, although such comparisons are admittedly difficult and often meaningless. The American separation of powers system is practically the only one that gives extensive powers on a day-to-day basis to a popular legislature; mid-term legislative elections provide an occasion for popular input at intervals more regular than that found in any other democratic system; and candidates for party nominations are selected for the most part in popular primaries (a unique arrangement).

> Ceaser claims that the U.S. is largely democratic in its procedures and backs this up by describing how.

Federal judiciary

If there is one reason to hesitate in proclaiming the democratic character of the American regime, it surely has to do with the role played by the federal judiciary, which has ventured deeply into the policymaking process, in ways never intended by the Framers, to make many policies that have often been opposed by local or national majorities. Curiously however while Dahl decries time and again the "pseudo-democratic imperial presidency," he never once criticizes the policymaking authority of the judiciary, even though it would seem to present a formidable "impediment" to procedural democracy.

> Ceaser concedes that the interference of the federal judiciary in policymaking is undemocratic.

The fact that the American regime is so democratic however is not necessarily a cause for rejoicing. Dahl readily concedes that "pseudo-democratic" developments do not always produce good government; perhaps the same could be said sometimes of real democratic developments. While there are clearly elements of the American regime that have been improved by democratization, there may be facets of the regime for which the opposite is true. Is it clear for example that we have improved our system by every cause in recent decades that has marched under the banner of democratic reform?

Even to begin to make such judgments of course requires abandoning the modern prejudice that equates the good exclusively with the democratic. It requires instead a search for the principles of good government itself. Not a bad place to begin would be a genuine encounter with the American tradition, and in particular with the Founders.

> Make lists of the good and bad points of democracy. Is democracy always "good"?

Summary

These articles present two competing answers to the question: Is the United States truly democratic? Robert Dahl argues that the United States is not truly democratic. According to him, such constitutional devices as separation of powers and checks and balances, which enable the president, for example, to veto laws supported by a popular majority, reflect the antidemocratic bias of the American political system. Dahl thus advocates political reform in line with the standards of what he calls procedural democracy in order to ensure that the United States becomes truly democratic. James W. Ceaser responds to Dahl's argument by showing how the Founders designed the political system, with its antimajoritarian devices, with other particular advantages in mind. He argues that majorities do not always make wise choices and says that the bicameral system with its checks and balances exists to counter the eventuality of unwise decisions. Ceaser states that the American system is quite democratic in its procedures but admits that the system is not without its flaws. He suggests that the current system with its impediments would be preferable to Dahl's proposals for democracy. Ceaser finishes with a call to search for the principle of good government itself rather than always equating the good exclusively with the democratic.

FURTHER INFORMATION:

Books:

Barber, Benjamin R., *Strong Democracy: Participatory Politics for a New Age.* Berkeley: University of California Press, 1984.

Burnheim, John, *Is Democracy Possible? The Alternative to Electoral Politics.* Berkeley: University of California Press, 1985.

Diamond, Martin, *The Founding of the Democratic Republic.* Itasca, IL: F.E. Peacock, 1981.

Goldwin, Robert A., and William A. Schambra (editors) *How Democratic Is the Constitution?* Washington, D.C.: American Enterprise Institute, 1980.

Articles:

Tarcov, Nathan, "The Meanings of Democracy," in *Democracy, Education, and the Schools,* edited by Roger Soder. San Francisco: Jossey-Bass Publishers, 1996.

 Useful websites:

xroads.virginia.edu/~HYPER/DETOC/ home/html
Text of Alexis De Tocqueville's "Democracy in America."

www.thenation.com/issue/981026/1026/BARB.HTM
Article "More Democracy!" in *The Nation.*
Core Documents of U.S. Democracy.
www.access.gpo.gov/su_docs/locators/coredocs/index.html
www.dnet.org
The Democracy Network site has election coverage and candidates' statements.

The following debates in the Pro/Con series may also be of interest:

In this volume:

Topic 1 Is direct rule by the people better than representative democracy?
Topic 3 Are democracy and capitalism at odds with each other?
Topic 7 Does the two-party system adequately represent the people?

IS THE UNITED STATES TRULY DEMOCRATIC?

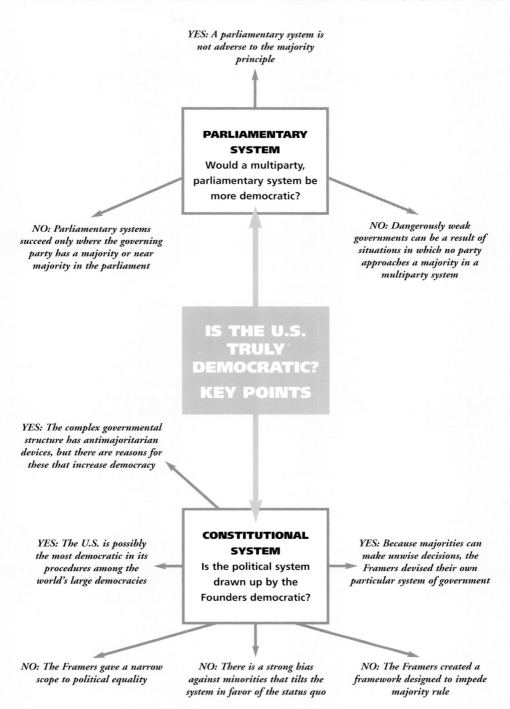

YES: A parliamentary system is not adverse to the majority principle

PARLIAMENTARY SYSTEM
Would a multiparty, parliamentary system be more democratic?

NO: Parliamentary systems succeed only where the governing party has a majority or near majority in the parliament

NO: Dangerously weak governments can be a result of situations in which no party approaches a majority in a multiparty system

IS THE U.S. TRULY DEMOCRATIC? KEY POINTS

YES: The complex governmental structure has antimajoritarian devices, but there are reasons for these that increase democracy

YES: The U.S. is possibly the most democratic in its procedures among the world's large democracies

CONSTITUTIONAL SYSTEM
Is the political system drawn up by the Founders democratic?

YES: Because majorities can make unwise decisions, the Framers devised their own particular system of government

NO: The Framers gave a narrow scope to political equality

NO: There is a strong bias against minorities that tilts the system in favor of the status quo

NO: The Framers created a framework designed to impede majority rule

RESEARCH SKILLS

Anyone who wants to write authoritatively on any subject must at some point attempt to do some research. It need not be too time-consuming or complicated. It can be as simple as reading an article like the one below.

Essential research tools

i. A dictionary—to check spelling and also provide definitions of words.

ii. A thesaurus—provides synonyms (words that are similar) in order to minimize the number of repeated and overused words.

iii. An encyclopedia—even one that is a few years old will contain a wealth of information and support your argument.

iv. A library—books can be expensive, so go to the library. There will normally be a quiet place to work and access to computers.

v. The Internet and World Wide Web—see opposite.

Time management

Keep your deadline in mind. Set aside time each day in which to work. Break down your project into small, manageable sections. Give each of them a heading, and break them down further if necessary. Once you have done that, estimate the time you can give each one in relation to your total time frame.

Space to work

It is important to have a clear, quiet space to work in. If possible, work on your project in the same place at the same time each day.

Taking notes

Before you start, make sure you understand the question properly. Look up any key words. If you are writing notes, make sure your writing is legible. If you're typing, make sure you spell words correctly. Note down your sources carefully, and credit any quotations, statistics, or material taken directly from an existing book, article, or from the Internet in your essay. Plagiarizing is illegal!

Collating, writing, and editing—main points

1. Collect all the notes you have made.

2. Draw a key/mind map to help you work out what the main points are and the order in which you want to address them in your essay/critique.

3. Try to word-process rather than write your work. Not only does it look better, but you will also find it much easier to edit the work later on.

4. Always save a copy of your first draft for later reference.

5. Keep your dictionary and thesaurus handy during the editing process.

6. Read through your draft. At the end of each sentence or paragraph ask: "Why have I written this?"

7. Delete any irrelevant material.

8. Get someone else to read the essay if necessary.

USING THE INTERNET

What is it?

The Internet is nothing more than a series of computers all interconnected and sharing some of their data globally. Users of the Internet publish their work on the World Wide Web—it is a series of graphic and text documents that are all interconnected through clickable "hypertext" links or "hyperlinks."

Why use it?

The World Wide Web (WWW) can be the largest library in the world. It can also be the most frustrating resource tool if not used properly. Because of its size and information capacity it is easy to become sidetracked by interesting but irrelevant information. Before using the WWW, write down exactly what it is you need to find out while online, and stick to this goal. Remember that articles used from the WWW must be cited as your source.

Search engines

The easiest and fastest way to find information on the web is to use a "search engine."

A search engine is software designed to help you look through the web. One way to access a search engine is to click the search button on your browser's toolbar. It will open up a window on the left of your screen where you can submit your "search query." A search query is simply a string of words relevant to your research—once you have entered a few words and clicked "search," the engine will bring back a list of sites that contain those words.

Metasearch programs

A more thorough way of searching is by using a metasearch program, such as www.metacrawler.com.

This is a search facility that uses 12 separate engines at the same time, thereby finding many more results. Standalone search programs such as Copernic 2000 (which can be found at www.copernic.com) do the same thing but run independently from your browser, using their own software.

Be specific

Using the Internet can be frustrating, so you should always be as specific as possible. For example, if you are searching for a specific person, such as George W. Bush, type in the whole name and not just the surname. Try to feed in as much information as possible.

USEFUL SEARCH ENGINES

www.altavista.com	www.askjeeves.com	www.dogpile.com
www.google.com	www.hotbot.com	www.lycos.com
www.northernlight.com		

PART 2
U.S. GOVERNMENT

Throughout our history prominent Americans have claimed that the United States represents a novel experiment in democratic government, an experiment that tests whether a nation conceived in liberty and dedicated to the proposition that all men are created equal can endure.

Features of the U.S. system

Many of the most distinctive features of U.S. constitutional government were designed to remedy the perceived problems of democracy without departing from the principle. The Constitution thus establishes, for example, a separation and checking of powers among three branches of government, an independent judiciary, the indirect rule of the people through their representatives, and a shared sovereignty between the federal government and the states. These institutional arrangements are not departures from democracy, those who drafted the Constitution believed, but rather modifications of democracy necessary for its long-term survival and success.

More than 200 years after its inception one might well ask: How successful has the American experiment in democracy been? The following articles by a number of respected authors raise several important issues that are central to this question.

Separation of powers

Unlike most other democracies today, the U.S. government operates under a system of the separation of powers. The Constitution vests national legislative power in Congress, executive power in the president, and judicial power in the courts. The Framers designed the U.S. system of government in this way because they believed "the accumulation of all powers, legislative, executive, and judiciary, in the same hands, whether of one, a few, or many, and whether hereditary, self-appointed, or elective, may justly be pronounced the very definition of tyranny."

This is the issue taken up by Lloyd Cutler and James Ceaser in Topic 8. Cutler argues that our system has produced policy gridlock that renders the government incapable of dealing with the important issues of our time; Ceaser responds by arguing that history has proven that the U.S. political system is in fact capable of overcoming policy gridlock. The issue in dispute between them remains an enduring one.

A too powerful president

Another feature of government that is controversial is the single executive. At the time of the nation's founding many people feared that a single executive was inconsistent with republican government. In order to remain true to republican principles, some people favored a plural rather than single executive. It was James Madison's view, though, that "energy in government requires … the execution of it by a single hand." Today many critics argue that the presidency is too powerful and must be curbed. This is the matter at issue between Arthur Schlesinger and Suzanne Garment in Topic 9. Schlesinger, writing at the time

Founders had disdain for parties, thinking of them as "factions motivated by ambition and self-interest." As a consequence, U.S. political history began without parties. However, parties emerged quickly as a major force in American life, influencing electoral politics and policy debates. An often-heard criticism of the party system today is that there is no real

---

"You cannot possibly have a broader basis for any government than that which includes all the people, with all their rights in their hands, and with an equal power to maintain their rights."

—WILLIAM LLOYD GARRISON, U.S. ABOLITIONIST AND REFORMER

---

of Watergate (1972–1975), is concerned about the rise of what he calls "the imperial presidency." Garment worries that continual attacks on the presidency have dangerously undermined the ability of the president to perform his constitutional duties.

Federalism v. centralization

Federalism is another important issue. In the U.S. context it refers to the idea of political authority being shared between the national and state governments. In recent years many Americans have come to believe that the national government has grown too powerful at the expense of the state governments. Jean Yarbrough and Samuel Beer provide very different opinions on this issue in Topic 6.

Parties and the system

It is also vital to ask how well political parties and the federal bureaucracy have served U.S. democracy. The

difference between the Democratic and the Republican parties. If this is true, can they be said to adequately represent the people? Edward Banfield and Gordon Black provide competing viewpoints on this question in Topic 12.

Federal bureaucracy

Another prominent feature of the U.S. government is the federal bureaucracy. The Framers must have anticipated the development of some kind of bureaucracy in the executive branch to help the president fulfill his constitutional responsibility to "take care that the laws be faithfully executed." But it is arguable whether they envisioned something as extensive as the bureaucracy that exists in the United States today.

Does the large American federal bureaucracy serve or threaten the U.S. experiment in democracy? George Roche and Dean Yarwood take opposite positions on this question in Topic 5.

Topic 5
IS THE FEDERAL BUREAUCRACY TOO BIG?

YES
"AMERICA BY THE THROAT"
FROM *AMERICA BY THE THROAT: THE STRANGLEHOLD OF FEDERAL BUREAUCRACY*
GEORGE ROCHE

NO
"STOP BASHING THE BUREAUCRACY"
PUBLIC ADMINISTRATION REVIEW, NOV/DEC 1996, VOL. 56
DEAN YARWOOD

INTRODUCTION

In his 1996 State of the Union address President Bill Clinton declared that "the era of big government is over."

Whether or not this was merely a rhetorical flourish (the fact that the federal government spends nearly $2 trillion a year suggests that it was), the enthusiastic response President Clinton received for saying it provided vivid illustration of the degree to which "big government" has become a pejorative term in American politics.

Advocates of reducing government frequently refer to a line in President Ronald Reagan's first inaugural address: "Government is not the solution to our problem; government is the problem." When Reagan spoke of "government," he was referring especially to the various departments and regulatory agencies in Washington, D.C., that make up the federal bureaucracy, such as the Department of Health and Human Services (HHS), the Food and Drug Administration (FDA), and the Occupational Safety and Health Administration (OSHA). In today's public discourse it is not uncommon to hear a politician rail against the federal bureaucracy for being wasteful, slow, confusing, rigid, or even oppressive.

The federal bureaucracy is part of the executive branch of the U.S. national government. It is not mentioned in the Constitution—indeed, the Constitution leaves the executive branch largely undefined—but it has been instituted over time by congressional statute in order to help the president fulfill his constitutional obligation to "take care that the laws be faithfully executed."

In the early part of our nation's history the federal bureaucracy was quite small. The State Department, for example, started with only nine employees. During the 19th century the largest department of government was the Post Office. From the Civil War to the Vietnam War each major conflict in American history has resulted in an increase in the number of the government's civilian and military employees. The federal bureaucracy as we know it today is largely the product of two major 20th-century events: the Great Depression and World War II.

During the Great Depression President Franklin D. Roosevelt's New Deal programs to promote economic prosperity and provide a safety net for those in need marked a significant expansion of the government's activities. In this period the federal government both assumed the responsibility of guaranteeing a basic level of income for the elderly through the Social Security program and made heavy use of federal income taxes on individuals and corporations to finance its war effort. As a consequence of this it was able to expand a variety of federal programs.

"Government is not the solution to our problem; government is the problem."

—PRESIDENT RONALD REAGAN

In the 1960s President Lyndon B. Johnson oversaw another significant expansion of the federal bureaucracy in his effort to build what he called a "Great Society," which resulted in the creation of the Medicare and Medicaid health-care programs and the establishment of several new federal departments (see box, page 70). Today the federal bureaucracy constitutes scores of departments and agencies, and employs more than three million people, a fact that has prompted critics to argue that the federal bureaucracy is now too big and needs to be scaled back.

The following articles present two very different answers to the question: Is the federal bureaucracy too big? George Roche's answer is made vividly clear by the title of his book, *America by the Throat: The Stranglehold of Federal Bureaucracy*. To Roche the federal bureaucracy reflects a trend toward an "all-powerful central government" that in his view is not only unconstitutional but is also a threat to personal freedom and the American dream. "Our energies as a free people are thwarted by the snarl of red tape," he writes. "Its cost is so great as to ennervate [sic] the most productive economy the world has ever seen."

Dean Yarwood calls on politicians to "stop bashing the bureaucracy." According to him, executive agencies always operate under the terms of some congressional statute, and therefore it is unreasonable for Congress to rail against what they themselves have helped create. As he, quoting James Q. Wilson, says: "For Congress to complain of agency red tape is akin to an architect complaining of a home owner who finds it necessary to walk up five flights of steps before he can get from his bedroom to his bathroom."

The "red tape" for which the federal bureaucracy is so much denounced helps promote the laudable goals of equity, access, and procedural due process. Far from being a threat to American democracy, Yarwood suggests, the federal bureaucracy helps ensure that American democracy is responsive to the needs of its citizens.

AMERICA BY THE THROAT
George Roche

Herbert Spencer (1820–1903) was an advocate of Social Darwinism. What is this concept?

☑ Herbert Spencer once noted that on any given day, you could read two stories in the papers about the failures of government programs—and three stories about pleas for new government programs to do even more for us!

That was over a hundred years ago, in England, but the point rings truer than ever for us today. The only difference is that now we see more stories about a certain kind of failure, one that seems to us mindless and mean. Such a story might read like this: "The Occupational Safety and Health Administration (OSHA) today ordered the University of Illinois to tear down the handrails alongside walkways on campus, and to install new handrails exactly 42 inches high. According to OSHA, the old handrails are several inches too low to comply with regulations."

Roche recounts a seemingly amusing example of bureaucracy but uses it to make a serious point about wasted expenditure.

The story happens to be true. And when we read it, we know at once here is the federal bureaucracy at work. It may even give us a chuckle—who else but a bureaucrat would be so boneheaded as to insist that handrails must be exactly 42 inches high, and not one inch higher or lower? But it is not so funny when you learn that Illinois had to pay over $500,000 to change those handrails. If it weren't for a petty bureaucratic rule, the money could have been used, say, to hire fifteen full professors, or build a dormitory wing, or add three thousand volumes to the school library.

The failure of government

It is precisely this sort of perverse and hurtful waste that increasingly marks the failure of government actions today. The problem is bureaucracy, and bureaucracy has become a national epidemic.

The federal bureaucracy has more than tripled in size in the last ten years. It is ten times as large and powerful as it was twenty years ago, at the beginning of the Kennedy-Johnson years. It has swollen a thousand-fold in power in the last half century. This titanic expansion of bureaucratic power is shattering the foundations of a free society and menacing the well-being of every citizen. The federal government, designed and intended to be the Servant of the people, now bids to become our Master.

Such is the problem I address, and it has already grown to proportions that are difficult to grasp. "Bureaucracy," in the abstract, is hardly a new concern. And if the problem were no more than a few harmless bumblers in dusty federal offices, we would have little to worry about. However a bureaucratic machine so swollen and powerful that it can hold sway over every citizen is indeed a new—and ominous—development in American life. How this situation came to be, what it portends, and what we can do about it, are questions every intelligent American ought to ponder. Soon.

How big is too big?

We are all aware that the federal government itself has grown immense in recent times. It is not as well understood, unfortunately, that as government grows, it necessarily becomes more and more bureaucratic and rigid—and authoritarian. The overweening bureaucracy that emerges is less an evil in itself than a reflection of this trend and a greater evil: the thrust toward an all-powerful central government. For fifty years and more, the dominant opinion in or near the seats of power has worked ceaselessly to erect a federal State on the Old World model: paternalistic, autocratic, and utterly alien to the American constitutional ideal. This effort has imposed on us the largest, most costly, most bureaucratic State in all of history, where once we had and long cherished the smallest.

Every extension of federal power has brought with it new bureaucratic controls and interferences in our lives. This is unavoidable. Bureaus are the handmaidens of political power. They are required by law as well as practical necessity to act as they do, however inflexible, small-minded, and destructive their actions may seem to the rest of us. Such are, and always have been, the consequences of the authoritarian State.

> "Paternalism" is a system under which an authority regulates or controls the conduct of its citizens. It comes from the Latin word for "father." Should the government be a "father" to its citizens?

Bureaucracy

It is in the nature of bureaucracy ever to work "by the book," reducing every aspect of our lives to suffocating rules and lifeless averages. Rulebook methods are the only way State power can be organized. There is no room for intelligent decisions and flexibility. The bureaucratic State, William F. Rickenbacker has written, is "...the very opponent and negation of human freedom and individuality. Men strive to excel, the State seeks after averages. Men covet novelty, the State extrapolates from yesterday. Men love to chaffer person to person, the State is a rule book. Men yearn to be free, the State is the sum of liberties lost."

COMMENTARY: President Ronald Reagan

Republican politician and 40th president of the United States (1980–1988), Ronald Wilson Reagan at a press conference.

Former Hollywood actor Ronald Reagan became the 40th president of the United States in 1981 and remained in power until 1989. Reagan envisioned a greater America with less government bureaucracy—in contrast to Lyndon Johnson (see page 70). He aimed to reduce the American people's reliance on the government. His form of economics became known as "reaganomics" and was aimed at protecting entitlement programs such as Medicare and Social Security, while eliminating "waste, fraud, and abuse." He supported legislation to curb inflation, stimulate economic growth, increase employment, and strengthen national defense. At the end of his two terms in office Reagan felt that he had fulfilled his campaign pledge to restore "the great confident roar of American progress and growth and optimism." However, any economic gain for the United States came at the cost of a massive annual deficit and national debt.

The bureaucracy has at its disposal one tool only, and that is force: coercive power. This tool has its purposes, but is totally unsuited to the direction of economic or private matters. Most applications of this power in the private sector, unfortunately, cause more harm than good.

Certainly much of the malaise America has suffered in recent years can be traced directly to the use of bureaucratic power where it does not belong. Our energies as a free people are thwarted by the snarl of red tape and rules. Our schools deteriorate year after year, in exact proportion to the growth of a gigantic educational bureaucracy. Business and industry, chained by literally millions of regulations, are less and less able to provide the jobs and goods we need. The poor, the aged, the disadvantaged, the hurt and handicapped, all supposedly the beneficiaries of government aid, instead become its victims, caught in an endless web of rules and frustrations. Our hopes of bettering our lives falter[s] under the burdens the bureaucracy imposes.

Roche wrote this piece in 1983. He blames America's malaise on red tape and bureaucracy. Is there still evidence of these problems in the economy?

The results

Half a century's experimentation with do-everything government has proven to be a monstrous, heart-breaking mistake. Instead of "solving" social problems, it has created new and far greater ones. Its ideas and programs go forward on their own momentum despite being repeatedly discredited by practical experience. Its cost is so great as to ennervate the most productive economy the world has ever seen. Its accumulated powers could emerge as totalitarianism in any severe crisis; and a crisis is sure to come if the statist trend continues.

www.whitehouse. gov, The White House site, explains Reagan's attempts to reduce the federal bureaucracy.

In the end, we too could face the fate that has marked every Old World State, every civilization before us: a progressive weakening of society by State exactions, leading to degeneracy, collapse, and death. No people before us who have made the same mistakes, who have chosen to put their faith in the State, have ever escaped this doom. Nor shall we.

STOP BASHING THE BUREAUCRACY
Dean Yarwood

NO

Yarwood uses a familiar, nonacademic phrase to make his point.

We live in a time when the federal bureaucracy seems to have reached a new low in public esteem. Bashing it is the order of the day.

As might be expected the Occupational Safety and Health Administration has come in for its share of criticism. In the House, a freshman member, Representative Charlie Norwood, R-GA, comments, "I continue to believe the best solution for OSHA is to close it down and spread every employee there out into the 50 states never to be allowed to return inside the Beltway." He continues, "A lot of these federal agencies have been in my life and in my pocket book and in my family's life and in my friends' life for a long time, and it gives one great pleasure to fight 'em back.'"

Should Yarwood make more of the fact that some of the criticism of OSHA is false?

Falsehoods

A story circulates (falsely) that OSHA bureaucrats have issued a regulation prohibiting dentists from giving extracted teeth to children, thus making the tooth fairy superfluous! Some of these members are not fixed on particular agencies but feel that the federal government itself has become too large and that it needs a general down-sizing.

This is the feeling of a dedicated group of Republican freshman members of the House. Calling themselves the "New Federalists," they have stipulated a great reluctance to vote for any budget resolution that does not eliminate cabinet level departments

Bureaucracy bashing in perspective

James Alexander McDougall (1817–1867) was U.S. Senator for California (1861–1867).

While times are difficult, this is not the first, nor will it be the last [time], for bureaucracy bashing by members of Congress. This diversion has a long history in the United States. As early as 1866 California Senator James A. McDougall proclaimed: "Our city of Washington is filled with officials who have new duties to perform, offices to be made for them. You may go to any of the departments of the government and walk through during business hours, and you will not find one clerk in five who has any business to do except smoke a cigar and enjoy conversation with his friends."

I do not begrudge a person of a good line that gets attention or draws a smile. However, there are several things wrong with the current bashing of the executive by Congress.

Reasons to stop bureaucracy bashing

First, it is not too much of a stretch to say that the bureaucracy as we know it is a creature of Congress. James Q. Wilson notes, "Congress certainly is the architect of the bureaucracy... For Congress to complain of agency red tape is akin to an architect complaining of a home owner who finds it necessary to walk up five flights of steps before he can get from his bedroom to the bathroom" (James Q. Wilson, 1989, pp. 236–237). And so is has ever been. As Francis Rourke recently reminded us in his Gaus address, from the beginning of the Republic, the question of, "Whose bureaucracy is this anyway?" has been answered by declaring the bureaucracy was under the joint custody of the president and the Congress

Find out who Francis Rourke is on www.libraryspot.com, which lists biography websites.

The reinventing government crowd notes that bureaucracy was created to fight the corrupt urban machines of 19th century America, but that it is not useful in dealing with modern problems However, focusing on Wilsonian bureaucracy does not get at the bureaucratic problems against which they rail and it is not appropriate for charting the role of Congress in creating that bureaucracy. It is more useful to think of at least two periods in the development of bureaucratization: the Progressive Period, lasting from the 1890s until the election of Warren Harding in 1902, and the period following 1920 until the present.

A concise statement on how you intend to structure your argument will help you make a clear and forceful case.

The progressive period

The progressive period of bureaucratization emphasized such values as efficiency, professionalization, merit appointment, discretion, and hierarchical accountability. The post-progressive period added to these values which were at times inconsistent with progressive values, including equity, access, and rules to assure procedural due process. Thus laws were passed to enhance veterans' preference in public employment, procedures to be used in cases of discipline and dismissal of federal employees, racial affirmative action goals and protections for genders, protections for those with disabilities, extensive rules to guide the letting of government contracts and making purchases, protections for domestic industries, rights to notification and hearing prior to promulgating administrative rules, freedom of information and rights to privacy, and so on.

COMMENTARY: President Lyndon B. Johnson

Following President John F. Kennedy's assassination on November 22, 1963, Lyndon B. Johnson was sworn in as president of the United States. Johnson believed in the idea of building a "Great Society" in which people would have a better standard of living through better education and health care, among other things. Johnson declared a war on poverty and was a strong advocate of equal rights. He established Medicare, a system of health insurance for the elderly, helped remove impediments to minority groups' voting, and set up two new departments—Housing and Urban Development and Transportation. All in all, President Johnson's policies supported a large and interventionist federal bureaucracy. However, they received a lot of criticism from his opponents, including Ronald Reagan.

American president Lyndon Baines Johnson addresses the nation on his first Thanksgiving TV broadcast from the executive offices of the White House.

For Woodrow Wilson and the Progressives the essence of good administration was giving professionals and managers the discretion to act, then holding them accountable for their choices. In the latter period the emphasis is on prescribing in detail the rules to which public servants must conform in making decisions rather than trusting their professional judgement. Thus a distinguishing characteristic of public administration in this latter period is decision making under-constraints-timidity, rather than decision making reflective of initiative and good judgment as is said to be more characteristic of private sector decision making. The point of all of this is that Congress, to be sure with complicity of the agencies, has been a full and equal participant in the creation of post-progressive bureaucracy. In his study of red tape, Herbert Kaufman noted the origin of rules and regulations [and the pluralistic sources of red tape]:

> The author makes the point that Congress, the leading critic of bureaucracy, helped create it.

The moment a government program for a specified group gets started, legislation and administrative directives and court battles proliferate … Procedures for requesting benefits, for processing such applications, for distributing the benefits, and for settling disputes with applicants over their entitlements must be established … Were we a less differentiated society, the blizzard of official paper might be less severe and the labyrinths of official processes less tortuous. Had we more trust in one another and in our public officers and employees, we would not feel impelled to limit discretion by means of lengthy, minutely detailed directives and prescriptions or to subject private and public actions to check after check. If our policy were less democratic, imperfect though our democracy may be, the government would not respond as readily to the innumerable claims on it for protection and assistance.

Positive change

It is entirely appropriate for Congress to periodically ask, "First, what can government properly and successfully do, [and] secondly, how it can do these proper things with the utmost possible efficiency." However, when it is finally through slashing budgets and cutting red tape … Congress will still need to work with officials of the bureaucracy. A proud and dedicated public service is a national treasure and is indispensible to a viable democratic policy process. So stop bashing the bureaucracy!

> Do you think it is possible to run a modern country without a public service?

Summary

George Roche and Dean Yarwood lay out important arguments for and against the federal bureaucracy. Roche gives powerful expression to the sentiment held widely today that the federal government has gotten so big that it threatens American freedom and prosperity. Roche echoes Ronald Reagan when he writes: "Half a century's experimentation with do-everything government has proven to be a monstrous, heart-breaking mistake. Instead of 'solving' social problems, it has created new and far greater ones." Yarwood strongly objects to this kind of "bureaucracy bashing." His article suggests that we should stop viewing ourselves as the helpless victims of a system that was created, after all, to address legitimate public policy concerns, such as racial and sexual discrimination. "A proud and dedicated public service is a national treasure," Yarwood concludes, "and is indispensable to a viable democratic policy process."

FURTHER INFORMATION:

 Books:

Parkinson, C. Northcote, *Parkinson's Law*. Boston: Houghton Mifflin, 1957.

Roche, George, *America by the Throat: The Stranglehold of Federal Bureaucracy*. Old Greenwich, CT: Devin-Adair Publishers, 1983.

Rourke, Francis E., *Bureaucracy, Politics, and Public Policy*. Boston: Little, Brown, 1984.

Wilson, James Q., and John J. Dilulio, Jr., *American Government*. 6th edition. Chapter 13. Lexington, MA: D.C. Heath and Co., 1995.

Wilson, James Q., *Bureaucracy: What Government Agencies Do and Why They Do It*. New York: Basic Books, 1989.

 Articles:

DeMuth, Christopher C., "Why the Era of Big Government Isn't Over."*Commentary*, April 2000, pp.23–29.

 Useful websites:

www.libraryspot.com
Useful reference site, includes biography sites, dictionaries, quotations, etc.
www. bioguide.Congress.gov
Biographical dictionary of U.S. Congress.

www.gi.grolier/com/presidents/ea/bios
The American Presidency site of *Encyclopedia Americana*.
www.politicalgraveyard.com
Site that lists of burial places of U.S. politicians, also supplies useful birth/death dates and biographies.
www.reagan.utexas.edu/ref/rrpres.htm
Analysis of the Reagan administration.
www.whitehouse.gov
The White House site.

The following debates in the Pro/Con series may also be of interest:

In this volume:

 Part I: Democracy and
Part II: U.S. Government.

 Research Skills,
pages 58–59.

IS THE FEDERAL BUREAUCRACY TOO BIG?

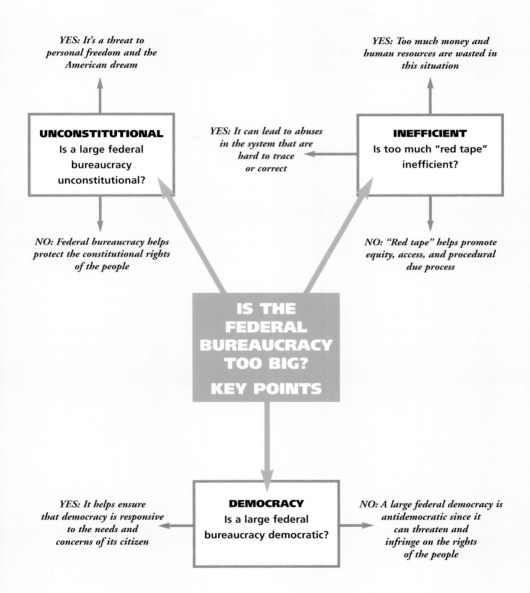

YES: It's a threat to personal freedom and the American dream

YES: Too much money and human resources are wasted in this situation

UNCONSTITUTIONAL
Is a large federal bureaucracy unconstitutional?

YES: It can lead to abuses in the system that are hard to trace or correct

INEFFICIENT
Is too much "red tape" inefficient?

NO: Federal bureaucracy helps protect the constitutional rights of the people

NO: "Red tape" helps promote equity, access, and procedural due process

IS THE FEDERAL BUREAUCRACY TOO BIG?
KEY POINTS

YES: It helps ensure that democracy is responsive to the needs and concerns of its citizen

DEMOCRACY
Is a large federal bureaucracy democratic?

NO: A large federal democracy is antidemocratic since it can threaten and infringe on the rights of the people

Topic 6
SHOULD MORE POWER BE GIVEN TO STATE GOVERNMENTS?

YES
"MADISON AND MODERN FEDERALISM"
FROM *HOW FEDERAL IS THE CONSTITUTION?*
JEAN YARBROUGH

NO
"THE IDEA OF THE NATION"
FROM *HOW FEDERAL IS THE CONSTITUTION?*
SAMUEL H. BEER

INTRODUCTION

One of the most enduring controversies in the political history of the United States concerns the relationship between the states and the national government. Should the "union" of the states enhance the power of the national government at the expense of states' rights and state powers? Or should the states retain significant rights and powers, thus weakening the national government?

The question goes to the heart of the intentions of the Framers of the Constitution and has been repeated at various stages throughout the history of the republic. In 1829 a famous exchange of toasts captured the fundamental issue at stake in the controversy. President Andrew Jackson and Vice President John Calhoun disagreed on the question of states' rights, particularly on the power of states to nullify or ignore certain national laws because they intruded on powers properly belonging to the states. Jackson was an advocate of national power and was an opponent of nullification; Calhoun was an advocate of greater states' rights, including the power to nullify national laws. Jackson embarrassed his opponents at a dinner they arranged by suggesting that they sought to destroy the Union. He said: "Our Union: It must be preserved." To which Calhoun quickly responded: "The Union: Next to our liberty, the most dear."

Is the Union a threat to our liberties or its greatest guarantor? Are the liberties of citizens most secure where the power of the states is greater, or where it is weaker? These issues divided Jackson and Calhoun in 1829, and they have been the source of much discussion ever since then.

At the time of the framing of the United States Constitution in 1787 the question of the relative power of the states and the national government was a subject of great debate. The

Constitution itself was a compromise between those who wanted to protect existing state powers under the Articles of Confederation and those who advocated a radical shift of power toward the national government. As part of this the states retained equal membership in the Senate. Every state has two senators, and this preserves the balance of power since small states have greater powers to defend themselves in the Senate than their population would otherwise allow. On the other hand, seats in the House of Representatives are apportioned to the various states by population, which has the effect of weakening those states that oppose the national consensus of most citizens around the nation.

"All government ... is founded on compromise and barter."

—EDMUND BURKE,

STATESMAN AND PHILOSOPHER

Similarly, the Constitution establishes a national government that has limited powers delegated to it by the people and the states. This has the effect of limiting the power of the national government to intrude on powers traditionally belong to the states (for example, the power to regulate education or to provide for prosecution under criminal laws).

However, the power to decide how far those limited powers extend is assigned by the Constitution to the national government, and especially to the Supreme Court, which has the effect of ensuring that the national government will usually be able to prevail in disputes with the states. In this respect the Constitution was a compromise in 1787 between advocates of strong national government and advocates of strong state governments. As *The Federalist* put it, the "federal system in America" provides a "double security ... to the rights of the people. The different governments will control each other."

The political history of the U.S. is the story of the gradual but almost uninterrupted ascendance of the nationalist party over the party of states' rights. Today the balance between national and state governments is more favorable to the national government than it was in 1787. Perhaps the most important reason for this development is that government was compelled to intrude on the traditional powers of states in order to defeat the evil of slavery (in the 19th century) and to promote civil rights (in the 20th century).

Today people wonder whether the increasingly unlimited power of the national government is not in itself a threat to civil liberties. They argue, if more power goes to Washington, it will be more difficult for citizens to govern themselves in their local communities where they best understand their own problems. They may in turn be overlooked by an overly busy national government. Since democracy is likely to be most fully achieved in small communities, some fear that the rise of the national government at the expense of the states will also weaken democracy in America.

The following two extracts by Jean Yarbrough and Samuel H. Beer put this debate in context.

MADISON AND MODERN FEDERALISM
Jean Yarbrough

 Are there any advantages to be gained from a renewed respect for the federal principle?

Arguments for federalism

Listing your points clearly will help you structure your argument.

Let us consider briefly the three arguments made on behalf of federalism. First, throughout most of its history, federalism has been important for its role in promoting civic virtue. According to the republican tradition, which stretched from ancient Greece and Rome through the Renaissance republics to the 17th-century English commonwealth and up to America in 1776, the primary purpose of federalism was to secure the advantages of a small republic while providing for defense through confederal association. It was thought that republican governments had to remain small in order to secure civic virtue. By civic virtue was meant a willingness to sacrifice private interests for the sake of the common good. This individual dedication to the whole was achieved in part through the active participation of the citizens in public affairs; direct democracy taught them to care for what they held in common. Federalism made direct democracy possible by allowing the republic to remain small; consequently, federalism was essential to the republic because it promoted civic virtue.

Is "civic virtue" still a valid criterion for judging society, or do you think it is out of date?

James Madison and the Framers

This aspect of the republican tradition [James] Madison and the [F]ramers of the Constitution consistently and emphatically rejected.

Indeed Madison's defense of the American republic in *Federalist 10* rested upon precisely the opposite assumption: it was not smallness but largeness that would rescue republican government, and it would do so by substituting representation for direct participation.

As Madison explained in *Federalist 63*, "The true distinction between … [the ancient republics] and the American governments lies in the total exclusion of the people in their collective capacity from any share in … their government." He then adds: "This distinction however qualified must be admitted to leave a most advantageous superiority in favor of the United States. But to ensure to this advantage its full effect, we must be careful not to separate it from the other advantage, of an extensive territory. For it cannot be believed that any form of representative government could have succeeded within the narrow limits occupied by the democracies of Greece."

The large republic, based on representation and modern federalism, may be superior to the small republic, but not because it promotes civic virtue in the traditional sense. Although modern federalism does bring the government "closer" to the people (and thus encourages civic virtue in a looser sense), it does not provide the citizens with an active and continuing opportunity to participate in public affairs. Direct democracy is no more possible at the state level than it is at the national level.

Is this true? See Topic 10 on the use of ballot initiatives, such as referenda.

Local government

The one place where direct democracy is possible in the extended republic is in the localities. Local governments have always been schools for civic virtue. By providing ordinary citizens with the opportunity to share in the activities of the republic within their competence, these political associations mitigate the worst effects of liberal individualism. Moreover, these self-governing communities put teeth into the claim that the people are the source of all political power, for alone among the institutions of the republic they allow men and women to exercise political power and responsibility jointly with their fellow citizens. But the federal system extends only to the constitutional division of sovereignty between the states and the national government; it does not include the localities, which are legally "creatures of the states." Consequently, federalism promotes civic virtue in this sense only indirectly, by further decentralizing political power to the localities. Moreover since the localities have no constitutional power to resist state encroachments, even the indirect role of federalism in promoting civic virtue is problematic.

Yarbrough argues that true democracy exists only at a level beneath that of the state. Do you agree?

Federalism as embodied in the American Constitution cannot, then, be understood primarily within the framework of the classical republican tradition, though it continues to promote such ends in an attenuated way. Rather, modern federalism must be judged by its role in preserving the liberal republic, with its commitment to the protection of individual liberty through largeness and diversity. In other words, modern federalism must be judged by how well it promotes pluralism on the one hand and liberty on the other.

COMMENTARY: *The Federalist*

The Federalist papers were published in several New York state newspapers between October 1787 and August 1788. They aimed to persuade New York voters to ratify the Constitution. James Madison (see box, page 106) and Alexander Hamilton (see page 81), with help from John Jay, were the authors of 85 essays written to explain and defend the Constitution. They combined insights into human nature and clear explanations of the ways in which the proposed government would operate, and they attacked the Articles of Confederation. Although the authorship of some of the articles is in dispute since they were all signed "Publius," James Madison is generally thought to have contributed 28 articles, Alexander Hamilton the majority at 52, and John Jay the remaining five. Although there were additional pro-federalist commentaries published at the time, *The Federalist* papers are the most articulate and coherent. Today they remain one of the best primary sources on political theory for this period. They are available online. See page 84, Useful websites.

James Madison, fourth president of the United States, from an 1828 painting by Gilbert Stuart (1755–1828).

Modern federalism strengthens diversity, by providing the different cultures generated in the large republic with the political power to preserve their social, moral, and political differences. It is federalism that makes possible the astounding diversity of state laws on gambling, drinking, marriage, the family, divorce, education, and criminal law, to name some of the more important areas reserved to the states. Thus, federalism permits Nevada's liberal laws on gambling, drinking, and divorce to coexist with the stricter views of neighboring Utah, without offending the dominant culture of either [one].

What reasons might lead to neighboring states having different laws? Is this a good thing?

Public policy
Closely related to the role of federalism in preserving our national diversity is the opportunity it affords the states to experiment in public policy, thereby confining the damage if unsuccessful, and serving as a model if successful. This experimentation does not preclude some degree of federal oversight to ensure that the constitutional rights of individuals are not violated, but it does require the national government to respect the heterogeneity and experimentation generated by the federal principle as essential elements of preserving the extended republic.

Should successful policy initiatives in states be adopted by the national government?

Federalism and republican government
Finally, and most important, modern federalism is necessary for republican government because it helps prevent the concentration of political power in the national government. For, to a much greater degree than Madison recognized when he warned against the dangers of consolidation, the nationalization of public policy has shifted political power from elected representatives in Congress to an unelected bureaucracy within the executive and to the courts.

Yarbrough's final argument is a traditional one: That it is vital to avoid creating an overly strong central government.

This is because "it is hard for Congress, owing to its clumsy and complex procedures, to control implementation of legislation by the executive, and it is impossible for Congress to control the interpretation by the judiciary of that implementation." Consequently, we have national policy increasingly made by unelected officials, often against the wishes of the majority. Seen in this light, the rediscovery of the federal principle (though not necessarily in the form of the New Federalism) is long overdue. Federalism, to be sure, does not guarantee the protection of individual rights. Those who oppose federalism because they fear a majority tyranny in the states, however, are advised to consider that a national tyranny is also possible—and more dangerous.

THE IDEA OF THE NATION
Samuel H. Beer

President Reagan was antifederal bureaucracy. See page 66.

NO

I have a difference of opinion with President Reagan.

We have all heard of the president's new federalism and his proposals to cut back on the activities of the federal government by reducing or eliminating certain programs and transferring others to the states. He wishes to do this because he finds these activities to be inefficient and wasteful. He also claims that they are improper under the U.S. Constitution—not in the sense that the courts have found them to violate our fundamental law, but in the larger philosophical and historical sense that the present distribution of power between levels of government offends against the true meaning and intent of that document.

The author quotes from Reagan's inaugural address and then uses academic sources to discredit Reagan's statement about federal government. This is a useful device to give your argument credibility.

Reagan and the Constitution

In justification of this conclusion, he has relied upon a certain view of the founding of the republic. In his inaugural address he summarized its essentials when he said: "The federal government did not create the states; the states created the federal government."

This allegation of historical fact did not pass without comment. Richard Morris of Columbia took issue with the president, called his view of the historical facts, "[a] hoary myth about the origin of the Union," and went on to summarize the evidence showing that "the United States was created by the people in collectivity, not by the individual states."

No less bluntly, Henry Steele Commager of Amherst said the president did not understand the Constitution, which in its own words asserts that it was ordained by: "We, the People of the United States," not by the states severally.

We may smile at this exchange between the president and the professors. They are talking about something that happened a long time ago. To be sure, the conflict of ideas between them did inform the most serious crisis of our first century—the grim struggle that culminated in the Civil War. In that conflict, President Reagan's view—the compact theory of the Constitution—was championed by Jefferson Davis, the president of the seceding South. The first Republican president of the United States, on the other hand,

COMMENTARY: Alexander Hamilton

"Those who stand for nothing fall for anything."
—ALEXANDER HAMILTON

Alexander Hamilton (1755–1804) was born in the British West Indies. He was only 45 years old when he died, but he managed to accomplish a great deal in his short life. He fought tirelessly for ratification of the Constitution and played a vital role in defining governmental processes for managing the national economy. Yet Hamilton, unlike Jefferson or Lincoln, does not immediately spring to mind as one of the men key to the shaping of the United States' Constitution, even though he drafted the call for a constitutional convention and strongly believed that the United States would be a global power stabilized by capitalism.

Federalist

From 1782–1783 Hamilton served as a member of the Continental Congress. He also served in the New York Legislature and went to the Philadelphia Convention in 1787, which studied and adopted the Constitution on September 2, 1789. He produced a series of articles with John Jay and James Madison called *The Federalist* (see page 78), which aimed to explain and defend the Constitution. It is for this and his role as the first Secretary of the Treasury under President Washington that Hamilton is best remembered. Hamilton believed in the importance of an energetic federal government. This government would, he believed, assume responsibility for the country's debts, standardize and control the country's currency through a national bank, encourage domestic manufacturing, and maintain a good relationship with Britain. He believed in a centralized economy—and his ideas have provided the basis for the financial system still in existence in the United States today.

Financial concerns

Hamilton's financial program was innovative and carefully planned, and yet it received plenty of criticism from his peers, including Jefferson and Madison. On January 14, 1790, Hamilton published a "Report on the Public Credit." His financial proposals provided for domestic and foreign debts and strongly recommended the assumption of the states' debts by the federal government.

Hamilton also advocated import and export duties to raise revenues. His ideas were met with staunch resistance, particularly by the Republicans. But Hamilton did not even try to appease his opponents. On July 11, 1804, he was fatally injured in a duel. He died the following day.

espoused the national theory of the Constitution. "The Union," said Abraham Lincoln, "is older than any of the states and, in fact, it created them as States … The Union and not the states separately produced their independence and their liberty … The Union gave each of them whatever of independence and liberty it has."

The author uses this quote by Abraham Lincoln to argue that ultimate power lies in the United States.

The national idea of authority

As stated by President Lincoln, the national idea is a theory that ultimate authority lies in the United States. It identifies the whole people of the nation as the source of the legitimate power of both the federal government and the state governments. The national idea, however, is not only a theory of authority but also a theory of purpose, a perspective on public policy, a guide to the ends for which power should be used. It invites us to ask ourselves what sort of a people we are, and whether we are a people, and what we wish to make of ourselves as a people. In this sense the national idea is as alive and contentious today as it was when Alexander Hamilton set the course of the first administration of George Washington.

See page 81 for more information on Alexander Hamilton.

Hamilton and government

Like the other Founders, Hamilton sought to establish a regime of republican liberty, that is, a system of government which would protect the individual's rights of person and property and which would be founded upon the consent of the governed. He was by no means satisfied with the legal framework produced by the Philadelphia convention. Fearing the states, he would have preferred a much stronger central authority, and, distrusting the common people, he would have set a greater distance between them and the exercise of power. He was less concerned, however, with the legal framework than with the use that would be made of it. He saw in the Constitution not only a regime of liberty but also, and especially, the promise of nationhood.

The author uses Hamilton and Jefferson to argue that a strong centralized government is important.

Hamilton's nationalism did not consist solely in his belief that the Americans were "one people" rather than thirteen separate peoples. The father of the compact theory himself, Thomas Jefferson, at times shared that opinion, to which he gave expression in the Declaration of Independence. The contrast with Jefferson lay in Hamilton's activism, his belief that this American people must make vigorous use of its central government for the task of nation building. The Founders confronted the task of founding a nation-state. Our present exercise in nation building is no less challenging. What we are attempting has never before been attempted by any country at any time. It is to create within a liberal, democratic framework a society in which vast numbers of both black and white people live in free and equal intercourse—political, economic, and social. It is a unique, a stupendous, demand, but the national idea will let us be satisfied with nothing less.

The federal system that confronts Ronald Reagan is the outcome of these three great waves of centralization: the Lincolnian, the Rooseveltian, and the Johnsonian. By means of his new federalism President Reagan seeks radically to decentralize that system. Does the history of the national idea in American politics suggest any criticism or guidance?

By drawing on three great presidents—Lincoln, F.D. Roosevelt, and L.B. Johnson—the author adds weight to his argument that centralization is better for the United States than federalism.

Rhetoric is important. Words are the means through which politicians reach the motivations of voters and by which leaders may shape those motivations. Both the compact theory and the national theory touch nerves of the body politic. Each conveys a very different sense of nationhood— or the lack thereof. My theme has been the national theory, which envisions one people, at once sovereign and subject, source of authority and substance of history, asserting, through conflict and in diversity, our unity of origin and of destiny. Such an image does not yield a rule for allocating functions between levels of government. That is for practical men, assisted no doubt by the policy sciences. But the imagery of the national idea can prepare the minds of practical men to recognize in the facts of our time the call for renewed effort to consolidate the union. The vice of the compact theory is that it obscures this issue, diverts attention from the facts, and muffles the call for action.

The situation today

Today this issue is real. A destructive pluralism—sectional, economic, and ethnic—disrupts our common life. It is foolish to use the rhetoric of political discourse to divert attention from that fact. I would ask the new federalists not only to give up their diversionary rhetoric, but positively to advocate the national idea. This does not mean they must give up federal reform. A nationalist need not always be a centralizer. For philosophical and for pragmatic reasons he may prefer a less active federal government.

Is it true that states' rights are a threat to the statutes of the United States as a single nation and of its citizens as a single people?

The important thing is to keep alive in our speech and our intentions the move toward the consolidation of the union. People will differ on what and how much needs to be done. The common goal should not be denied.

Summary

Jean Yarbrough argues that "modern federalism must be judged by how well it promotes pluralism on the one hand and liberty on the other." Federalism—greater states' rights—can serve pluralism by making possible the "astounding diversity of state laws on gambling, drinking, marriage, the family, divorce, education, and criminal law." Nevada and Utah can exist side by side without either "offending the dominant culture" of the other. Perhaps more important, federalism can help prevent the concentration of too much power in the national government, which is increasingly government by an unelected bureaucracy. In this way federalism helps preserve the liberties of citizens. "Those who oppose federalism because they fear a majority tyranny in the states," she argues, should remember that "a national tyranny is also possible—and more dangerous." Samuel Beer argues that the Founders and their greatest successors—Abraham Lincoln, Franklin Roosevelt—established what he calls "the national idea." The national idea is above all the idea that we are one people, united by a shared aspiration to build a new nation: "It invites us to ask ourselves what sort of a people we are ... and what we wish to make of ourselves as a people." After two centuries we still face this task of nation building—"What we are attempting has never before been attempted by any country at any time"—to establish a multiracial liberal democracy, in which equality and freedom are achieved for all citizens. That "stupendous" aspiration can be achieved by one people, united and acting together toward a common purpose.

FURTHER INFORMATION:

Books:

Beer, Samuel, *To Make a Nation: The Rediscovery of American Federalism*. Cambridge, MA: Harvard University Press, 1988.

Diamond, Martin, *As Far as Republican Principles Will Admit: Essays by Martin Diamond*. Washington, D.C.: American Enterprise Institute, 1992.

Goldwin, Robert A., and William A. Schambra, *How Federal Is the Constitution?* Washington, D.C.: American Enterprise Institute, 1987.

Grodzins, Morton, *The American System*. Chicago: Rand McNally, 1966.

Useful websites:

www.mcs.net/~knautzr/fed/madison/htm
The Federalist online.
www.xroads.virginia.edu/~CAP/ham/hamintro.html
Detailed site on Alexander Hamilton.

The following debates in the Pro/Con series may also be of interest:

In this volume:

Topic 7 Does the two-party system adequately represent the people?

Topic 5 Is the federal bureaucracy too big?

Topic 8 Does the separation of powers produce ineffective government?

SHOULD MORE POWER BE GIVEN TO STATE GOVERNMENTS?

YES: Individual rights will be overlooked by bureaucrats who have no interest in the liberty of individual groups or local communities

YES: Since it might just result in national tyranny of the people

YES: It allows states to have very different customs and laws from one another without upsetting each other

LIBERTY
Will a powerful centralized government threaten the liberty of its citizens?

DIVERSITY
Does federalism preserve diversity?

NO: A strong central government is the only way to protect the rights and freedom of the people it serves

NO: Federalism allows individual states to impose their own codes of conduct and views on education and religion, for example

SHOULD MORE POWER BE GIVEN TO STATE GOVERNMENTS?
KEY POINTS

YES: A strong centralized government helps cement the idea of a multicultural democratic society

UNITY AND EQUALITY
Can a strong national government promote a united and multicultural society?

NO: The individual's rights and cultural diversity will be sacrificed to achieve this end

Topic 7
DOES THE TWO-PARTY SYSTEM ADEQUATELY REPRESENT THE PEOPLE?

YES

"IN DEFENSE OF THE AMERICAN PARTY SYSTEM"
FROM *POLITICAL PARTIES IN THE EIGHTIES*
EDWARD C. BANFIELD

NO

"THE POLITICS OF AMERICAN DISCONTENT"
FROM *THE POLITICS OF AMERICAN DISCONTENT: HOW A NEW PARTY CAN MAKE DEMOCRACY WORK*
GORDON S. BLACK

INTRODUCTION

It is quite unusual for a nation as large and culturally diverse as the United States to have only a two-party system. Throughout Europe democratic political systems are structured in such a way that it is normal for more than two parties to have a chance of winning an election. In the United States, however, a two-party system is very much the norm and has been since around 1800. The main reason for that can be found in its history, which is rooted within the opposition of the Federalists and Non-Federalists. Although there are other "third-party" political parties, for the most part populist parties, they exist as a voice for minority or ethnic groups and do not command a significant percentage of the vote. Therefore perhaps of greatest importance today is the two parties' gift of self-perpetuation.

To a certain extent the issue of political identity is hereditary. Children learn that their parents are either Democrats or Republicans at an early age, and that has a great influence on their own political views and opinions. Of course, as children mature and develop their own identities, they often clash with those of their parents. In the political sense this often leads to an individual moving across from one party to the other.

The Republican and Democratic parties, while nominally right and left leaning respectively, both contain a variety of opinion. They seem to be more centrally based, and many voters worry that in reality there is little difference between them. While other parties of course exist, the hold that the Republicans and Democrats (see box on page 91) have over the electorate is such that a vote for a "third" party is often considered at best a "protest" vote and at worse merely a "wasted" vote.

A third party is usually composed of dissatisfied groups that feel the need to break away from the major two parties. The Republicans and Democrats can look at third parties to gauge current political thought and feeling, using them as indicators of upcoming important political trends. The main parties can recognize that a segment of the electorate feels disfranchised from the formation of a new party.

Depending on how far removed these third-party views are from the thoughts and feelings already represented by the two major parties, hard-core supporters will decide how much of the third parties' issues are actually given voice.

It is often remarked that third-party groups are needed to act as a kind of safety apparatus, since they give a minority a course of action other than social upheaval or violence. One of the reasons cited when calling for the formation of a third party is that it is sometimes difficult to differentiate between the views or policies of the two major American political parties. This is despite their quite diverse supporters.

Independent voters, it seems, are on the increase as less of the population feels a strong affiliation to either the Republican or Democratic parties.

The closest contender to becoming a legitimate third party in the 2000 elections, for example, was the Green Party, although it still fell far short of both Republican and Democratic levels. It seems that in order for the two-party system to survive, relationships must be strengthened with the voters in order to change them from independent individuals into active party members.

Many Americans now believe that the recognition of a credible third party is needed in order to offer more choice to the electorate and therefore create more competition. It would force the major parties to be more receptive to the opinions of the American people. Others, however, think that the present system works well. So then why attempt to change it?

The following articles defend and attack the two-party system as a fair means of representing the people. Edward C. Banfield lists the criticisms that are commonly raised against the two-party system and then challenges each point. Gordon S. Black, however, argues that not only does the two-party system fail the electorate, but also that a third party that could realistically win a future election is required if democracy itself is not in threat.

COMMENTARY:
Election 2000 presidential candidates

Harry Browne, LIBERTARIAN
Patrick J. Buchanan, REFORM
George W. Bush, REPUBLICAN**
Albert Gore, DEMOCRAT

John Hagelin, NATURAL LAW
David McReynolds, SOCIALIST
Ralph Nader, GREEN
Howard Phillips, CONSTITUTION

**George W. Bush was elected 43rd President of the United States.

IN DEFENSE OF THE AMERICAN PARTY SYSTEM
Edward C. Banfield

Banfield begins his argument by spelling out the criticisms of the U.S. party system and then discussing them.

The American party system has been criticized on four main grounds:

1. the parties do not offer the electorate a choice in terms of fundamental principles; their platforms are very similar and mean next to nothing;

2. they cannot discipline those whom they elect, and therefore they cannot carry their platforms into effect;

3. they are held together and motivated less by political principle than by desire for personal, often material, gain, and by sectional and ethnic loyalties; consequently party politics is personal and parochial; and

4. their structure is such that they cannot correctly represent the opinion of the electorate; in much of the country there is in effect only one party, and everywhere large contributors and special interests exercise undue influence within the party.

These criticisms may be summarized by saying that the structure and operation of the parties do not accord with the theory of democracy or, more precisely, with that theory of it which says that everyone should have a vote, that every vote should be given exactly the same weight, and that the majority should rule.

Everyone has the right to vote, but do certain groups exercise it less than others? If so, why?

Does the two-party system work?

"It is a serious matter," says Maurice Duverger, a French political scientist who considers American party organization "archaic" and "undemocratic," "that the greatest nation in the world, which is assuming responsibilities on a world-wide scale, should be based on a party system entirely directed towards very narrow local horizons."

Using quotes from other sources can lend weight to your argument.

[Duverger] and other critics of the American party system do not, however, base their criticisms on the performance of the American government. They are concerned about procedures, not results. They ask whether the structure and operation of the parties is consistent with the logic of democracy, not whether the party system produces—and maintains—a good society, meaning, among other things, one in which desirable human types flourish, the rights of individuals are respected, and [finally] matters affecting the common good are decided, as nearly as possible, by [the] reasonable discussion [of those involved].

If they were to evaluate the party system on the basis of results, they would have to conclude that on the whole it is a good one. It has played an important part (no one can say how important, of course, for innumerable causal forces have been at work along with it) in the production of a society which, despite all its faults, is as near to being as good one as any and nearer by far than most; it has provided governments which, by the standards appropriate to apply to governments, have been humane and, in some crises, bold and enterprising; it has done relatively little to impede economic growth and in some ways has facilitated it; except for the Civil War, when it was, as Henry Jones Ford said, "the last bond of union to give way," it has tended to check violence, moderate conflict, and narrow the cleavages within the society; it has never produced, or very seriously threatened to produce, either mob rule or tyranny, and it has shown a marvelous ability to adapt to changing circumstances.

Not only has the American party system produced good results, it has produced better ones than have been produced almost anywhere else by other systems. Anyone who reflects on recent history must be struck by the following paradox: those party systems that have been most democratic in structure and procedure have proved least able to maintain democracy; those that have been most undemocratic in structure and procedure—conspicuously those of the United States and Britain—have proved to be the bulwarks of democracy and of civilization.

Making parties "responsible"

Some [people] think that the American party system can be reformed without changing its nature essentially. Several years ago, a Committee on Parties of the American Political Science Association proposed making certain "readjustments" in the structure and operation of the party system to eliminate its "defects." [This committee discussed the "effectiveness" of parties entirely in terms of procedure.]

These readjustments, the Committee said, would give the electorate "a proper range of choice between alternatives" in the form of programs to which the parties would be committed and which they would have sufficient internal cohesion to carry into effect. Thus, the two-party system would be made more "responsible."

Banfield's argument is that the system is OK because it works. Is that the only standard that is important, or do principles and procedures matter too?

Henry Jones Ford wrote The Rise and Growth of American Politics, New York. Macmillan, 1900.

Britain is, like America, dominated by two parties—the leftish Labour Party and the rightish Conservative Party.

What this means is unclear. "Responsibility" here seems to be a synonym for accountability, that is the condition of being subject to being called to account and made to take corrective action in response to criticism. In the case of a party, this can mean nothing [other than] going before an electorate, and in this sense all parties are by definition responsible.[As William Graham Sumner remarked,] "A party is an abstraction; it cannot be held responsible or punished; if it is deprived of power it fades into thin air and the men who composed it, especially those who did the mischief and needed discipline, quickly reappear in the new majority."

William Graham Sumner (1840–1910) was an influential sociologist and educator.

Leaving aside both the question of what "responsibility" means when applied to a party and the more important one of whether as a matter of practical politics such "readjustments" could be made, let us consider how the political system [c]ould be affected by the changes proposed.

The issue of "valid choice"

The hope that the two-party system might be made to offer a choice between distinct alternatives is illusory for at least two reasons. [The first] is that a party which does not move to the middle of the road to compete for votes condemns itself to defeat and eventually, if it does not change its ways, to destruction.

But even if this were not the case, the parties could not present the electorate with what reformers think of as "a valid choice." The reason [for this] is that the issues in our national life are such that there does not exist any one grand principle by which the electorate could be divided into two camps such that every voter in each camp would be on the "same" side of all issues.

Should voters expect to support every policy of any political party?

Without a grand principle which will make unities, [or rather] opposed unity of the party programs, the electorate cannot be offered "a valid choice." A choice between two market baskets, each of which contains an assortment of unrelated items, some of which are liked and some of which are disliked, is not a "valid" choice in the same sense that a choice between two market baskets, each of which contains items that "belong together" is a "valid" one.

Comparing political choice to shopping choice is a useful analogy.

In the American party system, most items are logically unrelated. This being so, "valid" choice would become possible only if the number of parties was increased to allow each party to stand for items that were logically related, if one issue became important to the exclusion of all the others, or if, by the elaboration of myth and ideology, pseudo-logical relations were established among items.

COMMENTARY: The two parties

The Democratic Party

The Democratic Party was founded by Thomas Jefferson in 1792. It was established in opposition to the elitist Federalist Party and also to fight for the Bill of Rights. Also known as the "party of the common man," it officially became the Democratic–Republican Party in 1798. Thomas Jefferson became the first Democratic President of the United States in 1800. Jefferson served two terms and was followed by James Madison in 1808. Following the contested election of John Quincy Adams in 1824, the popular Andrew Jackson emerged as national leader. Under his guidance the Democrats developed a national convention process and the party platform. In 1844 the party became simply the Democratic Party. The party embraced immigration, women's suffrage, and the direct election of senators, among other things.

The Democrats have produced several progressive presidents, including Franklin Roosevelt (1933–1945), whose New Deal helped bring the United States out of the Great Depression, John F. Kennedy (1961–1963), and more recently, Bill Clinton (1993–2001).

The Republican Party

Also known as the Grand Old Party (GOP), the Republican Party is the other significant political party in the United States. The earliest meeting of this political group can be traced to October 1853. However, it was at a convention in Jackson, Michigan, in July 1854 that the Republican Party was formally launched.

At the first national convention in 1856 the party held that Congress had the right to abolish slavery in a territory and ought to do so. That was a popularly held view in the North, where the party quickly became the dominant one in the region, a fact proven when Abraham Lincoln, the party's second presidential candidate, became president in 1860. The secession of the Southern states led to a Republican domination of federal government; however, the Civil War weakened Lincoln's popularity.

After his death and the end of the war a long period of Republican domination occurred, which was partly due to the party's support of protective tariffs and big business. Of the 18 presidential elections held from 1860 to 1932, 14 were won by Republican candidates. However, Herbert Hoover's failure to deal adequately with the chaos caused by the Depression gave the Democrats the boost they needed, and the Republicans were kept out of office for the next 20 years.

One of the most famous Republican presidents was Richard M. Nixon (1969–1974), whose name is synonomous with Watergate (see pages 172–173). In 2000 George W. Bush was elected the 43rd U.S. President, following in the footsteps of his father George H. W. Bush (1989–1993).

THE POLITICS OF AMERICAN DISCONTENT
Gordon S. Black

Posing a rhetorical question is a good way to start your argument.

Why do we invest so much hope in the promise of a new party? After all, few political commentators have cast a critical eye on the role of the political parties in the decline of American democracy. Debate about problems instead usually centers either on the responsibility of individual voters and their failure to throw the bums out, or on the pernicious role of organized groups. The media plays a good game of documenting partisan bickering but has been virtually silent on the role of the political parties in the debacle of the budget crisis, for example.

The role of political parties

If the parties have been neglected, this is probably because they have failed to live up to their potential in almost every respect. An examination of the comparison between the theory of the role of parties in a democracy and the reality of the contemporary American two-party system reveals that the two parties are, in fact, the great under-achievers of American politics—so much potential, so little performance. Professor James Sundquist provides a succinct description of the party system as it is supposed to operate:

> *Political parties are formed because groups of people, each sharing a philosophy and a set of goals, desire governmental power in order to carry out their programs. In competition with one another, they present [them] to the people in an open and free election. The party or coalition that wins the support of a majority of the people gains control of the government and enacts its program. The minority party or parties form an opposition, with the power to criticize, debate, and delay but not to block. After a few years, the voters in another election render a verdict on the majority's stewardship. If they approve what has been done, they return the ruling party or coalition to office. If they disapprove, they turn the incumbents out and entrust power to an opposition party or combination of parties. The party is the glue that unites the disparate institutions that make up the government.*

This clearly is not the way our two-party system has been functioning. As 40 years of Democratic domination of the House demonstrates, even if the public at large disapproves of the stewardship of the party in power, changing the leadership is no simple matter. Moreover we have a minority party that often offers only rhetoric as opposed to effective alternatives, largely because it has so little expectation of governing Congress, now or in the foreseeable future.

American political parties have never really fulfilled their ideal role, [however,] the trends of the past 30 years have exacerbated their failings. Prior to the late 1950s the electoral system and the leadership of Congress were responsive to the changing political and economic conditions of the day. After the late 1950s, however, there is little relationship between shifts in public sentiment and the control of Congress. The implication is that no matter how badly Congress performs in the current context, the House as an institution will not suffer serious political consequences from its performance.

Having provided the reader with an ideal definition of the party system, the author uses it to show that theory and practice are very different.

Another party, another option

We believe that the only way to ensure that the broader interests of the public are given priority over the narrow special interests is to create a new party to represent these broader interests and introduce real competition into Congressional races. The only democratic institution capable of fundamentally altering the cost/benefit structure of politics is the political party. The reason [for this] is simple: political parties define the political marketplace; they offer the candidates that voters can choose and they can thereby define the political agenda.

Go to the White House website. Which party had the third largest votes? Do you think it provides a realistic option to the two main parties?

The current condition of the Democrats and Republicans is similar to that of General Motors, Ford, and Chrysler in the mid-1970s. The automobile manufacturers had grown lazy. For half a century, with relatively little foreign competition, they had controlled the domestic market, vastly limiting the choices of the American people. What happened? The Japanese started to export a better product, and each year, a larger and larger percentage of American [people] were buying the better product, despite their loyalty to the American manufacturers.

Do you see parallels between the way big business works and the way government runs?

At the beginning, the American automobile manufacturers ignored the new products streaming in from Japan. They said that the American people wanted big cars—Buicks, Oldsmobiles, and Cadillacs—and the American people didn't care about safety or gas mileage. They were wrong. After a

Republican vice president Richard Nixon and Democratic senator John F. Kennedy take part in a televised debate during their presidential election campaign.

while, they could no longer ignore the imports, which were eating up more market share every day. The Japanese were producing a strikingly better product at a lower price. Next, the automobile companies cried: "Foul!" They said that they were poor, misbegotten victims of unfair trade practices and cheap foreign labor. They wanted higher tariffs in order to artificially and institutionally limit the choices of the American people. However, that plan didn't work either.

In the end, there was no one to blame but themselves. When this realization occurred, a remarkable thing happened—the American automobile manufacturers decided to make better cars. To do so, they completely redesigned their enormous, fat, slow bureaucracies into new, leaner organizations that served the wishes of their customers. And although the story is not over, they are making better cars today and are successfully competing with the Japanese

Black makes a common argument for free capitalism.

on their own terms. While they haven't stemmed the tide, they have certainly made strides in the right direction. In the process, the winner has been the consumer, who has better choices and better prices from all the manufacturers.

What the research in this analysis proposes is that we unleash the same type of competitive forces that caused the revolution in the automobile industry into the political arena. If a new political party can provide a set of proposals more in line with the needs of the voters, the other parties will be forced either to adapt or die.

If the electorate had more political choice, would that limit abuses of power by politicians?

A third party, by this argument, would improve the other two parties.

The reality of a two-party system

The failures of the two-party system have created a chasm in the electorate: a large group of voters distinctly different from partisan Democrats and Republicans. These voters are liberal or moderate on social issues, profoundly conservative on fiscal issues, and disturbed by the loss of their democratic influence. They are committed to the novel idea that the government should be open, fair, honest, accountable, and balance its books. Ideologically, they are the center of American politics. They don't fit in anywhere, and their voting mobility makes them a crucial factor in any statewide or nationwide coalition.

Do low election turnout figures in the United States support this argument?

Every four years, the two major parties scheme and plan how to convince these voters to temporarily enter the party fold. But, once in power, the party officeholders are free to serve the interests of the partisan core that is their political base. The result: the socially moderate, fiscally conservative political reformers are always the bridesmaids and never the brides. They are treated with respect, only to be given a mere taste of what they want. The choice is simple. This group of voters can continue begging for scraps at the existing partisan plate, or they can pursue the option of serving themselves by creating a party that will represent their interests.

Using a familiar phrase can help make a point more memorable.

[T]here [currently] exists a market for a very different type of political party, with a very different message for the American people. If an organization can be created that will provide the right set of proposals and will be free from the demands of special interests, [our] research demonstrates consistently that the voters are ready to buy the new political product.

If this occurs, the other parties will be forced to improve their own product in order to compete. In the process, voters will get real choice and [consequently] our democracy will be strengthened.

Would more political parties really improve voter choice?

Summary

Edward C. Banfield believes in a two-party system but gives voice to the current system's detractors. He views their arguments as flawed because they criticize procedures rather than results. Based on the latter, the two-party system works, resulting in a humane, strong, and adaptive system of government that others have failed to match. In answer to claims that the current system is undemocratic and therefore flawed he states that: "Those party systems that have been most democratic in structure and procedure have been proved least able to maintain democracy" and vice versa. To make the system more "responsible" would deprive it of power, ultimately destroying it. In conclusion Banfield sees the idea of a "valid choice" for voters as an illusion because it is impossible to position all political principles into one camp or another.

Gordon S. Black believes that a third party is needed to represent those voters who have no democratic voice. He sees the two parties at present as underachieving, not only in their promises, but also in their potential. Problems noted include the complicated process of changing the leadership of a party, even if the majority of the public wishes to see such a change. An alternative party would provide representation to "broader interests and introduce real competition into Congressional races."

Without this competition Black believes that the system will stagnate. He sees a gap that needs to be filled if it is not going to grow and engulf the current system, which at present only recognizes these independent voters once every four years.

FURTHER INFORMATION:

Books:

Bobby, John L., and Maisel, L. Sandy, *Two-Parties—Or More?* Cambridge, MA: Westview Press, 1998.
Committee on Political Parties of the American Political Science Association, *Toward a More Responsible Two-Party System.* New York: Rinehart, 1950.
Duverger, Maurice, *Political Parties.* New York: Wiley, 1954.

Useful websites:

www.whitehouse.gov
Official White House site.
www.ipl.org/ref/POTUS
Internet Public Library (IPL)
Good reference site, with a comprehensive
U.S. president guide that includes web links.

The following debates in the Pro/Con series may also be of interest:

In this volume:

Topic 9 Is the president too powerful?

Topic 12 Does the primary system produce the best president?

See *The Watergate Affair,* pages 172–173 and *The Case of President Clinton,* pages 200–201.

DOES THE TWO-PARTY SYSTEM ADEQUATELY REPRESENT THE PEOPLE?

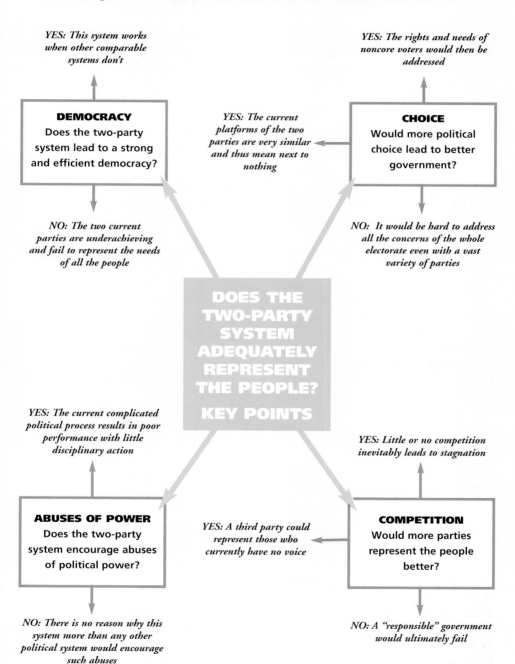

YES: This system works when other comparable systems don't

DEMOCRACY
Does the two-party system lead to a strong and efficient democracy?

NO: The two current parties are underachieving and fail to represent the needs of all the people

YES: The current platforms of the two parties are very similar and thus mean next to nothing

CHOICE
Would more political choice lead to better government?

YES: The rights and needs of noncore voters would then be addressed

NO: It would be hard to address all the concerns of the whole electorate even with a vast variety of parties

DOES THE TWO-PARTY SYSTEM ADEQUATELY REPRESENT THE PEOPLE?
KEY POINTS

YES: The current complicated political process results in poor performance with little disciplinary action

ABUSES OF POWER
Does the two-party system encourage abuses of political power?

NO: There is no reason why this system more than any other political system would encourage such abuses

YES: A third party could represent those who currently have no voice

COMPETITION
Would more parties represent the people better?

YES: Little or no competition inevitably leads to stagnation

NO: A "responsible" government would ultimately fail

Topic 8
DOES THE SEPARATION OF POWERS PRODUCE INEFFECTIVE GOVERNMENT?

YES
"TO FORM A GOVERNMENT"
FROM *SEPARATION OF POWERS: DOES IT STILL WORK?*
LLOYD N. CUTLER

NO
"IN DEFENSE OF SEPARATION OF POWERS"
FROM *SEPARATION OF POWERS: DOES IT STILL WORK?*
JAMES W. CEASER

INTRODUCTION

The single most distinctive feature of the American national government is its separation of powers. The first three articles of the U.S. Constitution vest the national legislative power in Congress, the executive power in the president, and the judicial power in the courts. This system of government contrasts sharply with the more widely favored alternative among democracies in the world today, the parliamentary system. In our presidential (or separation of powers) system the president is elected independently of the legislature; yet in the British parliamentary system of government, for example, the prime minister is chosen by the majority party in parliament and remains in office only with the support of that majority. As a result, the British parliamentary system avoids the problem of divided government—that is, a government in which one party controls the presidency, and a different party controls one or both houses of

Congress. Divided government has been a common feature of American national politics for much of the past half century. This has prompted many to argue that our system of separated powers produces nothing but partisan bickering and policy gridlock.

It is true that the separation of powers does not facilitate easy passage of legislation. But that was the purpose of the Framers of the Constitution, who intentionally designed a system of government to prevent what they most feared, legislative tyranny. As James Madison warned in one of the essays that he wrote in defense of the Constitution, "it is against the enterprising ambition of [the legislative] department that the people ought to indulge all their jealousy and exhaust all their precautions."

The primary way in which the U.S. Constitution, protects against the danger of legislative tyranny is the separation of powers. As a consequence of the separation of powers, laws passed by the legislative branch require the approval of the executive branch before they become effective because the president has the power to veto legislation that he disapproves of. Furthermore, the judicial branch has the power to review and strike down laws that it finds unconstitutional. The power of veto and of judicial review are part of the system of checks and balances that allows each branch to check the powers of the other branches. This results in an "invitation to struggle" among the various branches of government. The question is, did the framers of the Constitution design a system of government that is so divided that it is unable to deal adequately with the problems facing contemporary society?

The following two articles provide starkly different answers to this question. Lloyd Cutler, who was an adviser to President Jimmy Carter, argues that the separation of powers produces policy gridlock. He writes, "The separation of powers between the legislative and executive branches, whatever its merits in 1793, has become a structure that almost guarantees stalemate today." As an example of what he has in mind, Cutler points to the Carter administration's failure to secure the constitutionally required support of two-thirds of the Senate for ratification of an important arms control treaty (SALT II) that it had signed with the Soviet Union. Under the British parliamentary system, Cutler suggests, Carter would not have faced this problem. After all, the prime minister's party always has a majority in parliament (if he or she did not, then someone else would be prime minister). And more importantly, given

that the British prime minister is chosen by parliament itself, he or she is confident that any major piece of legislation submitted to parliament will be approved. The American system's separation of the executive and legislative powers, Cutler argues, makes adoption of the president's legislative program structurally difficult. This problem is compounded when the president's party does not even hold the majority of the seats in the legislature. He therefore calls on Americans to begin thinking about reforming the Constitution from a presidential system to something closer to a parliamentary system, thereby enabling our elected leaders to "'form a government' [that can] propose, legislate, and administer a balanced program for governing."

James Ceaser opposes any such reform of the American system. In identifying a set of criteria for judging the relative merits of a separation of powers system and a parliamentary system, he says that the former is superior. He denies that the U.S. system is not efficient. He concedes that under certain circumstances a parliamentary system has the capacity to adopt quickly a legislative program, but points out that the greater complexity of the U.S. system ensures that the effects of any proposed policy are thoroughly debated before it is adopted.

Ceaser suggests that the U.S. system of government produces wiser public policies. And, he does not agree that the U.S. system is incapable of overcoming policy gridlock. He points to critical elections in the past (1932, 1964, and 1980) that brought into office strong presidents, backed by unified parties, and that resulted in significant changes in the direction of public policy.

TO FORM A GOVERNMENT
Lloyd N. Cutler

YES

Our society was one of the first to write a constitution. This reflected the confident conviction of the Enlightenment that explicit written arrangements could be devised to structure a government that would be neither tyrannical nor impotent in its time and to allow for future amendment as experience and change might require.

We are all children of this faith in a rational written arrangement for governing. Our faith should encourage us to consider changes in our Constitution—for which the Framers explicitly allowed—that would assist us in adjusting to the changes in the world in which the Constitution must function. Yet we tend to resist suggestions that amendments to our existing constitutional framework are needed to govern our portion of the interdependent world society we have become and to cope with the resulting problems that all contemporary governments must resolve.

A system designed for stalemate?

A particular shortcoming in need of a remedy is the structural inability of our government to propose, legislate, and administer a balanced program for governing. In parliamentary terms one might say that under the U.S. Constitution it is not now feasible to "form a government." The separation of powers between the legislative and executive branches, whatever its merits in 1793, has become a structure that almost guarantees stalemate today. As we wonder why we are having such a difficult time making decisions we all know must be made and projecting our power and leadership, we should reflect on whether this is one big reason.

We elect one presidential candidate over another on the basis of our judgment of the overall program he presents, his ability to carry it out, and his capacity to adapt his program to new developments as they arise. We elected President Jimmy Carter, whose program included, as one of its most important elements, the successful completion of the SALT II negotiations that his two predecessors had been conducting since 1972. In June 1979 President Carter did complete and sign a SALT II treaty, which he and his cabinet regarded as very much in the national security interests of the United States. Notwithstanding subsequent events, the president and his cabinet continued to hold that view—indeed they believed the mounting intensity of our confrontation with the Soviet Union made it even more important for the two superpowers to adopt and abide by explicit rules about the size and quality of each side's strategic nuclear arsenal. Because we do not form a government, however, it was not possible for Carter to carry out this part of his program.

Importance of the two-thirds majority

Of course the constitutional requirement of Senate advice and consent to treaties presents a special situation. The case for the two-thirds rule was much stronger [when the Constitution was framed] in 1793, when events abroad rarely affected this isolated continent and when "entangling foreign alliances" were viewed with a skeptical eye. Whether it should be maintained in an age when most treaties deal with such subjects as taxation and trade is open to question. No parliamentary regime anywhere in the world has a similar provision. But in the United States—at least for major issues like SALT—there is merit to the view that treaties should indeed require the careful bipartisan consultation essential to win a two-thirds majority. This is the principle that Woodrow Wilson fatally neglected in 1919. But it has been carefully observed by recent presidents, including President Carter for the Panama Canal treaties and the SALT II treaty. For each of these there was a clear record of support by previous Republican administrations, and there would surely have been enough votes for fairly rapid ratification if the president could have counted on the total or nearly total support of his own party—if, in short, he had truly formed a government, with a legislative majority that took the responsibility for governing.

The U.S. Senate failed to ratify the Versailles Treaty at the end of World War I because President Wilson refused to make the amendments it had requested.

Treaties may indeed present special cases, and I do not argue here for any change in the two-thirds requirement. But our inability to form a government able to ratify SALT II is replicated regularly over the whole range of legislation required to carry out any president's overall program, foreign and domestic. Although the enactment of legislation takes only a simple majority of both houses, that majority is very difficult to achieve. Any part of the president's legislative program may be defeated or amended into an entirely different measure, so that the legislative record of any presidency may bear little resemblance to the overall program the president wanted to carry out. Energy and the budget are two critical examples. Indeed, SALT II itself could have been presented for approval by a simple majority of each house under existing arms control legislation, but the administration deemed this task even more difficult than achieving a two-thirds vote in the Senate. This difficulty is of course compounded when the president's party does not even hold the majority of the seats in both houses, as from 1946 to 1948, from 1954 to 1960, and from 1968 to 1976—or almost half the duration of the seven administrations between 1946 and 1980.

Cutler uses statistical evidence to illustrate how frequently presidents have been left without a majority of seats in both houses.

In such a case the Constitution does not require or even permit the holding of a new election, in which those who oppose the president can seek office to carry out their own program. Indeed, the opponents of the various elements of the president's program usually have a different makeup from one element to another. They would probably be unable to get together on any overall program of their own or to obtain the congressional votes to carry it out. As a result the stalemate continues, and because we do not form a government, we have no overall program at all. We cannot fairly hold the president accountable for the success or failure of his program, because he lacks the constitutional power to put that program into effect.

Advantages of parliamentary system

Cutler compares the U.S. system to the kind of parliamentary system he thinks works better.

Compare this system with the structure of parliamentary governments. A parliamentary government may have no written constitution, as in the United Kingdom. Or it may have a written constitution, as in West Germany, Japan, and Ireland, that in other respects—such as an independent judiciary and an entrenched Bill of Rights—closely resembles our own. Although it may have a ceremonial president or, as in Japan, an emperor, its executive consists of those members of the legislature chosen by the elected legislative majority. The majority elects a premier or prime minister, and he or she selects other leading members of the majority as members of the cabinet. The majority as a whole is responsible for forming and conducting the government. If a key part of its program is rejected by the legislature or if a vote of no confidence is carried, the government must resign, and either a new government must be formed, or a new legislative election must be held. If the program is legislated, the public can judge the result and can decide at the next election whether to reelect the majority or turn it out. At all times the voting public knows who is in charge and whom to hold accountable for success or failure.

Do you think the American public knows who is in charge of the government?

I am not blind to the proven weaknesses of parliamentary government or to the virtues that our forefathers saw in separating the executive from the legislature. In particular, the parliamentary system lacks the ability of a separate and vigilant legislature to investigate and curb the abuse of power by an arbitrary or corrupt executive. Our own recent history has underscored this virtue of separating these two branches.

Moreover, our division of executive from legislative responsibility also means that a great many more voters are represented in positions of power, rather than as mere members of a "loyal opposition." If I am a Democrat in a Republican district, my vote in the presidential election may still give me a proportional effect. If my party elects a president, I do not feel—as almost half the voters in a parliamentary constituency like Oxford must feel—wholly unrepresented. One result of this division is a sort of permanent centrism. While this means that no extreme or Thatcher-like program can be legislated, it also means fewer wild swings in statutory policy.

This is also a virtue of the constitutional division of responsibility. It is perhaps what John Adams had in mind when, at the end of his life, he wrote to his old friend and adversary Thomas Jefferson that "checks and ballances, Jefferson … are our only Security, for the progress of Mind, as well as the Security of Body."

These virtues of separation are not without their costs. I believe that the costs have been mounting in the past half-century and that it is time to examine whether we can reduce the costs of separation without losing its virtues.

President Richard Nixon (1969–1974) was found guilty of such an abuse of power. See The Watergate Affair *(pages 172–173) and the box on* Independent Counsel *on page 205.*

British prime minister Margaret Thatcher passed a controversial program of legislation while in office (1979–1989).

John Adams (1767–1848) was sixth U.S. president, and Thomas Jefferson (1743–1826) was third U.S. president.

IN DEFENSE OF SEPARATION OF POWERS
James W. Ceaser

NO

English philosopher John Locke (1632–1704) influenced theories of liberal democracy.

The French changed from a parliamentary system to a more presidential one.

Only once in recent history has a major democratic regime changed its basic institutional structure with the clear aim of remaining a democracy. That change occurred in France in 1958, when Parliament could not form an effective government in the face of the Algerian crisis and the imminent threat of a military coup. While Parliament fiddled, Paris nearly burned. France had lost the sine qua non of any functioning government: the power—let us call it, with John Locke, the "executive power"—to act with energy and discretion to save the nation from conquest or disintegration.

To remedy this fatal flaw, the founders of the 5th French Republic, drawing heavily on the American presidential model of government, instituted a unitary and independent executive elected outside Parliament and endowed by the constitution with a broad grant of power. The new office was designed to ensure that there would always be a force to act for the state, even in the event of a stalemate among the political parties on the normal policies of governing. The nation's heart would never cease to beat.

"It is with infinite caution that any man ought to venture upon pulling down an edifice which has answered in any tolerable degree for ages the common purposes of society."
—EDMUND BURKE, STATESMAN AND PHILOSOPHER

Today in the United States several prominent persons are urging the American people to undertake a similar act of constitution making. Oddly enough, however, while many in this group proclaim their desire to strengthen the executive office, they are recommending the opposite course from that taken in France in 1958; they are calling for a change from a presidential (or separation of powers) system to something akin to a parliamentary system. They propose this change not because the United States faces an immediate crisis but because the government does not function as well as it might—because, in Lloyd Cutler's words (see pages 100–103), we are unable to "'form a Government' [that can] propose, legislate, and administer a balanced program for governing."

Although members of this group acknowledge possible risks in changing institutions, they can scarcely be accused of operating with a sense of the fragility or precariousness of constitutional forms. Self-proclaimed "children of the Enlightenment," they judge political life not from the somber perspective of what can go wrong but from the sunny perspective of what can be improved.

Criteria for judging

Let us look briefly at the criteria for judging [these two systems of government.]

Security No democratic system better meets the objective of security than the separation of powers system, for it ensures, no matter what else happens, the integrity of the essential executive power.

Liberty The debate between separation of powers and its critics has been as much about what liberty means as about how it can be obtained. The critics have taken the view that liberty is threatened more by society than by government, while some, but not all, defenders have taken the opposite position. This debate has now been overtaken by historical developments: we now have a welfare state that was built under a separation of powers system. Given the existence of liberty in systems that do not have a separation of powers system in the precise form in which it is found in America, it would clearly be foolish to assert that separation of the executive and the legislative powers is essential for the preservation of liberty. That is not to say, however, that it is not helpful as an additional check; and it may be precisely in welfare state systems, where political control is already so great, that this additional check is most needed.

Accountability Critics claim that a parliamentary system provides greater democratic accountability because of the concentration of power. Yet this accountability can be fictitious where the government rests on a party having the support of less than a majority. Furthermore, except in the

Ceaser lists the criteria for judging the two systems. He clearly spells out each argument in favor of the separation of powers. It often helps to arrange an argument in a series of shorter points.

rare cases in which governments in stable parliamentary systems fall, the voters may be compelled to live with government "mandates" for a period of up to five years. In the United States, by contrast, although the president holds his term for four years, a new sounding is taken every two years, and a president can lose influence in policy matters if his party suffers a severe setback in the midterm election.

Satisfaction of ambition   A political system is more than a cold mechanism that processes inputs and outputs. It is made up of live human beings, some of whom seek the honor and recognition of being able to serve as powerful political figures. Under a parliamentary system power is held by a

COMMENTARY: James Madison

James Madison (1751–1836) is the Founder most often credited with including the separation of powers in the American Constitution. He once said of the doctrine, "No political truth is certainly of greater intrinsic value."

Born in 1751, Madison was brought up in Orange County, Virginia, and he studied history, government, and law at the College of New Jersey (later Princeton). On his return to Virginia in 1774 Madison became involved in state government. In 1776 he participated in the framing of the Virginia Constitution and became a leader in the Virginia Assembly. Madison was a primary figure at the Constitutional Convention of 1787. He stressed the need for strong central government and was instrumental in later adding the Bill of Rights. His significant contributions led to him being called "the Father of the Constitution," although he protested that the document was "the work of many heads and many hands."

Although Madison initially aligned himself with the Federalists Alexander Hamilton and John Jay, he later moved to the Republican side. He served as President Jefferson's Secretary of State (1801–1809) and was elected in 1809, at the age of 58, the fourth president of the United States. During his administration the country was led inexorably to war with Britain in 1812. The young nation was not ready for war and was especially humiliated by the British entering Washington and setting fire to the White House and Capitol buildings. However, several notable victories such as General Andrew Jackson's triumph at New Orleans led to an increase in nationalism, and Madison left office in 1817 still enjoying popularity. From his retirement in Orange County Madison spoke out against the forces that threatened to shatter the Federal Union. On his death in 1836 a note left by him was found. It said: "The advice nearest to my heart and deepest in my convictions is that the Union of the States be cherished and perpetuated."

relatively small number of officials. In the United States, by contrast, the existence of an independent legislature provides an institution that can satisfy the desire for political honor for a much larger number of people. The United States is the world's second largest democracy, and the number of people yearning for a place in the sun is accordingly much greater than in Britain, France, or Denmark.

The separation of powers system might not be as efficient at putting a program into action, but it does allow for decision making based on the fullest information. Is this a worthwhile trade-off?

Efficiency Efficiency consists of at least two elements: (1) the capacity to act energetically to put a program into effect; and (2) the ability to make decisions with as much relevant information at hand as possible. A parliamentary system (under certain circumstances) certainly possesses greater efficiency in the first sense than the American system. In the second sense, however, the opposite may be true. The growth of complexity in government in recent years, involving more interests and trade-offs in most decisions, has been such that the relevant information may not be discernible by someone "studying the facts" from on high. On the contrary, it may be that the information relevant to making decisions can best become known under a system of multiple checks that allows the effects of any proposed policy to be gauged in an intensely political process. The greater complexity in governing today seems to cut both ways: it creates a need for both more and less hierarchy, and it is by no means clear that the separation of powers system is, on balance, less efficient than a parliamentary system.

Capacity for change Every system must have a capacity to avoid deadlock. Although this capacity may be less important in policy matters than in crises, stalemate in the policy process can have harmful consequences that can lead to crises. A political system that responds too quickly to proposed changes or initiates changes when they are unnecessary can itself become the source of problems.

The separation of powers system, as modified by the advent of political parties, has enabled strong presidents, backed by coherent parties and impressive electoral mandates, to institute relatively coherent changes in the direction of public policy. That happened after the elections of 1932, 1964, and 1980, as well as after some of the realigning elections in the 19th century. The critics of separation of powers, it would seem, have overlooked the phenomenon of critical elections and realignments as not only instances of electoral change but also mechanisms to effect minirevolutions in the direction of public policy.

Summary

The articles by Lloyd N. Cutler and James W. Ceaser present two very opposing answers to the question about the effectiveness of the separation of powers.

In Cutler's view contemporary America faces a number of significant domestic and foreign policy challenges that require national attention. Unfortunately, the separation of powers makes it quite difficult for the federal government to meet these challenges. According to Cutler, the separation of powers "almost guarantees stalemate today." He therefore advocates reducing the separation of powers and moving in the direction of a parliamentary system so as to sidestep the problem of gridlock.

Ceaser concedes that the American system of separated powers and checks and balances is complex, but he denies that it is ineffective. The greater complexity in the American system of government, he argues, may make quick and easy adoption of policies more difficult, but it does not make American government inert or ineffectual.

Ceaser draws our attention to significant policy initiatives undertaken by U.S. governments to deal with issues like the Great Depression and civil rights as evidence that the current system of government is fully capable of meeting the challenges that are faced in contemporary American society.

FURTHER INFORMATION:

 Books:

Fisher, Louis, *The Constitution between Friends: Congress, the President, and the Law*. New York: St. Martin's Press, 1978.

Goldwin, Robert, and Art Kaufman (editors), *Separation of Powers: Does It Still Work?*. Washington, D.C.: American Enterprise Institute, 1986.

Vile, M.J.C., *Constitutionalism and the Separation of Powers*. Oxford: Oxford University Press, 1967.

 Articles:

Diamond, Martin, "The Separation of Powers and the Mixed Regime," *Publius: The Journal of Federalism* 8: 3.

 Useful websites:

www.parliament.qld.gov.au/education/history/separpow.htm
Provides definition and the origins of the separation doctrine.
www.encarta.msn.com/index/conciseindex/03/00391000.htm
For Encarta encyclopedia article on separation of powers.
www.etext.lib.virginia.edu/jefferson/quotations/jeff1050.htm
Jefferson's political views on the separation of powers.

The following debates in the Pro/Con series may also be of interest:

In this volume:

 Topic 6 Should more power be given to state governments?
Topic 7 Does the two-party system adequately represent the people?
Topic 9 Is the president too powerful?

DOES THE SEPARATION OF POWERS PRODUCE INEFFECTIVE GOVERNMENT?

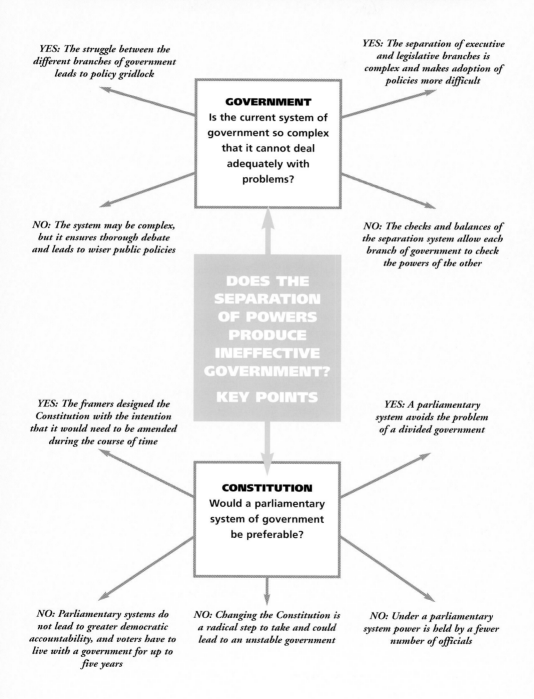

YES: The struggle between the different branches of government leads to policy gridlock

YES: The separation of executive and legislative branches is complex and makes adoption of policies more difficult

GOVERNMENT
Is the current system of government so complex that it cannot deal adequately with problems?

NO: The system may be complex, but it ensures thorough debate and leads to wiser public policies

NO: The checks and balances of the separation system allow each branch of government to check the powers of the other

DOES THE SEPARATION OF POWERS PRODUCE INEFFECTIVE GOVERNMENT?

KEY POINTS

YES: The framers designed the Constitution with the intention that it would need to be amended during the course of time

YES: A parliamentary system avoids the problem of a divided government

CONSTITUTION
Would a parliamentary system of government be preferable?

NO: Parliamentary systems do not lead to greater democratic accountability, and voters have to live with a government for up to five years

NO: Changing the Constitution is a radical step to take and could lead to an unstable government

NO: Under a parliamentary system power is held by a fewer number of officials

Topic 9
IS THE PRESIDENT TOO POWERFUL?

YES

"THE RUNAWAY PRESIDENT"

THE ATLANTIC, NOVEMBER 1973, VOL. 232

ARTHUR M. SCHLESINGER

NO

"TALKING ABOUT THE PRESIDENT"

FROM *THE FETTERED PRESIDENCY: LEGAL CONSTRAINTS ON THE EXECUTIVE BRANCH*

SUZANNE GARMENT

INTRODUCTION

Throughout American history few aspects of U.S. constitutional government have sparked as much debate as the issue of presidential power. At the time of the nation's founding, for example, the idea of a single executive (as opposed to an executive council) was one of the most controversial features of the new government. While supporters of the Constitution regarded this aspect of the presidency as essential to the defense of the nation and the execution of the laws, opponents identified it with monarchy—the very thing that the people who had participated in the Revolutionary War had fought against.

Before the Civil War the Democratic Party viewed the presidency as the tribune of the people, while the Whig Party was based on a shared opposition to a strong presidency. By the latter half of the 20th century, however, the presidency could be described as the most powerful political office in the world. This inevitably led to a new debate among the American people about whether a presidency as powerful as this was more harmful than good: whether, in fact, a president with so much power could threaten the liberties of the American people.

Concern about executive power reached a high point during the presidency of Richard M. Nixon (1969–1974). When Nixon came into office, he inherited a protracted and increasingly unpopular war in Vietnam. His handling of the war proved extremely controversial. Most notably, in an attempt to eliminate enemy supply lines, Nixon secretly expanded the war into the neutral country of Cambodia without prior or subsequent consultation with Congress—this was in spite of the fact that the Constitution gives the legislative branch alone the power to declare war.

The wave of dissent that followed this action prompted Nixon to use illegally various intelligence and law-enforcement agencies to acquire better information about those who were opposing him. Moreover, Nixon was involved in an attempt to cover up a number of illegal and unethical campaign activities, including a break-in at the offices of the Democratic National Committee in the Watergate Hotel, Washington, D.C.

The Watergate scandal eventually forced President Nixon to become the first president in American history to resign from office or else face almost certain impeachment and conviction.

> *"Watergate showed more strengths in our system than our weaknesses.... The whole country did take part in quite a genuine sense in passing judgment on Richard Nixon."*
> —ARCHIBALD COX, WATERGATE SPECIAL PROSECUTOR

Congress tried to reign in presidential power through the Ethics in Government Act of 1973, under which an independent counsel with investigative and prosecutorial powers is to be appointed whenever the attorney general concludes that a high-level executive official may have committed a crime. However, in the wake of public opposition to the zealousness with which independent counsel Kenneth Starr (see box on page 205) pursued his investigation into President Bill Clinton's personal relationship with former presidential intern Monica Lewinsky (see *The Case of President Clinton*, pages 200–201),

the independent counsel statute was allowed to expire.

The following articles by Arthur M. Schlesinger Jr. and Suzanne Garment, paint two very different pictures of presidential power in the United States.

Arthur M. Schlesinger Jr., writing at the time of the war in Vietnam and the Watergate scandal, speaks of "imperial presidency." According to the author, the Nixon presidency was not an aberration, but simply the culmination of an on-going trend in the direction of presidential tyranny. The origins of the imperial presidency lie in the aggrandizement of presidential power in foreign policy, he argues, but presidential imperialism has now moved into the domestic sphere. Schlesinger is particularly concerned about what he describes as the transformation of the restrained presidency of the Constitution into an unrestrained plebiscitary presidency—that is, an elected leader who personifies the majority, and any resistance to whom is considered to be undemocratic.

Suzanne Garment's description of presidential power contrasts sharply with that of Schlesinger. She argues that the perpetual legal scrutiny of the executive under the independent counsel statute has created an atmosphere of suspicion and distrust that has undermined the moral legitimacy of the presidency. In fact, the independent counsel statute passed by Congress has had the worrying effect of transforming political disagreements into criminal charges.

While in his article Schlesinger warns of the danger of executive tyranny, Garment, in contrast, warns of the danger of legislative tyranny in the United States.

THE RUNAWAY PRESIDENT
Arthur M. Schlesinger

Thomas Jefferson, "man of the people," was third U.S. president (1801–1809). James Madison, "Father of the Constitution," was fourth U.S. president (1809–1817). George Washington, "Father of his country" was first U.S. president (1789–1797).

"The tyranny of the legislature is really the danger most to be feared, and will continue to be so for many years to come," Jefferson wrote Madison six weeks before Washington's first inauguration. "The tyranny of the executive power will come in its turn, but at a more distant period."

On the eve of the second centennial of independence, Jefferson's prophecy appears almost on the verge of fulfillment. The imperial presidency, created by wars abroad, has made a bold bid for power at home.

The Nixon administration

The belief of the Nixon Administration in its own mandate and in its own virtue, compounded by its conviction that the republic has been in mortal danger from internal enemies, has produced an unprecedented concentration of power in the White House and an unprecedented attempt to transform the presidency of the Constitution into a plebiscitary presidency. If this transformation is carried through, the President, instead of being accountable every day to Congress and public opinion, will be accountable every four years to the electorate. Between elections, the President will be accountable only through impeachment and will govern, as much as he can, by decree. The expansion and abuse of presidential power constitute the underlying issue, the issue that Watergate has raised to the surface, dramatized, and made politically accessible.

A "plebiscite" is a vote by which the people of an entire country or district express an opinion for or against a proposal, especially on a choice of government or ruler. Try and find a recent example of this.

U.S. v. the British parliamentary system

Oddly, the crisis of the imperial presidency has not elicited much support for what at other times has been a favored theory of constitutional reform: movement in the direction of the British parliamentary system.

List the main differences between the U.S. and British political systems. Which do you think is better?

This [fact] is particularly odd because, whatever the general balance of advantage between the parliamentary and presidential modes, the parliamentary system has one feature the presidential system badly needs now—the requirement that the head of government be compelled at regular intervals to explain and defend his policies in face-to-face sessions with the political opposition. Few devices, it would seem, are better calculated both to break down the real isolation of the latter-day presidency and to dispel the spurious reverence that has come to [be associated with] the office.

The proposal that Cabinet members should go on to the floor of Congress to answer the questions and take part in a debate, "far from raising any constitutional difficulties," as E. S. Corwin once observed, "has the countenance of early practice under the Constitution. [In fact,] in his last annual message President William Howard Taft suggested that Cabinet members be given access to the floor in order, as he later put it, "to introduce measures, to advocate their passage, to answer questions, and to enter into debate as if they were members, without of course the right to vote."

William Howard Taft, 27th president, 1909–1913. Find more information on Taft on the POTUS section at www.ipl.org

The issue of presidential excess

Nixon's continued invocation, after Watergate, of national security as the excuse for presidential excess, his defense to the end of [the concept of] unreviewable executive privilege, his defiant assertion that, if he had to do it over again, he would still deceive Cambodia—such unrepentant reactions suggest that he still has no clue as to what his trouble was, still fails to understand that the sickness of his presidency is caused not by the over-zealousness of his friends or by the malice of his enemies, but by the expansion and abuse of presidential power itself. [T]he issue is more than whether Congress and the people wish to deal with the particular iniquities of the Nixon Administration. It is whether they wish to rein in the runaway presidency. Nixon's presidency is not an aberration but a culmination. It carries to extremes a compulsion toward presidential power rising out of deep-running changes in the foundations of society.

See Useful websites on page 120. The Richard Nixon page in Encyclopedia Americana *explains the background to the Cambodia crisis.*

In a time of the acceleration of history and the decay of traditional institutions and values, a strong presidency is both a greater necessity than ever before and a greater risk, [which is] necessary to hold a spinning and distracted society together, necessary to make the separation of powers work, risky because of the awful temptation held out to override the separation of powers and burst the bonds of the Constitution. The nation requires both a strong presidency for leadership and the separation of powers for liberty. It may well be that, if continuing structural compulsions are likely to propel future Presidents in the direction of government by decree, the rehabilitation of impeachment will be essential to contain the presidency and preserve the Constitution.

Look at the articles in the archive of www.cnn.com (the CNN site). Why was there an enquiry into President Clinton's conduct?

Schlesinger is writing at the time of the Watergate scandal.

Look at The Watergate Affair, pages 172–173.

Watergate is potentially the best thing to have happened to the presidency in a long time. If the trails are followed to their end, many, many years will pass before another White House staff dares take the liberties with the Constitution and the laws the Nixon White House has taken. If the nation wants to work its way back to a constitutional presidency, there is only one way to begin. That is by showing Presidents that, when their closest associates place themselves above the law and the Constitution, such transgressions will be not forgiven or forgotten for the sake of the presidency, but exposed and punished for the sake of the presidency.

If the Nixon White House escapes the legal consequences of its illegal behavior, why will future Presidents and their associates not suppose themselves entitled to do what the Nixon White House has done? Only condign [appropriate or deserved] punishment will restore popular faith in the presidency and deter future Presidents from illegal conduct —so long, at least, as Watergate remains a vivid memory. Corruption appears to visit the White House in 50-year cycles. This suggests that exposure and retribution inoculate the presidency against its latent criminal impulses for about half a century. Around the year 2023 the American people will be well advised to go on the alert and start nailing down everything in sight.

Does corruption "visit the White House in 50-year cycles"? Is this a fair comment? Can you find evidence to support this statement?

Strong and constitutional presidents

A constitutional presidency, as the great Presidents have shown, can be a very strong presidency indeed. But what keeps a strong President constitutional, in addition to checks and balances incorporated within his own breast, is the vigilance of the people. The Constitution cannot hold the nation to ideals it is determined to betray. The re-invigoration of the written checks in the American Constitution depends on the re-invigoration of the unwritten checks in American society. The great institutions—Congress, the courts, the executive establishment, the press, the universities, public opinion—have to reclaim their own dignity and meet their own responsibilities. As Madison said long ago, the country cannot trust to "parchment barriers" to halt the encroaching spirit of power. In the end, the Constitution will live only if it embodies the spirit of the American people.

Walt Whitman (1819–1892) was a poet, journalist, and editor. Whitman is one of America's best-known poets.

"There is no week nor day nor hour," wrote Walt Whitman, "when tyranny may not enter upon this country, if the people lose their supreme confidence in themselves, and lose their roughness and spirit of defiance, tyranny may always enter, the only bar against it is a large resolute breed of men."

President Richard Nixon gives the thumbs up after his resignation as 37th president of the United States.

TALKING ABOUT THE PRESIDENT
Suzanne Garment

It helps to begin your argument with a strong statement, just as Garment has.

X   If the institution of the American presidency has grown enfeebled over the past two decades, it is not only because of battles with its opponents over policies or institutional prerogatives. Its adversaries have also waged a crucial and more or less continuous attack on the underlying moral legitimacy of the office, its occupants, and the president's allies in the executive branch. The moral attack has not come from antipresidential partisans who deliberately set out to make war on the idea of federal executive power per se. Rather, it began as an incidental though large part of the ideological and policy struggles of the 1960s, especially the attack on the foreign policy pursued by U.S. presidents from World War II to Vietnam.

In a fight as bitter as this one has been, it is no surprise to find that the antipresidential troops have been using poisoned arrows or that our current national politics has become to a significant extent a politics of scandal and radical moral delegitimation. The changes that produced this state of affairs have been general. They affect more than the institution of the presidency, and their consequences cannot be reversed by narrow institutional changes. But institutional factors have placed a disproportionate burden on the executive branch and have helped perpetuate the current climate. Some of these [factors] can be altered if there is the political will to do so.

The Vietnam War (1955–1975) was an unsuccessful effort by South Vietnam and the United States to prevent the communists of North Vietnam from uniting North and South Vietnam under their leadership.

The president as victim?

Politics as usual finally collapsed almost entirely during the protests against the Vietnam War. Ideological resentment quickly turned into a pattern of violent personal accusation. Critics of the war did not limit themselves to objections on grounds of *realpolitik* or humanitarian moral concerns. Many took the next step and assaulted the war as illegal— indeed, criminal. They hammered away at quasi-criminal issues like the deception behind the bombing of Cambodia, the wiretapping, the illegal counterintelligence activity of the Federal Bureau of Investigation, and the attempted suppression of Pentagon papers. They treated the Vietnam War as a massive scandal, the U.S. government's pursuit of war as a huge illegal conspiracy, and the president as the chief conspirator. As in the early 1950s, an underlying ideological battle was joined to the traditional search for illegal or improper political behavior, and produced a politics of scandal that was unusually tense.

Watergate was the climax of this developing view that obnoxious American policies could continue in practice only because they were being foisted illegally on the nation by presidents who were criminals. By the end of the Watergate proceedings, the ideological and policy-related motives of Richard Nixon's adversaries had almost completely disappeared from public view, lost under the mass of talk about the threat posed by the executive branch to legality and institutional balance. Only amid this sort of confusion could an old-fashioned Southern politician like Senator Sam Ervin, who had voted against all the civil rights measures of the 1960s, become a liberal hero.

> *Carl Bernstein (1944–) and fellow Washington Post reporter Bob Woodward (1943–) unmasked the Watergate coverup. See the archive of The Washington Post.*

"When the president does it, that means it's not illegal."
—PRESIDENT RICHARD M. NIXON

> *Is this quote true? Can the president behave in any way he wants?*

Post-Watergate

The insistence that the crisis was institutional, a threat to the law on the part of the executive branch, produced a set of institutional remedies for what were really ideological and policy divisions. These remedies have increased public awareness of criminality and illegitimate acts by government officials. Because most of the remedies were devised for the executive branch alone, the executive has borne the brunt of this process of delegitimation.

The chain of events starts when someone asks the attorney general to investigate a matter that falls under the independent counsel statute. The attorney general is by law given 90 days to do the job, during which time he does not have subpoena power.

> *The attorney general appears in person to represent the government before the U.S. Supreme Court in cases of exceptional gravity or importance.*

After the 90 days he must either ask the court to appoint an independent counsel or write a report to Congress explaining why not. He is very unlikely, because of his limited time and tools, to be able to report with certainty—even in a dubious case—that there are no relevant questions left unanswered. He knows that if he tries there will be people in Congress and the press ready to question his competence and character.

If the attorney general does ask the court to appoint an independent counsel, he is in effect stating publicly and officially that he is dealing with a suspicious matter requiring further investigation. That is worth reporting. It is especially worth reporting because the independent counsel's office deals with high public officials. Moreover, calling the independent counsel into the case necessarily suggests that some high political authority would otherwise be interfering, or perhaps has already tried to interfere, in the matter. This last, unspoken story makes the start of independent counsel proceedings seem especially important.

Explain any complicated processes you mention. It will help you make a clear argument.

The process of the independent counsel creates impressions that affect the perceived legitimacy of the presidency as a whole, and it is through organizational differences like this one that Congress has its greatest advantage over the executive branch. There has been increasing comment in the past few years over the fact that Congress has legislated harsh ethics rules for the executive branch but more or less left itself out of the movement for reform and moral purity.

This is not to say that Congress has been scandal free during the post-Watergate years; on the contrary, because of all the changes that have taken place, post-Watergate scandals have involved Congress almost as much as the executive branch. What is missing in the Congress, though, is an institutional mechanism to drive a scandal forward, broaden its reach, and maximize its public impact and meaning. The House and Senate Ethics committees to which the task is given are not separate enough from the body as a whole and therefore do not have the proper incentives to do the job.

The author refers to other scandals after Watergate. Would it be helpful for her to list some of these as examples?

Congress and the constitution

The executive branch is distinctly limited in what it can do to combat this relative advantage that Congress holds. Where Congress clearly crosses a constitutional line, usurping or abridging some well-established presidential prerogative, the executive branch can certainly protest far more vigorously than it has done so far. There is every indication that at this time the courts will take executive branch arguments on such issues seriously. At the least a new administration might persistently question why Congress does not extend ethics legislation to its own members. People concerned about the larger problem posed by the politics of scandal cannot attack it, however, simply by contending that Congress is behaving in an unconstitutional manner. First, a good deal of what is continually putting the presidency on the moral defensive comes not from Congress but from cultural factors that affect all national political figures. Where congressional action is indeed the problem, the mechanisms Congress has established to eat away at executive branch authority are often perfectly constitutional, whether they are benign ideas or terrible ones. When Congress establishes new inspectors general in federal agencies, as it has done, or provides through legislation for special rewards to whistle blowers in the executive branch, or establishes a special public integrity section in the Justice Department, it is creating circumstances that cannot be simply changed in the courts.

> Garment argues that in modern U.S. culture public figures are relentlessly criticized.

This part of the executive branch's dilemma is nothing other than the old problem that the Constitution was designed to mitigate: Congress is indeed the most powerful, and therefore the most dangerous, branch. Government structures can be skillfully organized to mitigate the threat of legislative tyranny, and a clever president has many tools and stratagems at his disposal. But no other source of authority is as powerful as the law, because of the respect that its supposed neutrality engenders among all citizens. When a Congress starts using this respect in a tyrannical way—that is, when it starts using the laws to a significant degree in its own behalf, as weapons in its partisan struggles against opponents in the federal government or outside it—there is no way to avoid substantial damage.

The future

Improvement will come only when critical numbers of people in Congress begin to shift the focus of their legislative and investigative energy. It will come when talk about enforcing a higher ethical tone in the executive branch becomes less politically profitable than other issues— that is, when other themes stir constituents and opinion makers more deeply.

Discussion in the legal community of the office of independent counsel is by now skeptical. Issues from drugs to America's international competitiveness are beginning to stir the sort of widespread political anxiety that pulls politicians off one bandwagon and onto another. The moral attack on the executive in public discussion will end, as it began: with a shift of attention by the political elite, perhaps this time to issues and attitudes that place the president at [an] advantage in the executive-legislative tug of war.

Summary

Schlesinger warns of the rise of an imperial presidency overriding the constitutional limitations of presidential power. Good government, he concedes, requires a strong presidency; but he also recognizes that a presidency that is too strong threatens republican liberty. To counteract the encroachments of presidential power, Schlesinger calls for a reinvigoration of the Constitution's separation of powers and checks and balances. Thus, he argues, for example, that "the rehabilitation of impeachment will be essential to contain the presidency and preserve the Constitution."

Garment, writing after Watergate, worries that presidential authority has been dangerously undermined by the continual attacks on what she calls antipresidential partisans, bent on making war on the idea of presidential power itself. These attacks on the moral legitimacy of presidential power have been facilitated by the independent counsel statute, which has had the effect of deflecting congressional and public attention away from legitimate constitutional and policy issues and toward scandals. However, in conclusion, has distrust of executive power made it difficult for the president to perform his constitutional duties? See opposite for a key map on this subject.

FURTHER INFORMATION:

Books:

Bernstein, Carl, and Bob Woodward, *All the President's Men*. New York: Touchstone Books, 1994.

Cravitz, L. Gordon, and Jeremy A. Rabkin (editors), *The Fettered Presidency: Legal Constraints on the Executive Branch*. Washington, D.C.: American Enterprise Institute, 1989.

Schlesinger, Arthur M. Jr., *The Imperial Presidency*. Boston. Houghton Mifflin,1973.

Wildavsky, Aaron, *The Beleaguered Presidency*. New Brunswick, N.J.,1991

Articles:

Lind, Michael,"The Out of Control Presidency." *New Republic*, August 14, 1995, pp.18-23.

Useful websites:

www.washingtonpost.com
The Washington Post official website. Has a useful analysis of Watergate 25 years later.
www.grolier.com/presidents
The American Presidency site of *Encyclopedia Americana*
www.nixonfoundation.com
Official Nixon site with memorabilia and articles
www.cnn.com
Official site of CNN. Has useful archive and student/teacher separate page with lesson plans.
www.whitehouse.gov
Official site of White House.

The following debates in the series may also be of interest:

In this volume:

 Part 2: U.S. Government

Part 4: Politics and Morality

Topic 16: Can a sitting president be criminally indicted?

The Watergate Affair, pages 172–173.

IS THE PRESIDENT TOO POWERFUL?

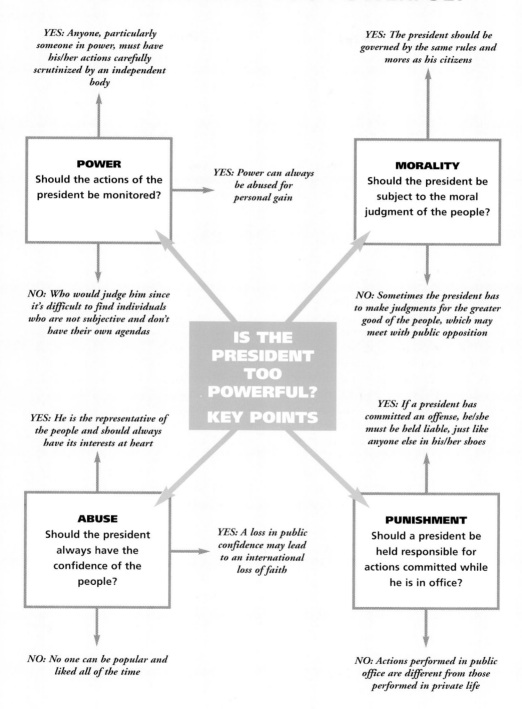

YES: Anyone, particularly someone in power, must have his/her actions carefully scrutinized by an independent body

YES: The president should be governed by the same rules and mores as his citizens

POWER
Should the actions of the president be monitored?

YES: Power can always be abused for personal gain

MORALITY
Should the president be subject to the moral judgment of the people?

NO: Who would judge him since it's difficult to find individuals who are not subjective and don't have their own agendas

NO: Sometimes the president has to make judgments for the greater good of the people, which may meet with public opposition

IS THE PRESIDENT TOO POWERFUL?

KEY POINTS

YES: He is the representative of the people and should always have its interests at heart

YES: If a president has committed an offense, he/she must be held liable, just like anyone else in his/her shoes

ABUSE
Should the president always have the confidence of the people?

YES: A loss in public confidence may lead to an international loss of faith

PUNISHMENT
Should a president be held responsible for actions committed while he is in office?

NO: No one can be popular and liked all of the time

NO: Actions performed in public office are different from those performed in private life

121

ELECTIONS

Elections are an important part of U.S. democracy. America has more elective offices and more elections than perhaps any other major democracy. Elections provide people with formal occasions for expressing their consent. The right of the people to consent to government is, according to the Declaration of Independence, a protection of individual rights to life, liberty, and the pursuit of happiness. In order to secure this right, elections were guaranteed by the American Constitution. Elections and the right to vote or run in them thus play a vital role in expressing the supremacy of the people over the government and in affirming the basic principles of American democracy.

Although Americans agree about the importance of elections, they disagree sharply about the purpose they want them to serve. This disagreement can be expressed in terms of the difference between procedures and results. Those who emphasize procedures ask whether the structure and operation of elections are sufficiently democratic; those who emphasize results ask whether elections produce desirable outcomes. The former evaluate elections in terms of their ability to produce officials who faithfully reflect the popular will, while the latter evaluate elections in terms of their ability to produce officials who are best able, as James Madison put it, "to refine and enlarge the public views." Proceduralists

would say that Madisonians do not pay enough attention to what the people think; Madisonians would respond by saying that proceduralists are too slavishly devoted to the people's will. The topics that follow help us reflect on this important debate on elections.

Electing the president

The presidency is the most important political office in the U.S. government. Throughout much of American history, selecting nominees for this high office was controlled by party leaders (or "bosses") who wielded great influence over the delegates to the presidential nominating conventions. In the 20th century political reformers denounced this method of selecting presidential nominees as corrupt and undemocratic. It was replaced by the present system of primaries, in which elections are held statewide prior to the general election, and it is the voters who select the candidates who will run on each party's ticket. Does this more democratic presidential selection process produce the best president? Robert DiClerico and Edward Banfield provide competing answers to this question in Topic 12.

The electoral college

The primary system is not the only controversial aspect of electing the president. Article II, section 1 of the Constitution prescribes an indirect method of presidential election. The electoral college is a group of people called "electors," selected by the voters in each state, that officially elects the president. There are 538 electoral votes in total; a candidate needs to receive 270 or more to win the presidency.

their lives. It has been limited thus far to state and local issues, but there have recently been calls for a nationwide initiative process. In Topic 10 Benjamin Barber supports such a plan on the grounds that the cure for democracy's ills is more, not less, democracy. But

---

"Our elections are free,
it's in the results where eventually we pay."
—BILL STERN

There have been many proposals to alter or abolish the electoral college, primarily on the grounds that it is undemocratic. A candidate can win the popular vote but still lose the electoral vote and thus the election, as occurred most recently in the election of 2000, when George W. Bush defeated Al Gore by a single electoral vote, even though Gore had won half a million more popular votes. This outcome sparked a renewed effort to abolish the electoral college by amending the Constitution. Should direct popular election of the president replace the electoral college? Opposing positions in this debate are taken by Senator Birch Bayh and Herbert Storing in Topic 13.

Direct legislation

An increasingly common aspect of state and local elections is ballot initiative—a procedure that enables citizens to vote directly on legislation or constitutional amendments. Ballot initiatives have been used to address many public policy issues. The initiative process is based on the idea that citizens should have the right to participate in making decisions on issues that directly affect

David Broder argues that the best form of democracy is not direct but representative. He also thinks that the initiative process provides yet another way for money to influence politics.

Money and politics

The influence of money on politics is a major public concern today. Many people think that money in the form of campaign contributions made by corporations and individuals decisively influences the outcome of elections. Indeed, a major political movement is currently underway to reform the way that campaigns are financed.

In 2000 Jon S. Corzine waged a successful campaign to represent the state of New Jersey in the U.S. Senate by spending $60 million of his own money—more than any other Senate candidate in the nation's history. David Adamany would take this as proof that the wealthy can buy their way into political office. But Alexander Heard argues that money alone cannot guarantee electoral victory. The issue debated here raises the issue that money can corrupt—both procedures and results (see Topic 11).

Topic 10

SHOULD PEOPLE BE ABLE TO LEGISLATE DIRECTLY THROUGH BALLOT INITIATIVES?

YES
FROM *STRONG DEMOCRACY: PARTICIPATORY POLITICS IN A NEW AGE*
BENJAMIN R. BARBER

NO
INTRODUCTION
FROM *DEMOCRACY DERAILED: INITIATIVE CAMPAIGNS AND THE POWER OF MONEY*
DAVID S. BRODER

INTRODUCTION

Ballot initiatives are a form of direct democracy whereby any citizen or group of citizens may draft a proposed law or constitutional amendment and, after gathering by petition the requisite number of signatures, have it referred directly to the voters for final approval or rejection. The initiative process has been used in various states for addressing a wide range of important public issues, such as taxes, government spending, affirmative action, abortion, gay rights, public morality, immigration, education, school vouchers, gun control, the medicinal use of marijuana, the regulation of business or labor, casino gambling, campaign finance, the minimum wage for workers, the environment, conservation, ballparks, auto insurance, hunting, animal rights, and methods of voting.

Ballot initiatives are growing increasingly popular. More than 100 years after South Dakota became the first state to allow citizens to vote directly on their laws, more measures were placed on more state ballots in the 1990s than in any previous decade. In 2000 voters in 42 states faced 204 initiatives or referenda (a procedure that enables voters to reject a measure adopted by the legislature); in Oregon alone, voters were asked to decide on 26 ballot initiatives.

The initiative process is based on the belief that ordinary citizens should take an active role in lawmaking. It has its roots in the beginning of the last century, when Populist and Progressive reformers advocated the ballot initiative as a means whereby citizens could vote directly on any proposed legislation, thereby bypassing the state legislature. At this time state legislatures and the political parties that controlled these institutions were widely held to be corrupt and unresponsive. Reformers therefore felt that it was important to provide citizens with the means to make policy themselves in order to advance the public good. Reformers hoped that the initiative process would make legislators and the parties they represented more responsive and, as a consequence, restore the faith of the people in the political system.

Over time, calls for this method of lawmaking have grown ever stronger. Although the United States is one of the few democratic countries that has never had a nationwide initiative, there have been calls in recent years for

---

"Referendum, n. A law for submission of proposed legislation to a popular vote to learn the nonsensus of public opinion."

—AMBROSE BIERCE,

THE DEVIL'S DICTIONARY

---

direct democracy at even the national level. In 1992 and 1996, for example, independent presidential candidate Ross Perot advocated what he called "electronic town meetings," in which citizens would be able to examine policy alternatives for themselves, deliberate about them, and convey their views to policymakers through the use of computer technology.

In light of the increasing popularity of national and state ballot initiatives and

referendums it behooves us to think about the pros and cons of such forms of direct democracy. The following two articles help us do just that.

In the first article political theorist Benjamin Barber argues for more active citizenship in order to correct the ills of American democracy. To this end, Barber favors a national initiative and referendum process. Such a process would have, according to him, the salutary effect of increasing citizen participation and civic responsibility, promoting civic education, and increasing public deliberation.

In the second article, the political columnist David Broder presents a strong case against the use of initiatives and referenda as substitutes for representative democracy. The initiative process, Broder argues, "has given the United States something that seemed unthinkable—not a government of laws but laws without government." Broder is troubled by the fact that the initiative process undermines the constitutional system of government established by the Founders—a system that is based not on a democratic but a republican principle, that is, on the idea that laws are to be made by the representatives of the citizens rather than by the citizens themselves. In addition, Broder contends that the initiative process provides a new way for money to influence politics and the policymaking process.

STRONG DEMOCRACY
Benjamin R. Barber

YES

Barber contrasts liberal democracy, which is how the U.S. system operates, with what he calls strong democracy, which has a higher level of direct citizen involvement.

Strong democracy requires unmediated self-government by an engaged citizenry. It also requires institutions that will involve individuals at both the neighborhood and the national level in common talk, decision-making and political judgment, and common action. Liberal democracy has many faults, but it also has a well-established and relatively successful practice. Strong democracy may derive from an attractive theoretical tradition, but it is without a convincing modern practice. Indeed modernity is frequently regarded as its nemesis and the scale and technological character of modern society are often offered as insurmountable obstacles to its practical implementation.

Our task [as contemporary democrats] is to place strong democracy in an institutional framework where its realistic potential as a practice can be assessed. Strong democracy entails both the intimacy and the feasibility of local participation and the power and responsibility of regional and national participation, and the reforms offered here are geared to both levels. This is not to say that strong democracy aspires to civic participation and self-government on all issues at all times in every phase of government, both national and local. Rather, it projects some participation some of the time on selected issues on both national and local levels of power. If all of the people can participate some of the time in some of the responsibilities of governing, then strong democracy will have realized its aspirations.

Strong government will not entirely replace liberal democracy.

National initiative and referendum process

See "Referendums and Plebiscites" at www.aceproject.org.

The initiative and referendum process has been widely used in the United States at the state and local level. It also has been critical to democracy in a number of other countries, most notably in Switzerland, where it remains the preferred method of national legislation. Putting aside the "plebiscites" conducted by totalistic regimes seeking unanimous approval of national decisions that have already been taken and the constitutional referenda on the founding documents of "new" countries, the initiative and referendum continue to be used in [the United States], Switzerland, Australia, New Zealand,

France, Scandinavia, and to a lesser extent, in Ireland and the United Kingdom. In the United States, 26 states, many of them in the West, have used the initiative and referendum process. South Dakota adopted it in 1898, Utah in 1900, and Oregon in 1902. More recently Wyoming adopted it in 1968, Illinois (which has a constitutional referendum only) in 1970, and Florida in 1972. But although in 1978 Senator James Abourezk proposed in Senate Joint Resolution 67 that an amendment to the Constitution establish a national initiative and referendum process, the proposal was never brought to a vote and the United States has [therefore] never had a national referendum process. Indeed even proposed amendments to the Constitution are voted on in the state legislatures rather than in a popular referendum.

The last referendum ballot in the United Kingdom took place in Wales on September 18, 1997, concerning the devolution of Wales from the United Kingdom—50.3% voted for it and 49.7% against.

Resistance to the referendum process

The resistance to a national referendum process derives in part from Madisonian fears of popular rule. These manifest themselves in the modern world as an anxiety about elite manipulation of public opinion, the power of image and money to influence the popular vote, the private-interest character of the balloting process, and the plebiscitary dangers of direct legislation. Now as earlier, even warm friends of democracy worry about popular obstructionism against progressive legislation, and about the civic incompetence of the "sovereign" people.

See box on James Madison, page 106— Does the Separation of Powers Produce Ineffective Government?—and Madison's views on republicanism on pages 46–47.

The dangers of elite manipulation in a mass society cannot be overestimated, but in fact the actual history of the referendum at the state level yields very little evidence of civic incompetence or obstructionism. Moreover it is foolish to think that a nation can be rescued from the manipulation of elites by reducing the potentially manipulable public's input into the democratic process. One might as well combat crime in the subways by keeping the public at home. Indeed it is more rather than less experience of government that will insulate voters against manipulation and prejudice.

A striking analogy, or comparison, is a memorable way to reinforce a point.

The more soothing reality

While Madisonian theorists have stood trembling at the prospects of a leviathan public running amok in schoolrooms filled with voting machines, students of the referendum's practical effects have been offering more soothing pictures. A commentator who reviewed the experience of Michigan writes: "There is quite as likely to be a judicious and rational decision on popular votes [by referendum] as on legislative votes." A student of the California referendum reports: "So far

President Harry S. Truman casts his vote during the Missouri primary election of 1948 at his home town of Independence.

as large problems of public welfare are concerned, [the public] is markedly more likely to reach a fair and socially valuable result." Of Oregon, a student writes: "The marvel is that this system of popular government, so vulnerable to apathy, indifference, and actual ignorance, has not only worked but has a considerable degree of constructive and progressive achievements to its credit."

A referendum legalizing physician-assisted suicide for terminally ill residents was passed in Oregon on October 27, 1997. The same bill was defeated in the Michigan referendum of November 1998.

Unfounded fears

The fear of obstructionism seems no better founded than the fear of popular prejudice. Early antinuclear referenda failed in a number of states, but similar referenda have succeeded in recent years. The Swiss use of the referendum has often favored tradition and opposed modernizing legislation, but in the Swiss case the "modernizing" legislation was being supported by the establishment and was defeated by a strong-willed and independently minded Swiss public that ignored pressures from big money and the media.

In Churchill County, Nevada, prostitution was legalized by referendum. Right-to-work legislation, generally considered conservative, has been defeated by referendum in several states. And Oregon led the way with progressive initiatives that abolished the poll tax and introduced female suffrage by popular ballot at the beginning of the century. (Oregon regularly draws higher turnouts at referenda than at elections for representatives.) More recently Michigan and Maine banned disposable soft-drink containers by popular vote, Colorado voted down an Olympics proposal for the state that had been widely supported by business and political elites, New Jersey introduced casino gambling by referendum, and bond issues have continued to win popular support for selected projects despite the increasing fiscal conservatism of the electorate.

Barber quotes examples to disprove the common belief that populist votes tend to be conservative rather than progressive.

Constructive uses outweigh disadvantages

In sum, the initiative and referendum can increase popular participation in and responsibility for government, provide a permanent instrument of civic education, and give popular talk the reality and discipline of power that it needs to be effective. Thus the constructive uses far outweigh the potential disadvantages—which history suggests are less alarming than critics believe in any case. It is therefore a crucial goal of the strong democratic program to institute a national initiative and referendum process as part of the effort to revitalize popular talk and public decision-making.

A clear and concise summary of your argument helps people understand the case you have made.

DEMOCRACY DERAILED
David S. Broder

NO

At the start of a new century—and millennium—a new form of government is spreading in the United States. It is alien to the spirit of the Constitution and its careful system of checks and balances. Though derived from a reform favored by Populists and Progressives as a cure for special-interest influence, this method of lawmaking has become the favored tool of millionaires and interest groups that use their wealth to achieve their own policy goals—a lucrative business for a new set of political entrepreneurs.

Exploiting the public's disdain for politics and distrust of politicians, it is now the most uncontrolled and unexamined arena of power politics. It has given the United States something that seems unthinkable—not a government of laws but laws without government. The initiative process, an import now just over 100 years old, threatens to challenge or even subvert the American system of government in the next few decades.

Government by initiative

In half our states—including the giant of them all, California—and in hundreds of municipalities, from New York City to Nome, policies are being made not by government but by initiative. In a single year, 1998, voters across America used the initiative process to pass laws or to amend state constitutions, achieving a wide variety of goals. They ended affirmative action, raised the minimum wage, banned billboards, decriminalized a wide range of hard drugs and permitted thousands of patients to obtain prescriptions for marijuana, restricted campaign spending and contributions, expanded casino gambling, banned many forms of hunting, prohibited some abortions, and allowed adopted children to obtain the names of their biological parents.

Not one of these decisions was made through the time-consuming process of passing and signing bills into laws—the method prescribed by the Constitution, which guaranteed the nation and each of the states "the republican form of government." Rather they were made by the voters themselves—or whatever fraction of them

See the Constitution at www.house.gov.

constituted the majority on Election Day. This is the new form of government—an increasingly popular one.

Government by initiative is not only a radical departure from the Constitution's system of checks and balances, it is also a big business, in which lawyers and campaign consultants, signature-gathering firms and other players sell their services to affluent interest groups or millionaire do-gooders with private policy and political agendas. These players—often not even residents of the states whose laws and constitutions they are rewriting—have learned that the initiative is a far more efficient way of achieving their ends than the cumbersome process of supporting candidates for public office and then lobbying them to pass or sign the measures they seek.

Broder suggests that although ballot initiatives seem democratic, they are open to manipulation by elites and pressure groups.

Necessary checks and balances

The founders of the American Republic were almost as distrustful of democracy as they were rebellious against royal decrees. They were steeped in the writings of philosophers such as John Locke, who proposed a social-contract theory to justify representative government against the claims of absolute monarchy, and Montesquieu, who urged the separation of legislative, executive, and judicial branches as a safeguard against abuse of power in a democracy. As their disciples, the writers of the Constitution placed the legislative branch first in their document—and preeminent in power—with independent executive and judicial branches providing the necessary checks and balances.

John Locke (1632–1704) was an English philosopher, whose theories about liberal democracy influenced the American and French revolutions.

See box on page18 for a biography of Montesquieu.

The founders were not naive. They recognized the potential danger that those elected to the national legislature might abuse power. So they divided that authority between two bodies, the House and the Senate—the first, numerous and of short tenure, to reflect short-term shifts in public opinion, and the latter, at one remove from the people and with a longer term, in order to apply a prudent check on those instant judgments by the House.

Further they created a role in legislative matters for the executive, by arming him with a veto power that could be over-ruled only by a two-thirds vote of the House and Senate. And implicitly, at least—or so John Marshall successfully argued—it empowered the Supreme Court to invalidate any legislation that contradicted the terms of the Constitution.

John Marshall, chief justice (1801–1835), established the doctrine of judicial review.

The great defense of that scheme of government can be found in the *Federalist* papers, written to persuade the states and their people to ratify the new Constitution. In *Federalist 10*, James Madison, one of the principal architects of the Constitution, gave the classic argument for its careful effort to balance democratic impulses with safeguards against heedless majorities.

[The founders'] reading of history had convinced them that the Greek city-states failed because they had tried to govern themselves by vote of the people. They also argued that while direct democracy might be appropriate for a small, compact civil society, it would be impractical, let alone inconvenient, in a nation the size of the United States. Yet, as children of the Enlightenment and believers in natural law, they were convinced that individual rights preceded the formation of the state and were superior to the edicts and laws of any ruler. They wanted the government they were creating to derive its powers from "the consent of the governed."

Representative government

Broder bases his argument on the precedent set by the founders. Is historical precedent necessarily correct?

Translating that phrase into reality became the great work of the Constitutional Convention. No one there argued for direct democracy. Instead their solution was representative government—based on election of officials who would exercise power within the limits set forth by the constitutions of the nation and the states and under the discipline of frequent elections, which would require them to defend their actions to their constituents and allow the people to replace them if they abused power or exercised it in ways that did not meet public approval. As Madison said at the 1788 Virginia ratifying convention, "I go on the great republican principle that the people will have the virtue and intelligence to select men of virtue and wisdom." Madison conceded that there was a risk that "men of factious tempers, of local prejudices, or of sinister designs, may, by intrigue, by corruption or by other means" come to office and abuse their powers. But that risk, he said, is reduced by the size and diversity of the American Republic.

Thus, the rationale for making the United States a republic, rather than a democracy, rested on a healthy apprehension of the dangers of direct democracy and the manifold risks of relying on simple majority rule. Direct democracy, Fisher Ames of Massachusetts wrote, would be "subject to factions and violence; decisions would often be made by surprise, in the precipitancy of passion.... It would be a government not by laws but by men." The threats, as the founders envisaged them, ranged from raids on the treasury and shifting of tax burdens from one constituency to another, to infringement of civil liberties, submersion of minority viewpoints and interests, and even destabilization of the entire political order.

Fisher Ames (1758–1808) was a U.S. statesman, writer, and orator.

The growing reliance on initiatives … where they are available is part of the increasing alienation of Americans from the system of representative government that has served this nation for over 200 years. As the new century begins, the reputation of elected officials … has rarely been worse. Our citizens always have had a healthy skepticism about the people in public office; the Constitution rests on the assumption that the exercise of power is a dangerous intoxicant; hence, those in authority must be checked by clear delineation of their authority and balanced against one another, lest anyone commandeer too much power.

What signs are there that Americans are alienated from representative government?

Public distrust of politics and politicians

But what we have … today goes well beyond healthy skepticism to a pervasive distrust of those we ourselves have elected to exercise temporarily the authority we have given them. As a young woman attending a session of the North Carolina Institute of Political Leadership—a wonderful skills-training program for community leaders who are preparing to enter elective politics—told me in 1999, "The reaction I get from people I've known for years is, 'You're such a nice person. Why would you want to go into politics?'"

See www.uncwil. edu/iopl for more information on the North Carolina Institute of Political Leadership.

The general disdain for politics and politicians is especially fierce when it comes to legislatures (including Congress) and their members. While many voters are prepared to exempt their own representative from the blanket indictment, the pervasive attitude is that our lawmakers are selfish, self-centered partisans, controlled by special interests and constantly on the lookout for ways to line their own pockets and pay off their pals and political sponsors.

One expression of that disdain has been the term-limits movement, which swept across the country during the last two decades, usually implemented by the mechanism of the initiative campaign. In that combination of initiatives and term limits, we have seen the clearest expression of the revolt against representative government.

The term-limits movement seeks to limit the term of elected public officials in order to curb self-interest and corruption. See www.termlimits. org/ustl.shtml for more information.

In every state I visited in my reporting, the initiative process was viewed as sacrosanct. In most of them, the legislature (even though term-limited) was in disrepute.

The argument [here] is that representative government is not something to be discarded quite so casually. We need to examine what really happens in direct legislation by initiative. And we must ask ourselves about the implications of a weakening of our republican form of government. Is California the model we want for the nation? Or is there enduring wisdom in the founders' design?

Summary

These two articles present important arguments for and against allowing the people to legislate directly through ballot initiatives. In Barber's view a national initiative and referendum process would help make the United States more democratic. "Strong democracy requires unmediated self-government by an engaged citizenry," Barber argues. "It requires institutions that will involve individuals at both the neighborhood and the national level in common talk, common decision-making and political judgment, and common action." To be sure, Barber does not advocate direct citizen participation "on all issues at all times in every phase of government, both national and local," but he does want to see all of the people participate at least some of the time on even selected national issues. A national initiative and referendum process would help realize this goal. While Barber looks forward to a national initiative process that fosters the virtues of active democratic citizenship, Broder fears the negative consequences of this kind of direct democracy. Relying on instant measures of majority opinion is dangerous, Broder argues, and that is why the American Founders established a representative democracy that would filter temporary popular passions through the process of prolonged deliberation and discussion. Broder therefore concludes by appealing to what he calls the "enduring wisdom in the founders' design."

FURTHER INFORMATION:

Books:

Barber, Benjamin R., *Strong Democracy: Participatory Politics for a New Age*. Berkeley, CA: University of California Press, 1984.

Broder, David S., *Democracy Derailed: Initiative Campaigns and the Power of Money*. New York: Harcourt, 2000.

Butler, David, and Austin Ramney (editors), *Referendums: A Comparative Study of Practice and Theory*. Washington, D.C.: American Enterprise Institute, 1978.

Haskell, John, *Direct Democracy or Representative Government?: Dispelling the Populist Myth*. Boulder, CO: Westview Press, 2001.

Article:

Verhovek, Sam Howe, "Oregon Ballot Full of Voter Initiatives Becomes Issue Itself." *The New York Times*, October 25, 2000.

Useful websites:

www.house.gov
U.S. House of Representatives site.

www.geocities.com/Capitol Hill/4821/Pros.html
Article on "Electronic Democracy: The Pros." Also provides other useful information on this subject.

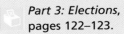

The following debates in the Pro/Con series may also be of interest:

In this volume:

Topic 1 Is direct rule by the people better than representative democracy?

Part 3: Elections, pages 122–123.

Topic 7 Does the two-party system adequately represent the people?

SHOULD PEOPLE BE ABLE TO LEGISLATE DIRECTLY THROUGH BALLOT INITIATIVES?

YES: It limits the role and influence of individual representatives

NO: It allows a new way for money and individuals to influence the policymaking process

YES: Such a process helps increase civic participation, responsibility, and education

ABUSE OF POWER
Does direct legislation help protect against self-serving and unresponsive elected representatives?

DEMOCRATIC IDEALS
Does the ballot initiative process make America more democratic?

NO: The process undermines the republican principle of representational government established by the Constitution

SHOULD PEOPLE BE ABLE TO LEGISLATE DIRECTLY THROUGH BALLOT INITIATIVES?

KEY POINTS

NO: The public is already protected by the checks and balances and the separation of powers that are written into the American Constitution

YES: The people are incompetent as lawmakers and will obstruct legislation because of mass fears and prejudices

YES: Although direct legislation might work in a small, compact society, it is impractical and cumbersome in a country as large as the United States

PROGRESS
Does direct legislation through ballot initiatives obstruct progressive and constructive legislation?

INEFFICIENCY
Is the ballot initiative process impractical and inconvenient in a country like the United States?

NO: Legislation passed through ballot initiatives has achieved such progressive outcomes as introducing female suffrage

NO: More experience of participating in government legislation will help insulate voters against apathy and prejudice

NO: Technological advances like the Internet have helped remove practical obstacles to large-scale citizen assembly by overcoming mass communication barriers

Topic 11

CAN THE WEALTHY BUY THEIR WAY INTO POLITICAL OFFICE?

YES

"DEMOCRACY AND DOLLARS"
FROM *POLITICAL MONEY*
DAVID W. ADAMANY

NO

"DOES MONEY WIN ELECTIONS?"
FROM *THE COSTS OF DEMOCRACY*
ALEXANDER HEARD

INTRODUCTION

Money has always been essential to political candidates. To wage a successful election campaign, one needs as much public exposure as possible, and it can be achieved through manipulation of the media and through advertising, among other things. In order to achieve maximum success, the candidate needs adequate financial backing, which in most cases comes in the form of donations from wealthy individuals or companies. Consequently, the source of these political donations has long been a subject of concern. Surely, critics ask, there must be a reason why a large company or bank, for example, is willing to commit funds to a particular political candidate? After all, as the saying goes, "There's no such thing as a free lunch."

As far back as 1825 the painter George Caleb Bingham depicted a voter being rewarded with whiskey outside a frontier polling office. Since then big

industry—U.S. railroad companies, banks, and the oil industry, among them—had financed its own candidates. More recently, according to data from the Federal Election Commission, the Democrats raised $513,059,203 and the Republicans $691,804,099 in the 1999–2000 election cycle. The main donors to the Republican fund included AT&T, Microsoft, and the National Association of Realtors. Similarly, apart from the unions, which included the AFL-CIO, Goldman Sachs and Citigroup were among the largest financial contributors to the Democrats.

A large percentage of these funds came from media organizations, such as Time Warner, Viacom, and Disney. Thus both the Democrats and Republicans heavily depended on financial contributions from large and economically important companies.

Since 1925 legislation has been passed to regulate political campaign financing. In 1939 the Hatch Act was passed (see box below); it was amended in 1940. The purpose of the Hatch Act was to control both the potential acquisition of political office and also the buying of political influence. The 1970s saw the Federal Election Campaign Act and its subsequent amendments. This major reform allowed corporations, labor unions, and other interest groups to set up Political Action Committees (PACs) to raise money for candidates. PACs can contribute up to $5,000 to each candidate in an election. Thus new means of financing political parties have evolved that escape the constraints of federal election law. "Soft money" is now raised to help fund general activities, such as voter education. Consequently, this means that corporations or individuals can now contribute millions of dollars, as long as the money does not feed directly into a single election campaign.

"Independent expenditures," not directly connected to a candidate's campaign, can also be made. These unregulated contributions are usually derived from PACs, like-minded individuals, or indeed, whole organizations. Therefore it is quite possible, and more importantly legal, for a candidate's campaign to receive a serious financial boost outside of his or her own expenditure.

"Bundling" is when a number of individuals hand over a single large contribution, usually made up of a combination of different maximum individual campaign contributions, thereby increasing their visibility to a candidate. Consequently, a single vote offered with no financial contribution is seen as being of less value than a substantial fiscal donation.

David W. Adamany and Alexander Heard in the following two extracts provide opposing arguments and viewpoints on this issue.

COMMENTARY: The Hatch Act

The Hatch Act was passed by Congress in 1939 and amended in 1940. It was named after its sponsor, New Mexico senator Carl Atwood Hatch (1889–1963). The act prohibited federal employees from engaging in specific types of political activity and placed a ceiling on campaign expenditure. It also made it illegal to coerce or intimidate voters in national elections, prevented civil service administrators from tampering with nominations or the election of candidates, and outlawed the solicitation of political contributions from relief recipients. In 1940 the amendments placed a $5,000 ceiling on annual contributions for any electoral candidate. A limit of $3 million per year was placed on the expenditure and acceptance of funds by political committees. The amendments also made it illegal to buy goods or use advertising to promote candidates for federal office. In 1993 the Hatch Reform Amendments made it possible for some federal and District of Columbia government employees to take an active part in political campaigns.

DEMOCRACY AND DOLLARS
David W. Adamany

Political power is so attractive that men have incessantly bought, stolen, coerced, and killed for it. Within modern democracies, killing, coercing, stealing, and many forms of buying have been outlawed as means to political power.

Today the ability of democratic societies to accommodate growing populations, external threats, ecological menace, economic crises, social and cultural change, and a host of other issues is in serious question. The future of democracy depends on how well its practitioners learn to adapt their processes to new and more difficult circumstances.

Definitions of democracy

Democracy is a system of government whose purpose is to implement the will of the people. Democracy is also a system for discovering what the will of the people may be and for ensuring that the government cannot act without frequent and regular reference to and control by that will. Intuitive or empathetic leaders, no matter how inspired or how carefully attuned to public opinion, cannot by themselves make democratic decisions. Decisions can be democratic only if in the decision-making process the participation of the people is critical and controlling.

In large political units, maintaining such participation is a problem—one that has been solved, for the most part through the institution of elections. [However] the worth of of a democratic system depends on putting questions to the people and on import and relevance of these questions. Democracy therefore requires electoral contests, in which the means are available to place alternatives before the people.

[For example] in a town meeting, the question of political finance has little significance. Issues are defined in common, and the voters and candidates know and have equal access to each other. The wealth or lack of it at a speaker's disposal may influence the degree of respect he is accorded, but it can hardly influence whether he is heard or affect his ability to say what he wants to say. [However] in a modern mass society, in which democracy must be representative rather than direct, the question of political finance can be of decisive importance.

Start your debate by stating why the issue is important. That will provide you with a base from which to build your argument.

It is important to clearly define important words and terms from the beginning. That will help others quickly understand the main points of your thesis.

Having defined his terms, Adamany then states that political finance can be of crucial importance in a modern mass society.

In the United States as in other democratic countries, political activity has traditionally been financed through private, voluntary contributions to parties and candidates. Since all citizens have an equal right to political participation, traditional democratic theory assumes that all interests and points of view will receive financial support and expression in proportion to the numbers of their adherents. In fact, however, since all persons do not have equal financial means, the views and interests of the wealthy are expressed far out of proportion to their numbers.

The author gives the traditionally accepted viewpoint and then disproves it in his next sentence.

Political resources

Financial means, of course, are just one of the inequalities in a democracy. Other political resources are also spread unevenly among individuals and classes. Specific traits—an imposing stature, attractive face, commanding voice, personal charisma, high energy level or intellect—aid one candidate or one citizen activist as against others. [Similarly] some political resources other than money are closely linked to the social and economic system.

Are any of the traits that the author lists more important than money for a politician?

Education helps one to understand issues and master the skills of politics. Leisure time gives one opportunities to engage in political activity. Prestige and community standing help one to be listened to attentively. Of course, incentives to political interest or activity are unequal. Money may affect even the cloudy realm of personal motivation. Those with family traditions of political activism, with a sense of personal effectiveness, [and those] with high needs for and expectations of ego satisfaction may be more likely than others to engage in political activity.

[A]t the outset inequalities of money are probably greater than inequalities in time, energy, education, and personal traits. Other political resources—though admittedly more widespread among the well-off—are also frequently found among other social and economic groups and, more important, can be more readily developed by activists within those strata. Those with money are more likely than those without it to participate in politics.

The author states that money is the most unequally distributed resource in a democracy.

The wealthy have continuing interests to defend, an understanding of the continuity of those interests, a quicker appreciation of the immediate and long-term advantages of political participation, and a social milieu that favors political activism. In other sectors of the society, political awareness and activism tend to be spurred by visible and exciting events, whereas the participation of the moneyed is linked to ongoing institutions and social structures.

Is the author suggesting that the wealthy make better politicians? Can you find examples to prove or disprove this point?

Money, unlike other political resources, is liquid. Dollars are easily moved from across the nation into, say, Alabama to assure that a senior senator, chairman of a powerful committee affecting national financial interests, will retain his seat in the world's greatest deliberative body and, therefore, the influential chairmanship that would otherwise go to the second-ranking majority party senator, perhaps a liberal mid-western maverick. The citizen outside Alabama who can give only his time, energy, or skills cannot easily use them to affect the Alabama senatorial election. [However,] dollars are legal tender anywhere in the United States.

Adamany now builds on his argument by giving an example of why money is more effective than the skills of the individual citizen in the acquisition of power.

"When wealth accumulates, men decay."

—OLIVER GOLDSMITH, IRISH PLAYWRIGHT

The liquidity of money

Adamany suggests that economic influence on politics can be secret and untraceable.

Money moves silently as well as easily. Cash leaves no tracks. Checks can be laundered—passed through intermediaries, individuals, or committees. Transfer payments among committees can obscure the original source of funds, whereas the citizen who serves on a political committee, canvasses his neighbors, posts a sign on his car or lawn, attends a caucus, or in other ways uses his time, energy, and skills can hardly conceal his attempt to influence politics. The public can evaluate who he is, what he wants, and what his support implies about his candidate or party.

He now shows that the liquidity of money is very important in buying noneconomic resources.

Finally, money can buy most noneconomic political resources. It can pay canvassers, or skilled campaign managers, or publicists, or researchers. It cannot endow a candidate with intelligence, but it can buy him a brain trust. It cannot change his voice or face, but it can hire a make-up man, a voice coach, and a clever film editor.

Those with money can buy virtually any of the resources that other citizens give directly. The inequality of wealth among citizens would by itself jeopardize democracy. But in a modern industrial society, financially powerful business, labor, and other organizations which have no standing as part of the electorate and to which no one has ever dreamed of extending the franchise have acquired, by deploying money, a kind of corporate citizenship. Much political giving today is not really private but institutional in character. Historically, the influence of money has been held in check by the press, public interest groups, social movements, and other noneconomic forces in society. But the final check has been the authority of voters and the vigor of opposition politicians to hold office-holders accountable in elections.

In recent years traditional voter loyalties, class identification, and political organizations have withered. Split-ticket balloting and highly unpredictable election outcomes reveal that voters are increasingly without electoral moorings. Long-accepted political leaders and institutions no longer influence voters. A better educated, highly mobile, and increasingly middle-class electorate receives its campaign information not from neighborhood precinct workers but from the communications media.

In politics a long-static pattern of organizations and institutions has been displaced by technology. Technology is for sale, at prices that stagger old-line politicians. Public opinion polls, broadcast media time, film producers and editors, computers and their attending armies of technicians, and advance men to organize the carnivals that gull newsgatherers are expensive.

The author contrasts the current situation to the past. Is politics so different today?

Having set the scene, Adamany now shows how other factors—in this case technology—have led to change. He uses this information to strengthen his argument.

Campaign expenses

Campaign costs have not only made politicians more vulnerable to pressures from those who have money, they have also made the wealthy more vulnerable to extortion by the politicians. Whether they want to or not, those who are regulated by or otherwise economically dependent on government—as is virtually every business and profession in a modern post-industrial society—often feel that they must contribute to politics when solicited.

Asked why he had authorized the illegal contribution of company funds to meet the solicitation of presidential money managers, the chairman of the board of one of the nation's largest corporations replied: "A large part of the money raised from the business community for political purposes is given in fear of what would happen if it were not given."

The author concisely summarizes his argument, reiterating his thesis that the wealthy can buy themselves or their chosen candidate into office.

DOES MONEY WIN ELECTIONS?
Alexander Heard

By widening the question, Heard immediately makes it clear that money isn't the only issue in elections.

The real question, of course, is what does win elections? Politicians campaign for the most part by instinct and shrewd guessing. Neither they nor laborious scholars can lay out a set of infallible rules for controlling the outcome of elections. Yet the notion is common that the side with more money has a better chance of winning. The belief is not discouraged by practical politicians who must pry campaign gifts out of their followers, but it springs initially from uncertainty as to what constitutes effective campaigning. Afraid to leave any stone unturned, campaigners usually expand the volume of electioneering until time and money run out. The calendar heeds no man, but somebody else always has more money, and may part with some of it.

The author spells out the other issues that have to be considered in order to see the complete picture.

No neat correlation is found between campaign expenditures and campaign results. Even if superiority in expenditures and success at the polls always ran together, the flow of funds to a candidate might simply reflect his prior popular appeal rather than create it. Our understanding of voting behavior is not so precise that all the financial and nonfinancial factors that contribute to success can be sorted out with confidence. Yet it is clear that under some conditions the use of funds can be decisive. And under others no amount of money spent by the loser could alter the outcome. The kinds of information available limit the analyses that can be made, but they do show clearly that financial outlays cannot guarantee victory in elections.

What wins elections?

He now examines the various ways in which money can be spent—emphasizing the point that other things have to considered.

The sheer volume of campaign expenditures is not necessarily decisive in the outcome of elections. After all, men must use judgment in spending money. They must decide what to use it for: for a larger office staff or more field agents; for a registration drive by mail or by personal contact; for more newspaper or more handbill advertising; for sending funds to this locality or to that; for a broadcast by this senator or that representative. In addition to decisions about the medium of expenditure are decisions about the content of the actions financed. The decision of Harry Truman in 1948 to ride his campaign on the record of the 80th Congress and the social and economic issues he generated from it apparently won him the election. The tables might have been turned had Governor Dewey chosen different tactics of debate. The significant use of campaign cash embraces not only its volume but also how it is spent. [An example of this is the Liberty League—see below—set up in the 1930s in opposition to Franklin Roosevelt.]

COMMENTARY: The American Liberty League

The American Liberty League was established by Conservative Democrats on August 22, 1934. Its aim was to "defend and uphold the Constitution and foster the right to work, earn, save, and acquire property." It was set up in opposition to the New Deal proposed by Franklin D. Roosevelt (U.S. president, 1932–1945). Roosevelt wanted to alleviate the problems caused by the Great Depression and to lessen the great divide between the nation's rich and poor. His policies alienated many wealthy individuals, such as former New York Governor Al Smith and former president and chairman of General Motors, Pierre S. Du Pont, who both joined the league's ranks, along with its president, Jouett Shouse, who was former Chairman of the Democratic National Executive Committee. There was, however, much public and media opposition to an organization that was financed largely by a rich minority, which was seen to be working to its own political agenda. The resulting backlash against the league worked to Roosevelt's political advantage. The league eventually disbanded in 1940.

[T]he judgment necessary in the use of money is only one of the "nonmonetary" elements—that is, something other than the volume of money—affecting both the given conditions of a campaign and the character and effectiveness of campaign activities. Many factors wholly unrelated to money influence the outcome of a campaign. Shrewdness in dealing with crucial state and local leaders, shrewdness in choice of campaign routes, and skill in campaigning and in energizing voluntary workers to get out the vote.

One of Senator Bilbo's old campaign managers in Mississippi used to say that if all other things were equal, money could win an election. But in Mississippi, as elsewhere, all other things are seldom equal, and Senator Bilbo himself was known for his reliance on personal campaign qualities. A colorful, magnetic, spellbinding, unscrupulous orator, the Senator had welded to himself over the years followers who voted and worked for him regardless

Money alone is not enough. Other factors also influence the outcome of a campaign.

Theodore Bilbo was Democratic governor of Mississippi (1916–1920, 1928–1930) and a senator (1935–1947). He died while Congress was investigating allegations against him of racism and taking bribes.

of the formal paraphernalia of campaign organization. His screams from the stump would be printed throughout his state without benefit of paid advertisements. Senator Bilbo depended on nonmonetary factors for success, more so than most of his contemporaries.

Another type of election will illustrate a different combination of factors that can prove decisive. In some states referenda are held. The issues are often novel to the voters and do not divide them along party or factional lines. The parties, in fact, may not become engaged at all.

A *"referendum" is a vote taken by the general public to directly decide an important legislative or policy issues.*

A referendum may become a contest between ad hoc combinations of fervent amateurs and miscellaneous oldsters. Under such circumstances the given conditions of a campaign probably exert less control on the outcome than in elections between party candidates for public office. Expenditures for organizational and communications purposes may thus more clearly determine the success of the campaign. Even in these circumstances volume of expenditures is not enough. Money can be used efficaciously or it can be wasted.

Is each election different?

Every election is different. The significance of money will differ in each. In closely balanced contests a tiny shift in any factor of campaign effectiveness can affect the outcome. The keen comment on a critical issue, the muddiness of roads to the polls, the absence of money in a key ward can prove decisive. But the situation is like a legislative vote carried by a margin of one. Sooner or later everybody on the winning side claims that his was the decisive vote. Actually, all of the individual voters acting together were decisive, and all campaign exertions that help victory constitute in combination [the sum of] the winning margin.

The author claims that each individual vote is decisive in winning a victory.

Essential costs and the choice of candidates

Seldom will nonfinancial elements of campaigning free a candidate from financial needs to the extent enjoyed by Senator Bilbo. This is especially unlikely when organized parties are opposing each other.

Regardless of the fluctuating significance of financial and nonfinancial elements from one campaign to another, in virtually all campaigns a basic amount of organizational work, communication through commercial media, and getting-out-the-vote must be accomplished if the candidate expects to compete seriously. [All of] these things require money.

Every candidate and every political campaign requires money.

Unless money to meet these minimum, essential expenses is available—regardless of how large or small the amount— contestants lacking it will be decisively handicapped. Many factors determine the sums required for conducting competitive elections under the diverse conditions prevailing in the United States. Despite a general financial inferiority, it cannot be argued convincingly that the Democratic party has lost a single presidential election in the 20th century for want of funds. If the facts could be known, the number of candidates at lower political levels whose defeat could be ascribed simply to a shortage of funds would probably be comparatively few. There are other consequences, however, of the need to meet minimum essential campaign costs. The need to do so, for example, takes heavy toll of the energies of party leadership, doubtless with an adverse effect on other campaign operations. Democratic leadership especially during a national election moves from one financial crisis to another, crises that divert the attention of even the top managers—especially of the top managers—from the serious business of debate, tactics, and action.

> *Heard asserts that the Democrats have never lost an election due to money. Look up the 1980 election at www.ipl.org— what factors led Democrat Jimmy Carter to lose?*

Election funds

The necessity for obtaining essential election funds has its most profound importance in the choosing of candidates. The monies can usually be assured, and often can be withheld, by the relatively small corps of political specialists whose job it is to raise money. If a prospective candidate cannot get assurances of the support necessary to meet the basic costs of a campaign, he may as well abandon hope of winning. If the assurances are not forthcoming, his party or faction will take note. As a consequence, money probably has its greatest impact on the choice of public officials in the shadow land of our politics where it is decided who will be a candidate for a party's nomination and who will not. There are many things that make an effective candidate, but here is a choke point in our politics where vital fiscal encouragement can be extended or withheld.

> *Heard states that the candidate lacking adequate financial backing is least likely to be nominated.*

The effect of money

This influence of important fund-raisers and of large contributors [in politics] is more persuasive with newcomers than with demonstrated vote-getters, more controlling with challengers than with champions.

[Thus, in conclusion] the effect of money in politics is probably more certain in determining who the candidates will be than in determining the outcome of elections.

> *In this last paragraph the author admits that money is important, but not in determining the outcome of an election.*

Summary

David W. Adamany believes that the nature of political power is so attractive that individuals will always use every available means to acquire it. While all citizens in a democracy have "an equal right to political participation," not all have an equal right to wealth; therefore a wealthy minority of the population is able to buy a louder voice. Despite other democratic inequalities, money is still the defining factor in gaining political office. Money becomes a political tool that is out of reach for the majority. He puts forward examples of the ease with which money can be used as leverage in a way that other resources cannot. The media now form a much more important part of the political process for the modern electorate than they have ever done before. To access this form of communication is expensive, and to manipulate it more costly still. He concludes that as money becomes a larger factor in the equation, it not only opens up the politicians to corruption via extortion, but also places them in a position to extort. Alexander Heard, however, argues that no "correlation is found between campaign expenditures and campaign results" and that no amount of money can guarantee victory. More important than the amount of cash contributed is the way that those monies are used or in some cases wasted. Other factors unrelated to finance influence a campaign's success. Too little or too much money is always a potential handicap, but has little to do with the actual outcome of a campaign.

FURTHER INFORMATION

Books:

Mieczkowski, Yanek, and Mark C. Carnes (editors), *The Routledge Historical Atlas of Presidential Elections*. New York: Routledge, 2001.

Overacker, Louis, *Money in Elections*. New York: The Macmillan Company, 1932.

Thurber, James A., et al. (editors), *Crowded Airwaves*. Washington, D.C.: Brookings Institute, 2000.

West, Darrell M., *Checkbook Democracy*. Boston: Northeastern University Press, 2000.

Useful websites:

www.opensecrets.org
Center for Responsible Politics site.
This organization tracks the use of money in elections and its influence on public policy.
www.ipl.org/ref/POTUS
Presidential site of Internet Public Library.

The following debates in the Pro/Con series may also be of interest:

In this volume:
    Part 2: U.S. government

Part 3: Elections

The Watergate Affair, pages 172–173
Research skills, pages 58–59

In *Media*
    Part 2: Advertising and the media.

CAN THE WEALTHY BUY THEIR WAY INTO POLITICAL OFFICE?

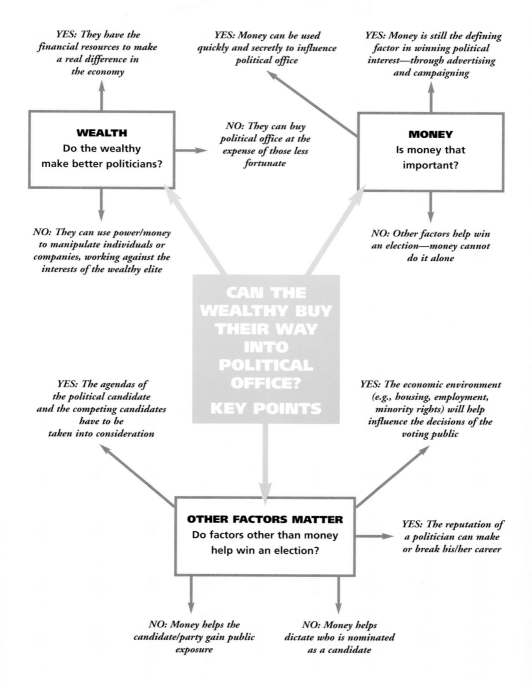

YES: They have the financial resources to make a real difference in the economy

YES: Money can be used quickly and secretly to influence political office

YES: Money is still the defining factor in winning political interest—through advertising and campaigning

WEALTH
Do the wealthy make better politicians?

NO: They can buy political office at the expense of those less fortunate

MONEY
Is money that important?

NO: They can use power/money to manipulate individuals or companies, working against the interests of the wealthy elite

NO: Other factors help win an election—money cannot do it alone

CAN THE WEALTHY BUY THEIR WAY INTO POLITICAL OFFICE?

KEY POINTS

YES: The agendas of the political candidate and the competing candidates have to be taken into consideration

YES: The economic environment (e.g., housing, employment, minority rights) will help influence the decisions of the voting public

OTHER FACTORS MATTER
Do factors other than money help win an election?

YES: The reputation of a politician can make or break his/her career

NO: Money helps the candidate/party gain public exposure

NO: Money helps dictate who is nominated as a candidate

Topic 12

DOES THE PRIMARY SYSTEM PRODUCE THE BEST PRESIDENT?

YES
"IN DEFENSE OF THE PRESIDENTIAL NOMINATING PROCESS"
FROM *CHOOSING OUR CHOICES*
ROBERT E. DICLERICO

NO
"PARTY 'REFORM' IN RETROSPECT"
FROM *POLITICAL PARTIES IN THE EIGHTIES*
EDWARD C. BANFIELD

INTRODUCTION

Presidential primaries are a familiar part of the year preceding a general election, with New Hampshire kicking off a whole series of primaries as early as February. The primaries are elections in which voters—usually but not always limited to members of the relevant party—select delegates to the presidential nominating conventions of the two major parties. Getting nominated for president requires winning enough votes at the party convention to get your name on the ballot in the general election. Although primaries seem to be an integral part of the U.S. political process, they are virtually unique. No other country has a directly equivalent system of selecting political candidates. Neither has the primary system always been used in the United States: Its first important use came only in 1903, in Wisconsin, though it then spread rapidly. Today virtually every state has adopted a version of the primary system.

Under the old presidential selection system political parties nominated their candidates for president at national conventions of delegates chosen by local party organizations around the country. The local party leaders who came together at these conventions wielded the greatest influence over deciding who would win their party's nomination. In the 20th century this method of selecting presidential nominees was attacked as being corrupt and undemocratic. It was eventually replaced by the primary system of selecting nominees.

The presidential primary system has weakened the grip of traditional party organizations in determining who gets nominated as their candidates for the presidency. Campaigns for the presidential nomination, for example, are no longer directed by regular party organizations but rather by each candidate's personal advisers and strategists. More importantly, a candidate can get nominated by his or her party simply by winning enough primaries—without needing also to win the support of the party's leaders. In this respect the presidential primary system has been described as "plebiscitary," meaning that it is characterized by candidates making direct popular appeals to win the support of the voters themselves, unmediated by party organizations.

The two major parties still hold national conventions, but they are no longer under the control of party bosses. By the time of the national conventions there is no doubt about who the nominees of each party will be—they are the candidates who have already won the presidential primary campaigns of their party.

The primary system of selecting presidential nominees does not have universal support. One common criticism of the primary system is that it does not guarantee that the best-qualified candidate will be chosen: Poor results in early primaries can knock a promising candidate out of the race even before he or she has a chance to put a case to a broader electorate.

The following articles present some of the most important arguments for and against the presidential primary system. Robert DiClerico admits that the primary system has its drawbacks, but he also contends that its critics "have undervalued the strengths of the president-by-primary process, while often overstating the benefits of the system it has replaced." DiClerico identifies four major areas in which the primary system is better than the system that it replaced. First, it produces more candidates and therefore provides voters with more choices. It also enables even those candidates who have little chance of winning their party's nominations the opportunity to influence the terms of the debate. Second, the long and tortuous primary system tests the candidates' toughness, temperament, and resilience; it forces them to connect with the American people; and it fosters some of the skills necessary to govern effectively, such as the ability to win public support, especially through the medium of television. Third, the primary system diminishes the influence of party elites and thus is a more democratic process. Finally, DiClerico says that the primary system may well serve an important function in preparing an incoming president for the demands of governing.

Edward C. Banfield argues against the primary system, claiming that "The 'new' system makes probable the election of a president who is radically unacceptable to a substantial majority of the electorate." Banfield argues that while party elites once exerted a moderating influence over the nominating process, the primary system is likely to produce "extremist candidates" who appeal to the party zealots voting in the primaries but not to average voters in a general election. Banfield also argues that the primary system, by separating candidates from their party and its institutional base in Congress, makes it difficult for a new president to govern effectively. The decline of the president's influence over Congress, Banfield argues, also creates opportunities for special interest groups to influence policymaking. Banfield worries that as a consequence of the primary system's effects on how the government works, "public confidence in and respect for government will decline."

IN DEFENSE OF THE PRESIDENTIAL NOMINATING PROCESS
Robert E. DiClerico

YES

Perhaps no feature of the American political process has been subject to more sustained and searing criticism over the last thirty years than the way we go about selecting the presidential nominees of each political party. From scholars, journalists, and public officials alike has come the charge that there is a great deal wrong with the presidential nominating process.... The dean of American political journalists (David Broder) finds the process to be a "recklessly haphazard way to choose the candidates for that demanding office." I will argue that the critics have undervalued the strengths of the president-by-primary process, while often overstating the benefits of the system it has replaced.

DiClerico opens his argument by stating his opponents' case and explaining how he will argue against it.

More candidates

Prior to the reforms of the seventies and the concurrent proliferation of primaries, presidential aspirants who were not looked upon favorably by the party elites stood little chance of winning the nomination—a reality that no doubt discouraged many from even attempting to run. But changes in the nominating process, in conjunction with campaign finance reforms, have made it possible for candidates to take their cases directly to the American people via the primaries. It should not be surprising, then, that we find more candidates running for the presidency after 1968.

The increase in the number of candidates running for the presidency is, on the whole, a healthy development in the nominating process. Within limits, more choice is better than less. Moreover those who may not necessarily stand much chance of winning nevertheless have some opportunity to enter the national debate and, particularly in candidate forums, compel other contenders to address their concerns.

In the 2000 presidential election candidates who influenced debate early in the primary process included John McCain and Steve Forbes for the Republicans and Bill Bradley for the Democrats.

With the party reforms and advent of the president-by-primary process, candidates must now take their case to a nationwide audience. This task, combined with the organizing that must be done to qualify for matching public funds, makes it virtually impossible to announce for the presidency six months before the conventions. On the contrary, candidates have been declaring anywhere from 12 to 18 months prior to their convention.

For the critics, what has just been described is precisely the problem. They assert that the president-by-primary process, though long and tortuous, does little to test candidates on the skills and qualities required in the presidency. Furthermore, the campaign itself has become such an ordeal that otherwise capable individuals are declining to run, thereby leaving the field to those less accomplished.

Several points should be noted in response to these indictments. First, the presidency is the most demanding and consequential public office in the world. Accordingly a nominating process with formal and informal stages that together consume the better part of two years does not seem inappropriate to determine who shall be the nominees for that office. Furthermore it is not unreasonable to assume that the longer we have to observe presidential candidates, the more of themselves they will reveal.

Second, Bill Bradley aptly observed that "When you run for President, you've got to get your arms around the country in a very fundamental way." Gruelling though it may be, the president-by-primary process is surely more successful than the old system in achieving that embrace, for it compels candidates to travel the length and breadth of the country, sensitizing them to its rich diversity as well as to issues on the minds of citizens in particular states and/or regions.

Third, to suggest that the skills required to compete and win have little to do with those necessary to govern is not wholly accurate. To be sure, some qualities many would value in a president, such as courage, decisiveness, or a sense of history, may not necessarily be tested; but then again, it is not altogether clear that they were under the old system either. Other qualities, however, get tested rather well—none more so than physical stamina and mental toughness. There are others too, including a candidate's ability to identify, organize, motivate, and manage talent as he or she goes about the task of assembling an elaborate organization charged with waging a nationwide campaign. Also tested will be a candidate's mental dexterity and grasp of the major issues confronting the nation, for to a far greater extent than was true under the old system presidential candidates are subject to having their views probed and questioned by those best positioned to do so—their opponents.

The current nominating process is also better suited than the old to preparing candidates for what has become an

> The kind of events to which DiClerico refers include the deaths of major world politicians, the outbreak of war, political scandal, or financial decline.

> Do you feel that presidential candidates would take much notice of local affairs were it not for the primary system?

increasingly "public presidency." It is more public in two respects, the first of which relates to exposure and the second to support.

Regarding the first, television has greatly expanded its commitment to news programming since 1963. Accordingly presidents are covered more closely than ever before, and far out-distance Congress as the lead story on the evening news programs. Moreover in the aftermath of Vietnam and Watergate that coverage has become more intensely probing and critical, requiring of those who hold the office a toughness, temperament, and resilience of a very high order. The scrutiny to which candidates are exposed in the presidential selection process comes closest to replicating that experience. The president has also become increasingly dependant upon *public* support as a means of exerting leverage over those he seeks to persuade—a development made necessary by the declining importance of parties within Congress and the electorate. Presidents who are particularly adept at projecting themselves on television (e.g. Reagan, Clinton) are also advantaged in their ability to generate that support. A television presence and skillful handling of the media is likewise of considerable importance to presidential candidates who, in the course of communicating with a host of primary electorates, must do so principally through the medium of television.

Diminished party elites

Of all the deficiencies ascribed to the president-by-primary process, none perhaps resonates more strongly with its critics than the diminished role of the party elites in the choosing of presidential nominees.

Once again, the critics have overstated their case, for the influence of the party elites, although undeniably reduced, can still make itself felt in the current nominating process. The important quality-control function they are presumed to have performed under the old system was actually less impressive than some would have us believe. A certain number of convention slots have been reserved for superdelegates—party officials and public office holders who, if they choose, may go to the Democratic National Convention uncommitted to any candidate. It should be noted that while superdelegates constituted 20 percent of all delegates to the 1996 convention, they represented fully 36 percent of the number needed for nomination. Thus, if united, superdelegates could make the difference in a close contest, as indeed they did in the 1984 nomination race.

The author uses statistics to argue that party elites still have an undue influence on convention decisions.

Fear that the demise of the party elites would invite self-starting, insurgent candidates with little experience … simply has not materialized. Furthermore if we compare the government experience of those chosen by the president-by-primary process to those elevated to the nomination under the old system, the former compare favorably with the latter.

Nominating and governing

Those harboring serious doubts about the efficacy of the current nominating process also insist that it complicates a president's ability to govern. Under the old system, it is argued, presidential candidates were required to forge alliances and reach accommodations with party elites—the very people they would have to share power with once they became president. With the demise of the party elites in the nominating process, according to the critics, presidential candidates are no longer obliged to take their views into account, which presumably renders more difficult their ability to govern.

That segment of the party elite most crucial to a president's success in governing is members of Congress, since most of what he wants to do will require their support in one way or another. Yet the critics have not provided much in the way of specifics as to how these alliances with members of Congress were forged under the old system, what accommodations were reached, and the implications of both for the president's policy positions. More importantly, recent evidence suggests that the disconnect between presidential candidates and the congressional wing of their party, presumed to be a consequence of the president-by-primary process, is not as apparent as the critics seem to suggest.

However a presidential candidate is chosen, DiClerico argues, he will have to work with Congress.

Conclusion

At bottom, there are two characteristics of the president-by-primary process that distinguish it from its predecessor. First, the selection of presidential nominees is placed in the hands of primary electorates rather than party elites, although the latter still have an opportunity to have an impact on the process. Second, expensive and demanding though it may be, the president-by-primary process subjects candidates to more protracted and intense scrutiny by the public, media, and even the party elites, than ever occurred under the old system. To be sure, this scrutiny does not guarantee that the most qualified candidate will be chosen. No system can. Yet it probably does a better job than the old system of ensuring that we do not select a very bad candidate.

How important is media scrutiny of presidential candidates? Is there any evidence that increased scrutiny before the presidential election is producing a morally "better" type of president?

PARTY "REFORM" IN RETROSPECT
Edward C. Banfield

The "old" party system and the "new"

Banfield argues that the old system required a candidate to have a wide variety of support at the state level.

In the days of the "old" party system—from Andrew Jackson's time to about the mid-1950s—both national parties were loose confederations of state parties that came alive every four years to nominate presidential candidates and then to wage campaigns for them. Some state parties existed in name only, but most were loose alliances of city machines, state and local officeholders, labor unions and other interest groups, and some wealthy individuals.

To be taken seriously as a contender for the presidential nomination, one had to be a leading figure in a major state party organization or have the backing of someone who was. The state leaders, many of whom were governors or senators, were political professionals who typically had worked themselves into positions of power by faithful service to the party. A few party leaders in each state, usually in some sort of convention—a "smoke-filled room"—chose the state's delegates to the national party convention. To win the presidential nomination therefore an aspirant had to put together a winning coalition of state leaders.

This famous phrase was first used to describe the nomination of Warren G. Harding at the Republican convention in 1920. When the nominating convention was deadlocked, party managers met at night and picked Harding as an unlikely compromise candidate. He was only nominated by the convention after 10 ballots.

More popular candidates?

That was the "old" party system. The "new" one is strikingly different. Today an aspirant for the presidential nomination need not be a state party leader or have the support of one. What is essential today is that he show promise of being able to win an enthusiastic, but not necessarily overwhelmingly large, popular following.

This change results from a sharp increase in the number of states having presidential primaries: from 17 in 1968 to 30 in 1976. Now nearly three-fourths of the Democratic and more than two-thirds of the Republican convention delegates are chosen in primaries. Even in the states that retain the convention system, party leaders are not as free as before to choose—and control—delegates. Obviously, a would-be nominee will court voters, not party leaders. If he does well enough with the voters, he may have the nomination won weeks before the convention is called to order.

His problem being to show that he can win primaries, the aspiring candidate will need to build an organization suitable for that purpose—one or two advisers with a talent for this sort of entrepreneurship, and several technical specialists: fund-raisers, pollsters, direct mail advertising experts, television and radio producers, organizers of volunteers, legal advisers, and so on.

Consequences for the political system

The party system is, of course, a component of the larger set of arrangements that is the political system. It is characteristic of any system that its elements are interrelated in such a manner that a change in the state of any one produces changes in all the others. "Reform" of the party system may therefore be expected to produce changes in features of the government that are in a sense remote from the parties themselves.

How has the political system been affected by the movement from the "old" to the "new" party? The question does not admit of a really satisfactory answer. For one thing, it is impossible to specify the particular causes, very likely many and diverse, that together have produced a particular effect; party "reform" was certainly a contributing cause of some changes, but how can one say whether its contribution was large or small? For another thing, the effects in question are seldom readily apparent; they may appear at unexpected places within the political system and at unexpected times: the most important may not appear for many years, until some unusual strain is put upon the political system.

Problems of the "new" system

Obviously, then the list that follows must be regarded with much caution. The "new" system makes probable the election of a president who is radically unacceptable to a substantial majority of the electorate. Under the "old" system, there was always the likelihood that mediocrities would be nominated: one could be confident however that they would be moderate mediocrities—the party professionals would see to that. Now it is likely that unrepresentative enthusiasts, voting in primaries, will produce extremist candidates in both major parties. Even if, under the pressures of office, the elected extremist adapts to the realities of the situation by moving toward the center, the consensual basis on which freedom and order so critically depend may in the meanwhile have been badly damaged.

Many commentators think that the U.S. political system tends to produce consensus and compromise. Do you see any signs that politics is being dominated by "extremists"?

The changes in the party system have decreased somewhat the power of the presidency in relation to that of the Congress. A president under the "new" system normally will not enter the White House as the leader of a coalition that includes principal figures in the House and Senate and, as often as not, he may be an "outsider." Under the best of circumstances, it takes some time for a new president to establish the basis of understanding and trust with the leaders of his party in Congress on which the success of his efforts at leadership depends. His position vis-à-vis Congress—indeed, vis-à-vis all those with whom he must deal—is much weakened by the fact that he may fail to win renomination: a president who has, say, a 25 percent chance of serving for eight years will presumably be taken only half as seriously as would one who has a 50 percent chance. The possibility of challenging the president for the nomination will be ever-present in the minds of some key figures in Congress. This will make it all the more difficult for the president to exert leadership there. Those who see themselves as possible challengers will refrain from supporting presidential positions they may later want to

> In reality parties tend to renominate sitting presidents— but not always without stiff competition.

A delegate waits for voting to begin at the 1992 Republican Convention. The primary system means that the candidate for president has been chosen long before the convention vote.

attack. The president, knowing that his strongest party associates are potential opponents, will avoid using them ways that might improve their standing in the polls.

The falling reputation of politics

The diminution of the president's influence with the leaders of Congress has opened new opportunities for the exercise of influence by special interest groups. This, in some measure, explains the phenomenal increase in the number of Washington lobbies in the past 30 years—from about 2,000 to about 15,000. (The main cause however has surely been the extension of federal intervention into every nook and cranny of national life.) Insofar as the competitive bidding of interest groups replaces presidential leadership, the policy outcome will be delay, stalemate, and contradiction. Government will be more "conservative," that is, less able to act, but the flood of special interest legislation will continue to rise. Presidential influence would be needed to stop it—more influence now than in the "old" days because congressmen who once depended upon the party label and party precinct captains to keep them in office must now look elsewhere for the large sums needed to court the issue-oriented voter. (The average House chairman received $45,000 from political action committees in the 1978 elections.)

Although this is an aside in Banfield's argument, it makes an important point and might be seen as weakening his case.

Public confidence in and respect for government will decline. The "new" system gives members of the president's party the incentive to undermine confidence in him and in his administration, in the hope of taking the nomination from him. There is a limitless supply of grounds (albeit mostly technical) for charging violation of the campaign financing laws and therefore "corruption." An "outsider" president will be unable to establish his ascendancy over other party leaders. There will be an appalling increase in the amount of special interest legislation and a relentless thrust of the bureaucracies toward self-aggrandizement. These and other causes will make the citizen ever more angry and frustrated with government and ever less disposed to think of it as the defender of liberty and justice.

Summary

Does the primary system produce the best president? The question is a complicated one, and the various arguments for and against primaries are complex. The question is of more than academic significance, however: It forces Americans to reflect on what qualities we expect in a president and whether the current system of selecting candidates for the presidency actually fosters those qualities.

According to DiClerico, the primary system, despite being long and tortuous for all involved—including the voters—does a good job of preparing candidates for the demands of the presidency. Moreover, it is more democratic than the previous process, which was dominated by party managers and backroom deals, and allows for the selection of a candidate even if he or she is not the choice of the party leadership. Banfield argues, in direct contradiction, that the primary system actually does a bad job in preparing candidates for the demands of this important office. Moreover, to the extent that it produces extremist candidates who do not appeal to the average citizen, he implies that it is actually less democratic than the previous party-dominated process.

FURTHER INFORMATION:

Books:

Barber, James David (editor), *Choosing the President*. Englewood Cliffs, NJ: Prentice-Hall, 1974.

Ceaser, James, *Presidential Selection*. Princeton, NJ: Princeton University Press, 1979.

Davis, James W., *U.S. Presidential Primaries and the Caucus-Convention System: A Sourcebook*. Westport, CT: Greenwood Press, 1997.

Davis, James W., *Presidential Primaries: Road to the White House*. Westport, CT: Greenwood Press, 1997.

DiClerico, Robert E., and James W. Davis (editors), *Choosing Our Choices: Debating the Presidential Nominating Process*. Lanham, MD: Rowman and Littlefield Publishers, Inc., 2000.

Kendall, Kathleen E., *Communication in the Presidential Primaries: Candidates and the Media, 1912–2000*. Westport, CT: Praeger, 2000.

Mayer, William G. (editor), *In Pursuit of the White House 2000: How We Choose Our Presidential Nominees*. New York: Chatham House Publishers, 2000.

Sanford, Terry, *A Danger of Democracy: The Presidential Nominating Process*. Boulder, CO: Westview, 1981.

Useful websites:

www.cnn.com/ELECTION/2000/primaries
CNN archive of the results of the 2000 election campaign.

www.washington-weekly.com/Primaries.html
Washington Weekly archive of the 1996 primary candidates and their main speeches.

www.thegreenpapers.com/index.html
Archive of recent U.S. elections.

The following debates in the Pro/Con series may also be of interest:

In this volume:

DOES THE PRIMARY SYSTEM PRODUCE THE BEST PRESIDENT?

YES: The long and arduous primary system is a good test of a candidate's stamina

YES: The primary system ensures that the media have a long time to scrutinize a candidate and that the candidate will be media friendly

YES: The primary system allows politicians to appeal directly to the people

PREPARATION
Does the primary system help prepare candidates for the office of president?

NO: The primary system means that good candidates are knocked out before the majority of the public has the chance to judge them

DEMOCRACY
Is the primary system compatible with the principles of democracy?

NO: Before the primary system presidential candidates had to establish a wide range of support at a local or state level. This was just as useful in preparing candidates for the presidency

NO: The primary system gives too much importance to the registered supporters of either party, not the great mass of regular voters

DOES THE PRIMARY SYSTEM PRODUCE THE BEST PRESIDENT?

KEY POINTS

YES: Candidates are tested more during a long primary process than otherwise, demonstrating their true abilities

YES: The primary system is plebiscitary, meaning that individual voters get the chance to have their say simply by being party supporters

QUALITY OF CANDIDATE
Does the primary system produce a better quality of presidential candidate?

CHOICE
Does the primary system give voters more choice?

NO: Many attractive candidates might be knocked out of the race early by bad results, by the enormous cost of campaigning, or by a reluctance to undergo constant media scrutiny

NO: Because party managers no longer play an important role in mediating the selection of candidates, they are more likely to be extremists with little appeal to most voters

NO: Primaries have produced ineffectual, weak, or corrupt presidents, just as the previous system did

Topic 13
SHOULD THE ELECTORAL COLLEGE BE ABOLISHED?

YES
"THE ELECTORAL COLLEGE AND DIRECT ELECTION OF THE PRESIDENT AND VICE PRESIDENT"
U.S. SENATE COMMITTEE ON THE JUDICIARY, JANUARY 27, 1977
SENATOR BIRCH BAYH

NO
"THE ELECTORAL COLLEGE AND DIRECT ELECTION"
U.S. SENATE COMMITTEE ON THE JUDICIARY, JULY 22, 1977
HERBERT J. STORING

INTRODUCTION

Among the most regularly and sharply criticized aspects of the American political system is the electoral college. Article II, section 1 of the Constitution provides that the president is to be elected not directly by the people but by "electors" appointed by the legislature of each state, "in such manner as the legislature thereof may direct." Each state is allotted as many electoral votes as it has senators and representatives in Congress. (The District of Columbia, however, gets three votes even though it has no members of Congress.)

In general, state laws provide that the winner of the popular vote within a state receives all of its electoral votes. To win the presidency, a candidate must receive a majority of electoral votes, or 270. If no candidate receives a majority of the electoral votes, the House of Representatives selects the president from those three receiving the highest number. In this process each state delegation has only one vote regardless of its number of representatives (thus giving the smallest state as much influence as the largest), and a majority of all states is required for election.

The electoral college method of electing the president was adopted at the Constitutional Convention in 1787 as the result of political compromise. A Commission on Electoral College Reform report on electing the president stated in 1967: "By allotting each state the same number of electors as it had senators and representatives, the electoral college allowed the Framers to settle the dispute between small states and large states, slave states and non-slave states, using the same principles and mechanisms they had used to settle their disagreements over representation in the legislature."

Though the electoral college was generally well received at the time of the Constitutional Convention, there have been numerous proposals throughout the history of the United States to alter or abolish this method of electing the president, a method that the American Bar Association once described as being "archaic, undemocratic, complex, ambiguous, indirect, and dangerous."

One of the most frequently expressed concerns about the electoral college is that, under this process of electing the president, a candidate could win the popular vote but not triumph in the electoral vote, as has happened several times in American history. In 1824 Andrew Jackson probably had more popular votes than his rivals, even though the House of Representatives chose John Quincy Adams as president after none of the candidates had received a majority of electoral votes. In 1876 Samuel J. Tilden won a majority of the popular votes, but Rutherford B. Hayes won the election when Congress awarded him disputed electoral votes. In 1888 Grover Cleveland received the larger popular vote, but Benjamin Harrison won the electoral vote to take the presidency. Most recently in 2000 Al Gore won the popular vote by more than 500,000 votes, and yet George W. Bush emerged as president with 271 electoral votes, just one more than the minimum necessary for victory.

The election of 2000, the nation's closest presidential race in more than a century, was ultimately decided through a bitterly fought legal battle over the 25 electoral votes of Florida. It was a fight that was ultimately decided by nine U.S. Supreme Court justices, who themselves split bitterly over the issue. That George W. Bush was able to win the presidency without winning the popular vote was decisive proof in the minds of its critics that the electoral college is undemocratic.

In 1977 Indiana Senator Birch Bayh proposed amendments calling for the abolition of the electoral college in favor of a nationwide popular vote for the president. In the event that no candidate received at least 40 percent of the popular vote, it provided for a run-off election between the top two candidates. After a decade of sporadic debate the proposal to scrap the electoral college died in the Senate. Although it had majority support, the bill did not have the two-thirds majority that it constitutionally required for constitutional amendments.

As chairman of the Senate Subcommittee on Constitutional Amendments, Senator Bayh held hearings on the proposal. What follows are excerpts from the hearings, which lay out arguments for and against abolishing the electoral college. While Bayh argues that the electoral college is "an affront to the principle of democracy," political scientist Herbert J. Storing responds by saying that the case against the electoral college is "superficially plausible and appealing, but fundamentally unsound and unpersuasive."

THE ELECTORAL COLLEGE AND DIRECT ELECTION OF THE PRESIDENT AND VICE PRESIDENT
Senator Birch Bayh

OPENING STATEMENT OF HON. BIRCH BAYH,
U.S. SENATOR FROM THE STATE OF INDIANA
AND CHAIRMAN, SUBCOMMITTEE ON
CONSTITUTIONAL AMENDMENTS

Today we begin hearings which I am confident will demonstrate the great need for direct popular election of the President and Vice President of the United States.

In the future, the American people—rather than the faceless, undemocratic electoral college—should choose the two highest officials in the land. For more than a decade, I and many of my colleagues have fought for enactment of a constitutional amendment to abolish the electoral college and to permit the American people to elect directly the President and Vice President.

> Bayh's argument has strong popular appeal since it is in favor of empowering the American people over an institution.

Bipartisan support

Many of my distinguished colleagues on both sides of the aisle are joining me in this bipartisan effort, and we intend to seek prompt action in the Senate this year. My distinguished colleagues, Senator Hubert Humphrey and Senator Robert Dole, will be the lead-off witnesses today. They have joined more than 40 of us in the Senate in sponsoring Senate Joint Resolution 1—the proposed direct election amendment—and they demonstrate the breadth of political support for this proposal. Hubert Humphrey has been a visionary on electoral reform. For more than 23 years, as a U.S. Senator, a Vice President, a Presidential candidate, and again as a U.S. Senator, he has been an eloquent spokesman for direct election.

Bob Dole more recently joined the ranks as one of the leading spokesmen for direct election. In 1973, as a U.S. Senator and former Republican National Committee chairman, he was our lead-off witness. Now he has witnessed from a very personal perspective the most recent test of the undemocratic electoral college in the 1976 Presidential and Vice Presidential election.

Partisan politics aside on this important issue, Hubert Humphrey, Bob Dole, and I join my distinguished friends, Senator Howard Baker, Senator Henry Bellmon, Senator Henry Jackson, and Representative Robert McClory, all of whom will testify today—and many other Members of both Houses of Congress—in urging prompt adoption of a direct election amendment.

We and a large bipartisan majority of the American people say that the electoral college must be abolished. The American people must be allowed to elect their President and Vice President directly.

Close-run elections

Only by sheer luck [in] November [1976] did [the American people] survive another round of electoral roulette with the popular will prevailing. The archaic electoral college came closer to defeating the popular will than it did in either of the close elections of 1960 and 1968. In fact not since 1888 has the present, outdated system come closer, percentage wise, to putting a President in office who came in second in the popular vote.

These elections involved John Kennedy and Richard Nixon in 1960, and Hubert Humphrey and Richard Nixon in 1968.

Even though President Carter's popular margin of victory was more than 10 times greater than President Kennedy's in 1960 and more than twice as great as President Nixon's popular vote margin over Senator Humphrey in 1968, a switch of only 9,245 votes in Ohio and Hawaii would have denied an electoral majority to President Carter.

That shift of popular votes, amounting to only about one-hundredth of 1 percent of the popular vote, would have denied the White House to President Carter in spite of a popular vote plurality of 1.7 million votes. President Carter's Southern strength, in particular, gave him millions of extra popular votes that were of no electoral value.

Undemocratic odds

Use specific examples—such as the 1976 election—to support broader points in your argument.

In close elections, such as the 1976 election and those in 1960 and 1968, statistical studies have shown that there is only a 50-50 chance that the winner of the popular vote will also be the winner of the electoral vote. Stated another way, in close elections there is a 50-50 chance that the candidate who receives the most votes will not be elected President.

That is, by simple definition, undemocratic. It is an affront to the principle of democracy—an affront which we tolerate, most ironically, only in the election of the two most important officials in our country.

As members of this great legislative body, one of our weightiest responsibilities is to preserve and, when necessary, correct flaws in the Constitution of the United States for present and future generations of Americans.

Bayh states what his credentials are for considering the idea of constitutional reform. This gives his argument weight.

This duty must be fulfilled with the greatest of care and deliberation. It has happened that, as chairman of the Subcommittee on Constitutional Amendments for nearly 14 years, I have been involved in Senate passage of two constitutional amendments, as well as the proposed 27th amendment which has already been ratified by 35 States.

But I do not take lightly the business of amending the Constitution. I do not propose to alter this nearly 200-year-old document casually. The long history of the study of electoral reform may establish this subject and the proposed direct election amendment as the longest considered, most carefully debated constitutional amendment in [our] history. For more

COMMENTARY: The votes that really count

Political theorists have been debating the question of the electoral college since it was created. Over the last 200 years, more than 700 proposals have been made to reform or abolish it. Changing the electoral college has been the most frequently proposed Constitutional amendment. The electoral college does involve a trade-off between direct democracy—where the majority rules—and representative democracy, where individuals are chosen to represent the whole people. Yet the system survives, and it seems that it will not be abolished easily.

The electoral college was invented by the Founders. At the time that they were drafting the Constitution, politics was strongly partisan at a local level. The Founders hoped to encourage national unity by giving each elector two votes and stipulating that at least one must be for someone not from his own state. The intention was that presidential candidates should appeal on a community basis—to a cross section of voters across different regions and with different interests—rather than centering on the needs of one bloc of voters. Electors are often state party officials or other loyal individuals chosen by the party. They have, however, been cases in which electors have voted for candidates that were not their party's nominee.

The outcome of a presidential election does not become final until a month after the election day. On the first Monday after the second Wednesday in December electors meet in each state to vote. The results are sent to Congress, where they are counted on January 6. On January 20 the candidate who received the largest number of electoral votes is inaugurated as president.

than a century and a half, we have recognized the perils of a system that leaves the choice of president to a group of electors—electors whose freedom to disregard the will of the people is presently guaranteed by the Constitution.

A Senate report published in 1826 noted that the free and independent electors had "degenerated into mere agents in a case which requires no agency and where the agent must be useless if he is faithful and dangerous if he is not." Yet more than 150 years later we still are subjected to the grave risks that the popular will of the people can easily be thwarted, either by the strange arithmetic of the electoral system or by the deeds of a handful of power brokers.

For more than two decades, the Senate Judiciary Committee has held hearings on electoral reform. Eleven years ago, the Subcommittee on Constitutional Amendments began the current study. Hearings on the election of the President began on February 28, 1966. In the following years, the record of the subcommittee's hearings on electoral reform totalled nearly 2,600 pages. In 1969, the House of Representatives approved a constitutional amendment for direct election by an overwhelming 339 to 70 vote. During Senate debate in 1970, we came within a handful of votes of breaking the filibuster which denied the American people even a vote on this crucial issue.

Bayh traces the history of hearings on electoral reform to try to suggest that change is becoming inevitable.

I have many times said that nothing is more important to the confidence of the American people in our political system and to the permanency and stability of our Government than the just and equitable selection of the President and Vice President.

Power of the people

An overwhelming majority of the American people—more than 80 percent according to a Gallup poll—favor direct popular election. The American people look to us now to assure that in future elections their popular vote will elect the President without the present risk that the will of the people can be thwarted by the electoral college. This proposed constitutional amendment should wait no longer. The confidence of the American people must no longer be suspended on such a narrow reed.

I look forward to the testimony of Senator[s] Humphrey and Dole, and the other witnesses who will participate in these hearings as important contributions to the culmination of this sub-committee's long and thorough study of electoral reform. I am confident that we are taking important historic steps toward adoption of the amendment by this Congress.

THE ELECTORAL COLLEGE AND DIRECT ELECTION
Herbert J. Storing

NO

Storing gets straight to his argument and says that direct popular election is against tradition and threatens democracy.

I want, basically, to make three points. In the first place, it seems to me that the case for direct popular election of the President rests on a simplistic notion of American democracy—a notion that is contrary to our tradition, that is unsound, and that is dangerous. Second, I think that the present constitutional system of electing the President supports a mode of Federal politics characterized by our two great state-based political parties that secures, to a great extent, the benefits we want in an electoral system. And, third, the alleged danger to democratic legitimacy arising from the present electoral college system and the superiority of direct popular election in fostering legitimacy are false.

Simplistic democracy

Explain the terms of your argument. The author clearly spells out what he means by "simplistic democracy."

I think that simplistic democracy has two elements. First, it assumes that government is good just so far as it is responsive to public wishes. The business of government, in this view, is simply to do what the people want. The second element of simplistic democracy is that so far as elections are concerned, the only thing that counts is that the individual wanted by most of the people should be elected. Any other consideration is regarded as unfair and improper. The proposal for direct popular election of the President seems to me to grow out of this simplistic democracy, to a very large extent; and its adoption would, I think, strengthen it.

Now the question is not whether responsiveness is important and necessary. Everyone agrees that it is. But the great architectural principle of our Government, as it was understood by its framers, is that popular responsiveness is necessary but not sufficient. There are other qualities we want in government, such as competence, stability, and sensitivity to individual and minority rights which may sometimes be at odds with responsiveness. The great genius of the American Government is the way it seeks to achieve these other qualities in a government that is, at the same time, basically democratic or responsive. One of the most powerful results of the adoption of direct popular election of the president, it seems to me, would be to tend to strengthen this notion of simplistic democracy—this notion that responsiveness is all that counts. It is true that one could grant all I've said so far and still say, correctly, that that doesn't settle the question of electoral reform. It does, however, dispose of what has in fact been the main argument of the advocates of direct popular election; namely, that any incidence of nonresponsiveness, such as, for example, the election of a president who did not have a popular plurality, is necessarily bad.

Storing's central argument is that democracy is not only about responding to popular opinion. A government needs other qualities as well.

Electoral output

I want to emphasize a couple of points in defense of the present constitutional system for electing the president. The first one is a rather theoretical point, but I think it's terribly important. It is this: To see the value of the present system, it is necessary to shift one's perspective from the question of electoral input to electoral output. Most of this discussion—especially from the proponents of direct popular election—has been concerned with the question of input: who votes, the way to vote, and matters of that kind. I know that our Framers did—and I think that we ought also to— concern ourselves with the question of the product of any electoral system. An electoral system is a means to serve the ends. In order to judge the electoral system, then, we have to try to think of what are the ends we want to accomplish and whether this or that given electoral system is likely to accomplish it. One of the main ways to strengthen this whole discussion of proposals for reform would be more focus on results and more focus on output, rather than merely a focus on input.

Having argued against changing the electoral college, Storing now moves on to make a positive case for the system.

Looking to the Framers

If we ask the questions, then, what is it we want out of an electoral system for electing the president? What kinds of things do we want to achieve? Our Framers provide us with some very useful guidance. I would summarize the ends of the system of electing the president, as the framers generally saw them, as something like the following. They seem to me to be altogether pertinent and appropriate today.

First, it should provide for significant participation by the people at large. Second, it should foster political stability and avoid the excesses of partisanship and factionalism that tend to form around important elections. Third, it should give some special place of influence to some individuals who are especially informed of, and committed to, the process of government. Fourth, it should recognize that this is a Nation of States and should give some weight to the interests of States. Fifth, it should leave the president independent of any institution of government, so far as his election is concerned. Sixth, it should, of course, tend to produce presidents of respectable character and intelligence.

The two-party system

The two-party system is one in which the electorate mainly votes for two major parties, either of which can win a majority in the legislature.

It is very hard to say how a change in the constitutional system for electing the president would affect the way our present two-party system works. It is that two-party system through which most of these benefits are achieved today. My own feeling is that that very difficulty is a good reason for being cautious about introducing changes—the consequences of which are difficult to foresee. Without claiming that this is by any means the last word on this matter, my own judgment would be that the probable effect of changing to a direct popular election of the president would be in the direction of weakening, or further weakening, our traditional two-party system.

The tendency of minority groups to go directly into presidential politics, either in hopes of influencing a runoff election or with the intention of bargaining for other advantages or even to provide an organizational focus for interest group activities of a fundamentally nonelectoral kind, seems to me likely to increase under direct popular election. Similarly, the role of the States—and specifically the State party organizations, already weakened in various respects— seems likely to be further undermined.

Drawbacks of popular election

Storing does not claim that the current system is perfect, but he paints an undesirable picture of the likely alternative.

Direct popular election of the president would, I think, foster a more open, volatile system of national politics, less rooted in State political organizations, less influenced by professionals or quasi-professionals, dominated by shifting alliances of nationally oriented personalities, by ideologies, by interest group spokesmen, and by media specialists. We could anticipate a political system pulled in one direction toward fragmentation and public, rather than intraparty, factionalism. And pulled, in the other direction, toward plebiscitory unity—rooted not in party organizations but in an individual President's personality and standing. The present system, as it works, does, it seems to me, provide us with the kinds of benefits that we want out of an electoral system reasonably satisfactorily. Nobody is going to claim that it's perfect.

Question of legitimacy

Finally to come to the trump card of the proponents of direct popular election—and my third point—there is the question of legitimacy. Wouldn't it be an intolerable strain to the American political system, giving rise to popular outrage and contempt, if it should happen, as it doubtless will happen, that sometime again a man with fewer popular votes than his opponent is the electoral winner? I doubt it. I would expect, under such a situation, for business to proceed in American politics pretty much as usual, unless there was some other reason for loss of confidence in the government.

Did business proceed pretty much as usual after the 2000 election, when this was again the case?

The idea that election of a president with less than a plurality of popular votes would be shocking and deeply disturbing to our system rests, I think, on a shallow notion of what political legitimacy is all about. Legitimacy depends on much more than mere numerical preponderance. Legitimacy depends, for one thing on tradition. For all the criticisms that are levelled against it, the electoral college system is very much a part of the American political tradition.

Should tradition be taken as a strong argument in favor of the status quo?

Design of government

Legitimacy depends also on the possession by government of those other qualities that the Framers sought to provide for: competence, stability, diverse representation, and equity. I think the doctrine of simplistic democracy tends to endanger that. The present constitutional system for electing the president can be explained and popularly understood for what it is: a method of election that secures the benefits that the American Government is designed to secure—federalism, social diversity, governmental competence, stability, and fairness to individuals and to minorities.

Present system still the best

The present system does have what could be called legitimacy problems but these difficulties are likely to seem minor compared to the legitimacy problems that would arise out of a series of very close elections, bitterly fought by numerous narrowly based parties contending for the prize of numerical majority, which would be the only real claim to legitimacy and which would yet be forever out of reach. The case against the present constitutional system for electing the president remains, I think, what it has always been—superficially plausible and appealing, but fundamentally unsound and unpersuasive.

Summary

These excerpts lay out clearly arguments for and against abolishing the electoral college. Birch Bayh, speaking in support of a constitutional amendment to abolish the electoral college, is concerned about what he takes to be the profoundly undemocratic character of the present system. Under the electoral college, he says, "the popular will of the people can easily be thwarted." Were this to happen, he suggests, the American people would lose confidence in the legitimacy of our political system. Bayh thus argues strongly for direct popular election of the president to ensure that the people themselves rather than a group of independent electors determine who will hold the most important political office in our democracy.

Herbert J. Storing argues with as much conviction in favor of preserving the electoral college. Storing, whose arguments are more complex than Bayh's, makes three points in opposition to direct popular election of the president: that it is based on a simplistic notion of democracy which is at odds with the complex but effective system of government established by the Framers; that it would not serve what the Framers thought were the appropriate ends of the system of electing the president; and that it would undermine the constitutional system by overturning political tradition.

FURTHER INFORMATION:

Books:

Diamond, Martin, *The Electoral College and the American Idea of Democracy*. Washington, D.C.: American Enterprise Institute,1977.

Ellis, Richard J. (editor), *Founding the American Presidency*, (especially Chapter 5 on the electoral college). Lanham, MD: Rowman & Littlefield,1999.

Articles:

Hamilton, Alexander, "*The Federalist* No. 68," in *The Federalist*, edited by Robert Scigliano. New York: The Modern Library, 2000.

Longley, Lawrence D., "Yes The Electoral College Should be Abolished," in *Controversial Issues in Presidential Selection*, edited by Gary L. Rose. Albany: SUNY Press, 1994.

Slonin, Schlomo, "The Electoral College at Philadelphia: The Evolution of an Ad Hoc Congress for the Selection of a President." *Journal of American History* 73 (June 1986), pp.35–58.

Useful websites:

www.fed.gov/pages/ecmenu2.htm
History of the electoral college and useful bibliography.

The following debates in the Pro/Con series may also be of interest:

In this volume:
Topic 1 Is direct rule by the people better than representative democracy?
Topic 7 Does the two-party system adequately represent the people?
Topic 10 Should the people be able to legislate directly through ballot initiatives?

In *Media*:
Topic 11 Is there too much political advertising?

SHOULD THE ELECTORAL COLLEGE BE ABOLISHED?

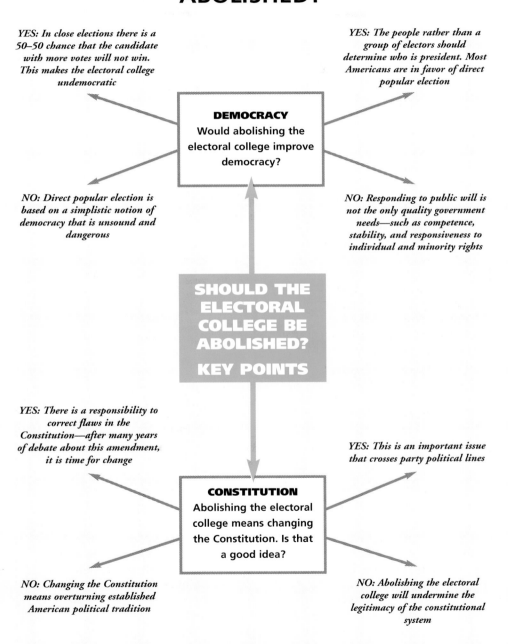

YES: In close elections there is a 50–50 chance that the candidate with more votes will not win. This makes the electoral college undemocratic

YES: The people rather than a group of electors should determine who is president. Most Americans are in favor of direct popular election

DEMOCRACY
Would abolishing the electoral college improve democracy?

NO: Direct popular election is based on a simplistic notion of democracy that is unsound and dangerous

NO: Responding to public will is not the only quality government needs—such as competence, stability, and responsiveness to individual and minority rights

SHOULD THE ELECTORAL COLLEGE BE ABOLISHED?

KEY POINTS

YES: There is a responsibility to correct flaws in the Constitution—after many years of debate about this amendment, it is time for change

YES: This is an important issue that crosses party political lines

CONSTITUTION
Abolishing the electoral college means changing the Constitution. Is that a good idea?

NO: Changing the Constitution means overturning established American political tradition

NO: Abolishing the electoral college will undermine the legitimacy of the constitutional system

THE WATERGATE AFFAIR

(1972–1975)

*"I was **under** medication
when I made the decision
not to burn the tapes."*

—FORMER U.S. PRESIDENT RICHARD M. NIXON

The Watergate affair (1972–1975) arose from revelations about illegal activities
carried out by the Republican administration of Richard M. Nixon during the 1972
presidential election campaign. What follows is a timeline of its key events.

January 20, 1969 Richard Milhous Nixon is
inaugurated as the 37th president of the
United States.

July 23, 1969 President Nixon first approves a
plan to expand the domestic activities of U.S.
intelligence services, including the FBI and
CIA. A few days later he goes back on this
decision and withdraws his approval.

June 13, 1971 *The New York Times*,
followed by *The Washington Post* only
a few days later, publishes the Defense
Department's secret history of the
Vietnam War, also known as the
Pentagon Papers. These documents
were allegedly leaked to both the
newspapers by Daniel Ellsberg, a former
defense analyst.

September 3, 1971 The office of Ellsberg's psychiatrist is burglarized by the White House "plumber's unit."

June 17, 1972 Five men break into the offices of the Democratic National Committee at the Watergate Hotel. They are arrested at 2:30 in the morning. One of the men claims to have worked for the CIA.

June 19, 1972 John Mitchell, former attorney general and head of the Nixon reelection campaign, denies any knowledge of the burglary after it's discovered that a GOP security aid is among the arrested men.

August 1, 1972 *The Washington Post* alleges that one of the burglars has a $25,000 cashier's check from Nixon's campaign in his account.

September 29, 1972 Allegations against John Mitchell. While serving as attorney general, Mitchell had a secret fund for financing intelligence-gathering operations against the Democrats.

October 10, 1972 The FBI establishes that the Nixon reelection effort and the Watergate break-in are linked.

November 7, 1972 Richard M. Nixon is reelected as president by a landslide—almost 60 percent of the vote.

January 30, 1973 G. Gordon Liddy and James W. McCord Jr. are found guilty of conspiracy, burglary, and wiretapping in the Watergate hotel. Five other men plead guilty.

April 30, 1973 Attorney General Eliott Richardson and senior White House officials H.R. Haldeman and John Ehrlichmann hand in their resignations. John Dean, the White House counsel, is fired.

May 18, 1973 Televised hearings show the findings of the Watergate committee. Archibald Cox is the Justice Department's special prosecutor for Watergate.

June 3, 1973 John Dean alleges that he discussed the Watergate coverup about 35 times with President Nixon.

June 13, 1973 Investigators find a memo addressed to John Ehrlichman. It describes plans to break into the office of Daniel Elisberg's psychiatrist. A former presidential appointments secretary reveals that Nixon has taped all conversations and telephone calls since 1971.

June 23, 1973 Nixon refuses to hand over the tapes to the Senate Watergate committee.

October 20, 1973 Nixon fires Cox and abolishes the office of special prosecutor. The attorney general and deputy attorney general resign. Members of Congress push for impeachment.

December 7, 1973 The White House cannot explain an 18.5 minute gap in one of the tapes subpoenaed.

July 27, 1974 The House Judiciary Committee passes the first of three articles of impeachment for obstruction of justice.

July 24, 1974 The Supreme Court rejects Nixon's claim of executive privilege and rules that he must turn over 64 tapes of White House conversations.

August 8, 1974 Richard M. Nixon resigns. He is the first U.S. president to do so. He is later pardoned by his successor, Gerald R. Ford.

To prevent further governmental abuses of power, the Ethics in Government Act was passed in 1978. *See page 205.*

PART 4
POLITICS AND MORALITY

One of the most distinctive but vexing features of American constitutional government is the executive. Defining the scope of executive power has been the subject of great debate throughout American history. Does the fact that the president is given the duty to "take care that the laws be faithfully executed" suggest that the proper meaning of executive power is merely to carry out the laws passed by the legislature? Or does executive power transcend this dictionary definition of "executive"?

Looking to the Constitution

That the latter alternative is the case derives some justification by a comparison of the so-called vesting clauses of Articles I and II of the Constitution. While the beginning of Article I states that "all legislative powers herein granted shall be vested in a Congress of the United States," thereby limiting the powers of Congress to those specifically enumerated in the remainder of Article I, the beginning of Article II implies no such limitation on the president's powers. It says that "the executive power shall be vested in a president of the United States." The implication is that "executive power" includes powers not specifically enumerated in the Constitution. This indicates that the Framers did not intend the executive to be merely subordinate to the laws passed by the

legislature, as the dictionary definition of executive might imply, but that they wanted the executive to have a certain flexibility, given the impossibility of providing by law for all necessities. This appreciation of the need for flexibility in the executive can be traced to the 17th-century political philosopher John Locke, who spoke of the need for what he called executive prerogative. According to Locke, the good of the society requires that the executive have the power to act according to his or her discretion, both where the law is silent and sometimes even against the law. But if we acknowledge this power of the executive, does it not force us to draw the troubling conclusion that the executive can act unconstrained by law and morality?

Limits of law and morality

To appreciate the limits of law and morality, and therefore the need for a doctrine of executive prerogative, but also the danger of such a doctrine, consider the following examples. Because Congress was not in session when the Civil War broke out in April 1861, President Abraham Lincoln did not hesitate to resort to "otherwise unconstitutional" measures to protect the Union and prosecute the war. He imposed a naval blockade on the southeast coast, employing a war power without the congressional declaration of war required by the Constitution.

He increased the size of the army and navy without congressional authority, and in order to empower government officials who were acting under the president's authority, he suspended the writ of habeas corpus, a constitutionally guaranteed civil liberty. Lincoln acted in the belief that in emergencies laws must give way to a discretionary executive power, i.e., on the basis of the doctrine of executive prerogative.

The case of President Nixon

Lincoln's actions were used by President Richard Nixon to justify the illegal actions that he considered taking against U.S. citizens opposed to his handling of the Vietnam War. When asked in an interview several years after he had resigned what he meant when he had said that the president can take actions on behalf of the national

The following topics force us to reflect on this tension between executive prerogative and the rule of law. In *Should moral principle matter in politics?* W.J. Cody and Richardson Lynn argue that all public officials must obey the law (see Topic 14). Niccolò Machiavelli, however, argued that since the law cannot anticipate changing circumstances, it would be dangerous for an executive to take one's bearings simply by what the law prescribes. In *Should the president be able to keep secrets?* (see Topic 15) Mark Rozell argues that the public's "right to know" must be balanced with the needs of national security and the president's need for candid advice from his advisers. But Raoul Berger insists that executive privilege is a constitutional myth, and it undermines democratic accountability. Since criminal

"A man who wants to make a profession of good in all regards must come to ruin among so many who are not good."
—NICCOLÒ MACHIAVELLI

interest that would otherwise be unlawful if taken by private persons, Nixon replied: "Well, what I had in mind I think was perhaps much better stated by Lincoln, during the War Between the States.... He said, 'Actions which otherwise would be unconstitutional, could become lawful if undertaken for the purpose of preserving the Constitution and the nation.' Now that's the kind of action I'm referring to." Nixon's use of Lincoln to justify illegal actions underscores the fact that exercising executive prerogative can set a dangerous precedent.

prosecution is an executive branch function, and since the U.S. Constitution declares that "the executive power shall be vested in a president," is it reasonable to consider the president subject to criminal prosecution?

In *Can a sitting president be criminally indicted?* (see Topic 16) Gary McDowell argues that since the Constitution does not expressly say otherwise, the criminal indictment of a president is permissible. However, Robert Bork argues that it would be unreasonable to subject the president to ordinary criminal prosecution.

Topic 14
SHOULD MORAL PRINCIPLE MATTER IN
POLITICS?

NO
CHAPTERS 15 & 18 FROM *THE PRINCE*
NICCOLÒ MACHIAVELLI

YES
"COMPETENT OR ETHICAL?"
AN ADAPTATION FROM CHAPTER 13 IN *HONEST GOVERNMENT: AN ETHICS GUIDE
TO PUBLIC SERVICE*
W. J. MICHAEL CODY & RICHARDSON R. LYNN

INTRODUCTION

In the wake of the massive antiwar demonstrations around the country that were provoked by the United States invasion of Cambodia in 1970, President Richard Nixon approved a plan that advocated the use of the Central Intelligence Agency, the Federal Bureau of Investigation, the Secret Service, and other police and intelligence agencies to acquire better information about the people who were opposing his administration, especially in its handling of the Vietnam War. Some of the means that were proposed for acquiring this information, such as burglaries, were clearly illegal. Although this plan was never implemented (FBI director J. Edgar Hoover opposed it), Nixon's approval of it was later listed in the articles of impeachment against him as an alleged abuse of presidential power. In an interview with David Frost several years after he had become the first president in American history to resign from office, Nixon tried to justify his approval of this plan on the grounds

that: "If the president approves something, approves an action, because of the national security, or in this case because of a threat to internal peace and order of significant magnitude, then the president's decision in that instance, is one that enables those who carry it out to carry it out without violating a law." Whether or not one accepts this as an adequate justification of Nixon's actions, it raises an important and enduring question: Are public officials justified in using immoral means in the pursuit of moral ends?

The issue of whether moral principle should matter in politics is a difficult one. Consider the following dilemma. We expect public officials to promote the interests of the people they represent, or, as W. J. Michael Cody and Richardson R. Lynn put it, "to maximize the benefits of government to all citizens." And yet we also want our public officials to be guided in their actions by moral principles. But what if, for example, a course of action that best serves the public interest does not conform to the moral principles we want our public officials to uphold, or vice versa? When faced with such a dilemma, should public officials take the course of action that is most advantageous but immoral or the one that is moral but less advantageous? Or, to pose this question from our own point of view as citizens, should we judge our public officials according to the standard of their ability to "get things done" or rather by their willingness to accomplish what they can within certain moral limits?

"Most of us are honest all the time, and all of us are honest most of the time."

—CHARLES McMATHIAS JR., U.S. CONGRESSMAN

The following selections present two diametrically opposed answers to the general question of whether moral principle should matter in politics. As the title of their book from which the following extract is taken indicates, *Honest Government: An Ethics Guide for Public Service*, Cody and Lynn believe strongly that public officials should be held to high moral standards. The authors concede that there is evidence that suggests that voters care more about "political effectiveness" than "ethical awareness." But they also believe that "there is a slow but steady trend toward public insistence on higher ethical standards for public officials." To elicit ethical behavior from those in public life, Cody and Lynn

argue, we should insist on a rigorous but workable code of public service ethics, including, for example, the insistence that public officials not lie, cheat, or steal, and that they obey the law. According to Cody and Lynn, abiding by such standards is not only morally right but also politically advantageous because politicians "become ineffective when they are caught using power illegally or if the public becomes dissatisfied with consistently unethical behavior."

An understanding of politics that subordinates politics to the demands of morality is strongly rejected by the 16th-century political philosopher Niccolò Machiavelli. To be sure, Machiavelli does not deny the importance of morality for politics. If for no other reason than to maintain the support of the people, who do care about morality, a public leader (or what Machiavelli calls a prince) must "appear merciful, faithful, humane, honest, and religious." But, as Machiavelli also argues, a successful public leader cannot afford to "observe all those things for which men are held good, since he is often under a necessity, to maintain his state, of acting against faith, against charity, against humanity, against religion." To succeed in politics, the good man must learn to overcome his moral inhibitions and practice deceit and betrayal when it is necessary for him to do so. "For," as he argues, "a man who wants to make a profession of good in all regards must come to ruin among so many who are not good." A political leader's deceit and betrayal will inevitably be judged by the good results it brings about. It is not without good reason that Machiavelli is identified with the view that in politics the end justifies the means.

THE PRINCE
Niccolò Machiavelli

NO

The author begins by announcing his intention to focus on what is true in reality rather than what is imagined.

It remains now to see what the modes and government of a prince should be with subjects and with friends. And because I know that many have written of this, I fear that in writing of it again, I may be held presumptuous, especially since in disputing this matter I depart from the orders of others. But since my intent is to write something useful to whoever understands it, it has appeared to me more fitting to go directly to the effectual truth of the thing than to the imagination of it.

And many have imagined republics that have never been seen or known to exist in truth; for it is so far from how one lives to how one should live that he who lets go of what is done for what should be done learns his ruin rather than his preservation. For a man who wants to make a profession of good in all regards must come to ruin among so many who are not good. Hence it is necessary to a prince, if he wants to maintain himself, to learn to be able not to be good, and to use this and not use it according to necessity.

Machiavelli suggests that princes, or leaders, need to learn how not to be good. Is this 16th-century viewpoint still applicable?

Qualities that bring praise or blame

Thus, leaving out what is imagined about a prince and discussing what is true, I say that all men, whenever one speaks of them, and especially princes, since they are placed higher, are noted for some of the qualities that bring them either blame or praise. And this is why someone is considered liberal, someone mean; someone is considered a giver, someone rapacious; someone cruel, someone merciful; the one a breaker of faith, the other faithful; the one effeminate and pusillanimous, the other fierce and spirited; the one humane, the other proud; the one lascivious, the other chaste; the one honest, the other astute; the one hard, the other agreeable; the one grave, the other light; the one religious, the other unbelieving, and the like. And I know that everyone will confess that it would be a very praiseworthy thing to find in a prince all of the above-mentioned qualities that are held good. But because he cannot have them, nor wholly observe them, since human conditions do not permit it, it is necessary for him to be so prudent as to know how to avoid the infamy of those vices that would take his state from him

Do you think Machiavelli has a high opinion of human nature?

and to be on guard against those that do not, if that is possible; but if one cannot, one can let them go on with less hesitation. And furthermore one should not care about incurring the fame of those vices without which it is difficult to save one's state; for if one considers everything well, one will find something appears to be virtue, which if pursued would be one's ruin, and something else appears to be vice, which if pursued results in one's security and well-being.

> Machiavelli argues that results are what counts.

Loyalty v. shrewdness

How praiseworthy it is for a prince to keep his faith, and to live with honesty and not by astuteness, everyone understands. Nonetheless one sees by experience that the princes who have done great things are those who have taken little account of faith and have known how to get around men with their astuteness; and in the end they have overcome those who have founded themselves on loyalty.

Thus, you must know that there are two kinds of combat: one with laws, the other with force. The first is proper to man, the second to beasts; but because the first is often not enough, one must have recourse to the second. Therefore it is necessary for a prince to know well how to use the beast and the man. This role was taught covertly to princes by ancient writers, who wrote that Achilles, and many other ancient princes, were given to Chiron the centaur to be raised, so that he would look after them with his discipline. To have as teacher a half-beast, half-man means nothing other than that a prince needs to know how to use both natures; and the one without the other is not lasting.

> Achilles and Chiron are characters from Greek mythology.

Using the beast in men

Thus, since a prince is compelled of necessity to know well how to use the beast, he should pick the fox and the lion, because the lion does not defend itself from snares and the fox does not defend itself from wolves. So one needs to be a fox to recognize snares and a lion to frighten the wolves. Those who stay simply with the lion do not understand this. A prudent lord, therefore, cannot observe faith, nor should he, when such observance turns against him, and the causes that made him promise have been eliminated. And if all men were good, this teaching would not be good; but because they are wicked and do not observe faith with you, you also do not have to observe it with them. Nor does a prince ever lack legitimate causes to color his failure to observe faith. One could give infinite modern examples of this, and show how many peace treaties and promises have been rendered

> The author is saying that the ends justify the means. Do you agree with him?

COMMENTARY: Niccolò Machiavelli

Niccolò Machiavelli, the Italian statesman and political theorist, was born in Florence in 1469. Although the family was among Italy's elite and was very wealthy, Machiavelli's father was one of the poorest members of the family. The young Niccolò lived frugally during his early life, of which little is known.

Years of influence

At the young age of 29 Machiavelli was made head of the second chancery of the Florentine republic. The position involved traveling to foreign states, and he made his first important trip to the French court in 1500, where he observed a strong nation under the rule of a single prince. On his return to Florence the republic was in danger of being ruined

This portrait of Niccolò Machiavelli was created in the 1500s.

by the ambitious Cesare Borgia. Machiavelli witnessed and wrote about the brutal political murders of Borgia in Sinigaglia in 1502. His early ideas of a "new prince" to redeem Italy were based on Cesare Borgia.

Under the chief magistrate Piero Soderini, Machiavelli gained favor and, inspired by his reading of Roman history, was instrumental in creating the citizen militia in 1510. After the Spanish invaded Tuscany in 1512, the Florentines deposed Soderini and allowed the Medici family to return to power. Distrusted by the Medicis, Machiavelli was dismissed from his position and, although innocent, was imprisoned as a conspirator.

Famous work

After his release Machiavelli was unable to redeem himself in the eyes of the Medicis, and living in poverty, he wrote his most famous work, *The Prince*. In this work he presents his vision of a strong leader who could forge a unitary state in Italy to push out the Spanish and French.

Many of the blunt maxims of *The Prince* were interpreted literally and gained Machiavelli the reputation of being an immoral cynic. In his desire for a "new prince" to save Italy, Machiavelli describes the means that were compatible with the conditions of the time. He described the world of politics as he saw it in reality rather than as how others thought it should ideally be. Machiavelli died in 1527. *The Prince* has greatly influenced principles of modern government and political theory, so much so that the term "Machiavellian" is now part of the English language.

invalid and vain through the infidelity of princes; and the one who has known best how to use the fox has come out best. But it is necessary to know well how to color this nature, and to be a great pretender and dissembler; and men are so simple and so obedient to present necessities that he who deceives will always find someone who will let himself be deceived.

Being evil when it is necessary

Thus, it is not necessary for a prince to have all the above-mentioned qualities in fact, but it is indeed necessary to appear to have them. Nay, I dare say this, that by having them and always observing them, they are harmful; and by appearing to have them, they are useful, as it is to appear merciful, faithful, humane, honest, and religious, and to be so; but to remain with a spirit built so that, if you need not to be those things, you are able and know how to change to the contrary. This has to be understood: that a prince, and especially a new prince, cannot observe all those things for which men are held good, since he is often under a necessity, to maintain his state, of acting against faith, against charity, against humanity, against religion. And so he needs to have a spirit disposed to change as the winds of fortune and variations of things command him, and as I said above, not depart from good, when possible, but know how to enter into evil, when forced by necessity.

Machiavelli is recommending that a strong leader needs to be deceptive and a "great pretender." Do you agree with him?

Machiavelli does not use the word "evil" until the finish. Does this give his argument more impact? Does a leader need to be evil if the circumstances dictate?

HONEST GOVERNMENT
W. J. Michael Cody & Richardson R. Lynn

YES

An "oxymoron" is a combination of contradictory words.

Our study of public service ethics brings us to this false dilemma, a choice between competent public servants or ethical ones. [We] dispute the view that *political ethics* is an oxymoron, like *jumbo shrimp* or *military intelligence*. Machiavelli believed that politics was amoral, merely a process of obtaining results through the effective use of power. However American government is not the best environment for his principles. Our best public servants are idealists who temper their idealism with pragmatism. Machiavellian "realists" become ineffective when they are caught using power illegally or if the public becomes dissatisfied with unethical behavior.

The authors state the premise of their argument: that politics can be ethical and that Machiavelli's ideas are not suited to U.S. government.

West Virginia Supreme Court Justice Richard Neely believes that voters are more pragmatic than idealistic. He wrote: "What voters really want in a politician is a lying, cheating, corrupt, thieving, wheeling-dealing bastard *who is their friend* and willing to place all his unethical skills entirely at their disposal. Only when such a creature can't be elected does the average voter become enchanted with "honest" government, which simply means that there is no lying, cheating, corrupt, thieving, wheeling-dealing bastard in office who is a friend of the voter's *enemies*."

What voters will tolerate

The authors quote statistics that back up their belief that voters will tolerate unethical behavior if they feel it is to their advantage.

Perhaps voters will tolerate most unethical behavior. Seventy-five percent of House members charged with ethics violations between 1968 and 1978 were reelected. More recent examples of indicted or convicted politicians reelected without opposition suggest that political effectiveness is more important to the public than ethical awareness. However we believe there is a slow but steady trend toward public insistence on higher ethical standards for public officials. The existence of well-defined ethics codes will help officials by giving them an excuse to refuse improper requests and avoid improper influences. A successful code of ethics must be realistic, recognizing that a political system requires compromise and that winning public office often requires an unusual toughness. The politician George Washington Plunkitt said: "A reformer can't

The authors present a solution to the problem: a well-defined ethics code.

last in politics. He can make a show of it for a while, but he always comes down like a rocket … He hasn't been brought up in the difficult business of politics and he makes a mess of it every time." If the proposed rules are naive or simplistic, they will be laughingly ignored. The ethical guidelines [outlined at the end of this article] are designed to set high but workable standards. Similar attempts at a statement of public service ethics should aim for the same goal.

Keeping good managers in government

[There] is a fundamental ethical duty to be competent, efficient, and a wise master of public resources. However critics of a rigorous set of public service ethics believe that tough ethics will drive out good managers. They argue that the best men and women in private life will be reluctant to enter government service because of disclosure requirements or restrictions on their postgovernment activities. They argue that the best career bureaucrats will leave government if a tough ethics code minimizes the perks, the free lunches, and junkets, or seems to be harshly judging them in hindsight.

If efficient public servants did leave because stringent ethics were imposed, it would be a hollow victory for ethics. Government does not need white hats on empty heads. Fortunately, there is no evidence that the enforcement of public service ethics would cause such a migration. Even if a few leave government for that reason, there are sufficient numbers of potentially great public servants who are entering government service at this time of heightened sensitivity to ethical issues. They will adjust to a new environment that clearly, emphatically requires higher standards for those in public life.

Difference between legality and ethics

As more issues of public service ethics become the subject of legislation, officials should not continue to think, as many do now, that if their conduct is legal, it is ethical. The politician who survives an investigation may claim, "I was exonerated." Usually, that claim merely means that a prosecutor found insufficient evidence to indict but has little to do with a declaration that the official acted ethically.

Even where ethics codes acquire the force of law, there will be unforeseen gaps in coverage or ethical dilemmas that the law does not address. For example, a law prohibiting gifts to an official may not explicitly prohibit the gift of expensive vacations or college tuition to the official's relative. An ethical public servant cannot be satisfied with obeying the law.

> The authors make an important distinction between public servants behaving legally and behaving ethically.

> The authors explain what they mean about the difference between legal and ethical behavior with an the example of accepting gifts.

The authors make a plea for ethical standards among the American people as well as public officials. Do you agree with their comments about participation in public life?

Rather, he or she will instinctually extend the basic principle of honoring the public trust to avoid the appearance of impropriety, as well as impropriety or illegality itself.

President Carter's wish for a government as good as the American people may have been for a less perfect government than he hoped. "We the people" are not always as good or as ethical in daily life as we should be. However high ethical standards in public service may result in a government as good as the American people should be.

Finally, Americans who are not public officials have ethical duties, also. We should be informed about governmental affairs. We should participate in discussions about government powers and policies, including the proper ethical standards for public officials. We should vote, not only because the outcome of elections is likely to be different, but also because voting leads people to increase their involvement in community affairs. In the 1990 congressional elections only 36.4 percent of the eligible voters voted.

Only 63 percent of eligible voters are even registered to vote. We have no right to hold public officials to high ethical standards unless we are willing to act responsibly as citizens.

An ethical premise

Public officials are obligated to render honest judgment, to work hard and efficiently, and to maximize the benefits of government to all citizens. This premise is the basis for all the remaining discussion about proper ethical standards for public officials. Each specific rule ought to be consistent with it. Public officials are defined as government employees, whether career or appointed, and elected officials at every level of government.

Basic principles

Based on that premise, there are certain self-evident rules of conduct for all public servants.

1. Public officials must not lie, cheat, or steal in any official capacity. They must obey the law. Public officials must always tell the truth to the public, other governmental bodies, and the press, except in extremely limited circumstances, such as war or national emergency, when a temporary deception serves a paramount purpose.

See page 188
Topic 15 Should the president be able to keep secrets?

2. Public officials must always avoid all conflicts of interest created by business, friendship, or family relationships and must always be careful to avoid the appearance of impropriety.

3. Public officials owe a fiduciary duty to taxpayers and all citizens to ensure that public funds are used efficiently. Officials and all public employees whom they supervise should be as productive as possible.

A "fiduciary duty" is a duty of trust.

4. Public officials must not allow zeal for their duties, including such duties as tax collection or law enforcement, to cause them to violate citizens' legal rights. Public servants should not be rude or unresponsive when dealing with the public.

5. Public officials should cooperate with other officials and agencies to maximize the public good, rather than acting out of cronyism or advancing the interests of politicians or a political machine.

6. Public officials should perform their duties based solely on the public good, rather than what is in their best political interests. They should not pressure public employees to assist in the official's political career or reelection efforts.

"Cronyism" means being partial to friends and contacts, especially in relation to appointing them to office regardless of their qualifications.

Summary

These selections lay out two starkly alternative answers to the question of whether moral principle should matter in politics. Cody and Lynn argue that a public servant who is entrusted with public office should be expected to act according to a set of high moral standards.

Machiavelli argues, contrary to Cody and Lynn, that what matters most in politics are results. Indeed, he would argue that holding the president, for example, to a strict set of moral guidelines restricts his ability to do whatever may be necessary to preserve law and order or protect national security. To be sure, Cody and Lynn do make an exception in allowing public officials the right to withhold the truth from the public when it may be expedient to do so in times of war or national emergency. But Machiavelli would argue that this alone does not go far enough in allowing public officials the necessary latitude to act as circumstances may require.

FURTHER INFORMATION:

 Books:

Cody, W. J., Michael and Richardson R. Lynn, *Honest Government: An Ethics Guide for Public Service.* Westport, CT: Praeger, 1992.

Gutmann, Amy, and Dennis Thompson (editors), *Ethics & Politics: Cases and Comments.* 2nd edition. Chicago: Nelson-Hall Publishers, 1990.

Machiavelli, Niccolò, *The Prince,* translated by Harvey C. Mansfield, Jr. Chicago: University of Chicago Press, 1998.

Articles:

Walzer, Michael, "Political Action: The Problem of Dirty Hands." *Philosophy & Public Affairs,* 1, Winter 1973, pp.160–80.

Weber, Max, "Politics as a Vocation," in *Max Weber: Essays in Sociology,* edited by H. H. Gerth and C. W. Mill, New York: Oxford University Press, 1958.

 Useful websites:

www.cfaba.org

Citizens for a Better America, an organization working to elect morality and values-based candidates.

www.jsonline.com/news/president/1001parents asp

www.washington post.com/wp-srv/politics/polls/ vault/ stories/values091198.htm

Articles about how the Lewinsky affair has prompted talks on morals and politics.

www.newsvote.bbc.co.uk/hi/english/talking-point/ newid-252000/252673.asp

BBC poll on "Does scandal matter?"

www.grtbooks.com

Online text of *The Prince.*

www.sas.upenn.edu/~pgrose/mach/

Index of the political thought of Machiavelli.

www.ctbw.com/lubman.htm

Biography of Machiavelli.

The following debates in the Pro/Con series may also be of interest:

In this volume:

 Topic 9 Is the president too powerful?

Topic 15 Should the president be able to keep secrets?

Topic 16 Should a sitting president be criminally indicted?

The Watergate Affair, pages 172–173.

The Case of President Clinton, pages 200–201.

SHOULD MORAL PRINCIPLE MATTER
IN POLITICS?

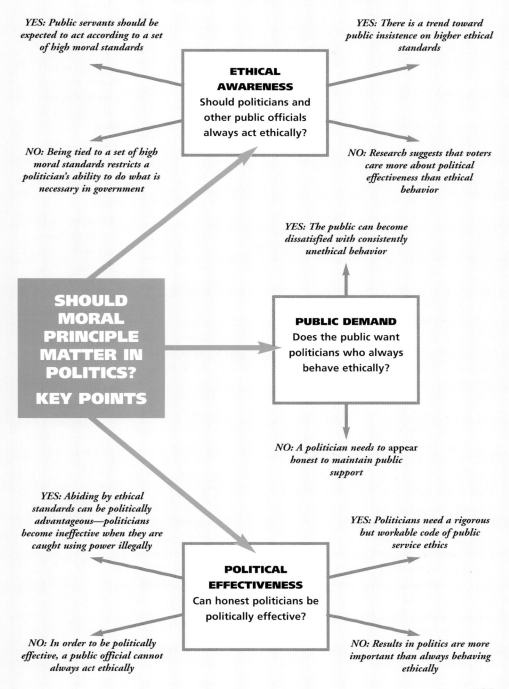

YES: Public servants should be expected to act according to a set of high moral standards

YES: There is a trend toward public insistence on higher ethical standards

ETHICAL AWARENESS
Should politicians and other public officials always act ethically?

NO: Being tied to a set of high moral standards restricts a politician's ability to do what is necessary in government

NO: Research suggests that voters care more about political effectiveness than ethical behavior

YES: The public can become dissatisfied with consistently unethical behavior

SHOULD MORAL PRINCIPLE MATTER IN POLITICS?

KEY POINTS

PUBLIC DEMAND
Does the public want politicians who always behave ethically?

NO: A politician needs to appear honest to maintain public support

YES: Abiding by ethical standards can be politically advantageous—politicians become ineffective when they are caught using power illegally

YES: Politicians need a rigorous but workable code of public service ethics

POLITICAL EFFECTIVENESS
Can honest politicians be politically effective?

NO: In order to be politically effective, a public official cannot always act ethically

NO: Results in politics are more important than always behaving ethically

187

Topic 15
SHOULD THE PRESIDENT BE ABLE TO KEEP SECRETS?

YES

"ARGUMENTS IN FAVOR OF EXECUTIVE PRIVILEGE"
FROM *EXECUTIVE PRIVILEGE: THE DILEMMAS OF SECRECY AND DEMOCRATIC ACCOUNTABILITY*
MARK J. ROZELL

NO

"INTRODUCTION"
FROM *EXECUTIVE PRIVILEGE: A CONSTITUTIONAL MYTH*
RAOUL BERGER

INTRODUCTION

Should the president be able to withhold information? The notion that the president has an executive privilege to conceal information is controversial. When President Bill Clinton argued, for example, that his discussions with top White House aides about the scandal surrounding his relationship with former presidential intern Monica Lewinsky were protected by executive privilege, critics responded by saying that Clinton was merely attempting to protect himself from personal embarrassment or perhaps even to thwart a criminal investigation into his conduct. In the view of its opponents executive privilege makes it difficult, if not impossible, to hold the president accountable for his actions (see *The Case of President Clinton*, pages 200–201).

The Constitution says nothing about whether the president has the right to withhold information from Congress, the courts, and ultimately, the public,

but presidents going all the way back to George Washington have exercised some form of executive privilege. In 1792 the Washington administration determined that it had the authority to withhold information requested by Congress if it was in the public interest to do so. This established a precedent that for almost 200 years was never seriously challenged.

The claim that executive privilege is an illegitimate exercise of power arose most prominently during the presidency of Richard Nixon. On July 17, 1972, five burglars secretly employed by Nixon's reelection committee were caught breaking into the offices of the Democratic National Committee in Washington, D.C.'s Watergate Hotel. The authorization for this break-in reached high into the Nixon administration. In June 1973 a former White House aide testified before a special Senate committee investigating President Nixon's possible abuse of power in the Watergate scandal that the president had installed a secret, voice-activated audiotaping system in the Oval Office of the White House. This revelation sparked a lengthy political and legal battle to secure the taped recordings of private Oval Office conversations as possible evidence of criminal wrongdoing on the part of the president. Several investigating bodies, including the Senate committee, the House Judiciary Committee, and the Watergate special prosecutor, subpoenaed a number of these tapes. Under intense political pressure Nixon released only transcripts of selected discussions. He argued that executive privilege justified his refusal to comply with any of the subpoenas.

Eventually, the dispute was resolved by the U.S. Supreme Court. It was the first time that the nation's highest court had addressed the issue of executive privilege directly. In the case of *United States v. Nixon* the Supreme Court, by a vote of eight to zero, held that Nixon must hand over the subpoenaed tapes. The transcripts of these tapes revealed Nixon's criminal involvement in the Watergate coverup. On August 8, 1974, Nixon became the first president in American history to resign from office. His attempt to use executive privilege to conceal evidence of his own criminal conduct diminished the legitimacy of the privilege in the public mind (see *The Watergate Affair*, pages 172–173).

The following two articles present the arguments for and against executive privilege very distinctly. Mark J. Rozell defends executive privilege on the grounds that national security often requires secrecy. He argues that foreign policy-making in the modern era makes the argument for executive privilege even more compelling, and that

Congress as an institution is not equipped to handle sensitive national security information or to make foreign policy decisively. Rozell refers to the *U.S. v. Nixon* case, when the Supreme Court for the first time recognized that the courts should grant a certain deference to the president when he claims executive privilege. Rozell says that historical events, such as World War II and the Cuban Missile Crisis, have confirmed the need for withholding information. Finally, he justifies the executive's right to secrecy because the legislative and judicial branches of government also practice secrecy.

As indicated by the title of the book from which his excerpt is taken— *Executive Privilege: A Constitutional Myth*—Raoul Berger denies the constitutional legitimacy of executive privilege. According to him, the doctrine of executive privilege undermines the legislative process, a process that must be based on informed judgment. Since Congress relies on the executive branch as the primary source of its information, executive privilege places a serious impediment in the way of the legislative branch's ability to pass wise legislation on the basis of having considered all relevant information.

Moreover, Berger argues, executive privilege undermines the president's accountability to Congress. After all, how can Congress be certain that the president is fulfilling his constitutional duty to execute the laws if it does not have full access to relevant executive branch information? Berger concludes that the notion that the president has the authority to keep secrets under the claim of executive privilege is profoundly undemocratic.

ARGUMENTS IN FAVOR OF EXECUTIVE PRIVILEGE
Mark J. Rozell

YES

The author opens with a fundamental point about executive privilege: That power has to involve the possibility of doing bad as well as good.

In defense of executive privilege

Although numerous presidents have exercised executive privilege, not all have done so judiciously. As with all other grants of authority, the power to do good is also the power to do bad. The only way to avoid the latter—and consequently eliminate the ability to do the former—is to strip away authority altogether. Chief Justice William Rehnquist has defended the need for executive privilege: "While reasonable men may dispute the propriety of particular invocations of executive privilege by various presidents during the nation's history, I think most would agree that the doctrine itself is an absolutely essential condition for the faithful discharge by the executive of his constitutional duties. It is, therefore, as surely implied in the Constitution as is the power of Congress to investigate and compel testimony."

Rozell sums up the points of his argument at the start. This enables him to develop his argument clearly and systematically.

The historical evidence for executive privilege is convincing and the reasons for its exercise compelling. Critics of executive privilege not only take a too narrow view of the Constitution; they have an unrealistic understanding of how America's governing system should work. The case for executive privilege is based on national security needs, the need for candid advice, the limits on congressional inquiry, historical necessities, and secrecy in other branches.

The author claims that the Framers of the Constitution recognized the need for secrecy. Would it help his argument to quote from the Constitution?

National security needs

Congress and the public's "right to know" must be balanced with the requirements of national security. Although the Constitution Framers recognized the importance of secrecy, unity, and dispatch to governing, the need to enhance those values in the modern era, particularly with regard to foreign policy-making, is more compelling than it was two centuries ago. Many of the crises faced by modern governments cannot be dealt with through open, lengthy, national deliberations. The pace of contemporary international events places a premium on rapid, decisive decision-making.

The presidency possesses the institutional capacities uniquely suited to responding to [crises]. The Framers recognized that, being one, rather than many, the president is more capable than Congress of acting with unity, secrecy, dispatch, and resolve.

In the realm of national security, an important matter of concern is the potential effect of public revelations of policy discussions. Such openness, for example, could lead to demands for the executive branch to act before it is prepared to do so. Consequently, the ability to deliberate carefully over time and to weigh options before making decisions could be compromised. In national security policy-making, it often is important to be somewhat removed from time and partisan pressures that may affect policy decisions.

Congress's failings as an institution

Executive privilege can be defended on the grounds that Congress, as an institution, is ill-suited to handling sensitive national security information and also is not capable of decisive foreign policy-making. Part of the problem of maintaining secrets in the legislature is that Congress lacks a central figure with ultimate control over the institution. Members of the institution are individual entrepreneurs in a place where generally no one exerts discipline on the membership. Numerous committees now claim the right of access to sensitive information, resulting in continual requests and struggles for executive branch information. Furthermore, the Constitution's speech and debate clause protects Congress from encroachment on legislative business by the executive or judicial branch. George C. Calhoun, former special counsel to the U.S. attorney general, explains "If members of Congress decide to make secret information public during a congressional debate, a court will not order them to stop and the speech and debate clause forecloses prosecution by the executive branch."

The Constitution says that Senators and Representatives "for any Speech or Debate in either House ... shall not be questioned in any other Place."

There is, therefore, a compelling case that national security often requires secrecy and that the right to exercise executive privilege is a necessary precondition for the chief executive to achieve national security aims. Additionally, the chief executive needs sound staff advice, and the quality of counsel depends ultimately on the degree of candor.

The need for candid advice

The president's constitutional duties necessitate his being able to consult with advisers, without fear of public disclosure of their advice. If officers of the executive branch

This argument suggests that a government is more effective if it formulates policy away from public pressure. Do you agree?

believed that their confidential advice could be disclosed, the quality of that advice would suffer serious damage. Indeed it would be difficult for advisers to be completely honest and frank in their discussions if their every word might someday be disclosed to partisan opponents or the public.

Indeed, in the *U.S. v. Nixon* case, the Supreme Court not only recognized the constitutionality of executive privilege, but the necessity of executive branch secrecy to the operation of the presidency. The Court therefore, has recognized that the need for candid interchange is an important basis for the constitutional doctrine of executive privilege. Although it is well recognized that Congress needs access to executive branch information to carry out its oversight and investigative duties, it does not follow that Congress must have full access to the details of every executive branch communication.

Why might presidential advisers be less "candid" if Congress had access to this communication?

Limits on congressional inquiry

Some scholars and members of Congress believe that Congress has an absolute, unlimited power, as the "Grand Inquest" of the nation, to compel disclosure of all executive branch information. [Democrat Congressman for Michigan] John Dingell asserts that members of Congress "have the power under the law to receive each and every item in the hands of the government." This expansive view of congressional inquiry is equally as wrong as the belief that the president has the unlimited power to withhold all information from Congress, regardless of his reasons for nondisclosure. This quest for constitutional absolutes obscures the fact that there are inherent constitutional limits on the powers of the respective governmental branches. The common standard for legislative inquiry has been whether the requested information was vital to Congress's lawmaking and oversight function. It is ironic that critics of executive privilege maintain that such a power lacks validity because it is not specifically granted by the Constitution, and then argue that Congress possesses an absolute, unlimited inquiry power despite a similar lack of such a constitutional grant.

John Dingell has served more consecutive terms than any other member of Congress in the House of Representatives.

Rozell picks up on a contradiction in his opponent's argument.

Historic necessities

Numerous historic incidents have confirmed that there are many good reasons for withholding information. For example, World War II, the crises over Berlin and Cuba, the long Cold War, and the war against Iraq have all confronted the United States with situations requiring rapid responses, as well as

Support your argument with real examples. Rozell refers to specific events that illustrate the need for withholding information

secret negotiations, thereby precluding full disclosure to Congress of military and diplomatic plans.

Congressional decision-making during the emergence of the nation's gravest crisis proved to be wholly inadequate. Therefore, a major defense of executive privilege rests on the proposition that Congress often does not discharge its duties in the national security realm with wisdom, and that legislative interference in international negotiations may have deleterious effects on the nation's security in crisis situations.

Practices in the other branches

Finally, executive privilege can be defended on the basis of accepted practices of secrecy in the other branches of government. Members of Congress receive candid, confidential advice from committee staff and legislative assistants. Congressional committees meet on occasion in closed sessions to "mark up" legislation. Congress is not obligated to disclose information to another branch. A court subpoena will not be honored except with a vote of the legislative chamber concerned. Congress has also exempted itself from disclosing information under the Freedom of Information Act. Members of Congress enjoy a constitutional form of privilege that absolves them from having to account for their official behavior, particularly regarding speech, anywhere but in Congress. As with the executive, this privilege does not extend into the realm of criminal conduct.

The Freedom of Information Act, passed in 1966, requires federal agencies to give copies of records to the public when asked unless the information sought falls within one of the act's nine exemptions.

Judicial privilege

Secrecy also is found in the judicial branch. It is difficult to imagine more secretive deliberations than those that take place in Supreme Court conferences. David M. O'Brien refers to secrecy as one of the "basic institutional norms" of the Supreme Court. "Isolation from the Capitol and the close proximity of the justices' chambers within the Court promote secrecy, to a degree that is remarkable …. The norm of secrecy conditions the employment of the justices' staff and has become more important as the number of employees increases." Members of the judiciary claim immunity from having to respond to congressional subpoenas. The norm of judicial privilege also protects judges from having to testify about their professional conduct.

Rozell finishes his defense of executive privilege by arguing that the judicial and legislative branches of government have their own forms of privilege for secrecy.

It is inconceivable that such a practice as secrecy, common to the legislative and judicial branches, should not be exercised by the executive. The executive branch is regularly engaged in a number of activities that are secret in nature.

EXECUTIVE PRIVILEGE
Raoul Berger

NO

"Executive privilege"—the President's claim of constitutional authority to withhold information from Congress—is a myth. Unlike most myths, the origins of which are lost in the mists of antiquity, "executive privilege" is a product of the 19th century, fashioned by a succession of presidents who created "precedents" to suit the occasion. The very words "executive privilege" were conjoined only yesterday, in 1958. Of late assertions of "executive privilege" have assumed swollen proportions, four realizing the extreme claim of Deputy Attorney General William P. Rogers that the President has "uncontrolled discretion" to withhold information from Congress.

Keeping Congress informed

Rogers [said] "We live in a democracy in which an informed public opinion is absolutely essential to the survival of our nation and form of government. It is likewise true that Congress must be well informed if it is to do its legislative job realistically and effectively." An "uncontrolled discretion" to refuse information to Congress, however, leaves Congress, and therefore public opinion, at the mercy of the President; they learn only what he considers they should know. " The country," said Woodrow Wilson, "must be helpless to learn how it is being served" unless Congress has and "use every means of acquainting itself with the acts and disposition of the administrative agents of the government."

Our democratic system is bottomed on the legislative process. "With all its defects," said Justice Jackson in rejecting a presidential power-grab, "men have discovered no techniques for preserving free government except that the Executive be under the law and that the law be made by parliamentary deliberation." Since lawmaking needs to be based on an informed judgment, this requires the widest access to information. With the help of Congress, the Executive has developed the greatest information-gathering apparatus extant; it is a national asset, not an exclusive executive preserve. To duplicate these worldwide facilities in order that Congress may obtain the information it [needs] for performance of its duties would be an intolerably costly folly.

Impeachment

The Constitution contemplates executive accountability to Congress, as the Article II, [section] 3 provision that the president "shall take care that the laws be faithfully executed" alone should show. Who has a more legitimate interest in inquiring whether a law has been faithfully executed than the lawmaker? So thought Montesquieu, the high priest of the separation of powers—the doctrine which is again and again invoked by the Executive branch in defense of executive privilege. The legislature, said he, "has a right [to examine] in what manner its laws have been executed". The accountability of the executive branch to Congress is underlined by the provision for impeachment of the president. Impeachment lies [ahead] for corruption, bribery, and other high misdemeanors, and for action contrary to law.

Berger quotes from Montesquieu's study The Spirit of the Laws. Baron Montesquieu (1689–1755) was a French jurist and philosopher. See box on page 18.

From early times it was preceded by parliamentary investigation. Such considerations were summarized by Woodrow Wilson: "Quite as important as legislation is vigilant oversight of administration; and even more important than legislation is the instruction and guidance in political affairs which the people might receive from a body which kept all national concerns suffused in a broad daylight of discussion." Performance of these functions has increasingly been made to run an executive gauntlet, and this on the basis of made-to-order "precedents" of very recent vintage.

"Impeachment" means to charge a public official with misconduct in office before a tribunal. Nixon resigned from office in 1974 rather than be impeached.

Congress's powers of investigation

But, as a critic of the McCarthy era pointed out, "If Congressional use of power to investigate produced occasional excesses, it also produced tremendous boons." Corruption and mismanagement repeatedly have been exposed over strenuous executive opposition only because of congressional investigation. The starting point, therefore, must be a congressional function which has proved its value over the years. Growing resort by the Executive branch to "uncontrolled discretion" to withhold information robs the country of the benefits which flow from legislative inquiry into executive conduct. That information is more frequently furnished than withheld is beside the point: investigation is hobbled at the outset if the Executive branch may determine what Congress shall see and hear.

Senator Joseph McCarthy (1908–1957) made sensational but unproved charges of Communist subversion in high government circles in the 1950s.

How can that determination safely be left to the object of investigation? That it cannot was pointed out by William Pitt in 1741: "This enquiry will produce no great information if those whose conduct is examined, are allowed to select the

William Pitt (1708–1788) was a British politician. He was a member of the Whig party, which sought to limit royal power and increase parliamentary authority.

evidence." Since 1954 it has become executive practice to refuse on the flimsiest grounds information which should underlie the appropriations of billions of dollars or the passage of legislation. Recoil from the McCarthean excesses has engendered a cure that is worse than the disease.

Widespread concealment

Only the tip of the iceberg is represented by the formal claim of executive privilege. Bureaucrats engage in interminable stalling when asked for information. The Secretary, and his underlings, of a Department which owes its very creation and continued existence to Congress, advise the senior partner in government, for so Congress was regarded by the Founders, that it is "contrary to the national interest" or "inappropriate" for it to see the requested information! Such refusals are merely part of a wider pattern of concealment: "executive agreements" which are suspected of making large-scale military and financial commitments are not disclosed to Congress or the people.

Do you agree that the president's ability to keep secrets might encourage others to keep secrets too?

Dangers of secrecy

The costs of such undercover presidential policy were evidenced by a massive revulsion against the Vietnam War. Whether President Lyndon Johnson candidly communicated his plans for escalation of American involvement in Vietnam, whether he advised Congress of all the relevant facts before requesting the Gulf of Tonkin Resolution is not nearly so important as the existence of a large body of opinion that he practiced concealment. Even the spokesman for the conservatives on military matters, Senator John Stennis, Chairman of the Senate Armed Services Committee, who long held up the arms of the President, stated in 1971, "Vietnam has shown us that by trying to fight a war without the clear-cut support of the American people, we ... strain the very structure of the republic." Vietnam teaches, to borrow the words of the Chairman of the Foreign Relations Committee, Senator Fulbright, that "secrecy and subterfuge are themselves more dangerous to democracy than the practices they conceal."

Back up your argument with concrete evidence. Berger uses the Vietnam War (1955–1975) to show the dangers of concealing information from Congress.

Presidential judgment

As if to temper Rogers' "uncontrolled discretion" claim, Assistant Attorney General (now Justice) William H. Rehnquist stated that the "President's authority to withhold information is not an unbridled one." But he immediately washed out this concession by asserting that "it necessarily requires the exercise of his judgment" whether disclosure "would be harmful to the national interest." Thus the president is "bridled," but it is a bridle that only he himself can check! Since Congress admittedly must "obtain information in order to aid it in the process of legislating," a conflict is presented with the president's claim of power to "withhold documents or information in his possession."

Boundaries of power

On this boundary dispute, Attorney General Rogers unabashedly asserted, "the president and heads of departments must and do have the last word"; a view reiterated by Assistant Attorney General Rehnquist in blander terms: the issue "necessarily requires the exercise of his [president's] judgment." Although Mr. Rehnquist quoted Madison's statement in *Federalist* No. 49 that "neither the executive nor the legislative can pretend to an exclusive right of settling the boundaries between their respective powers," he did not draw the conclusion that some other tribunal than one of the boundary disputants must therefore determine the issue. Madison merely followed the centuries-old law that no man may be judge in his own cause, not even the King, a rule that has the greater urgency when the executive judgment would render Congress subordinate and dependent.

Opposition to secrecy

Americans have a historical aversion to secrecy. There is a strong "public feeling against secrecy of any kind in the administration of the Government," stated President Polk; and that the feeling has endured is recognized in Assistant Attorney General Rehnquist's statement that "the claim of executive privilege is an unpopular one." The price of secrecy, as one who was within the inner circle of the Lyndon Johnson administration stated, is "an actual loss in public confidence in the Government itself," what has come to be known as the "credibility gap." At bottom, the issue concerns the right of Congress and the people to participate in making the decisions that affect the fortunes of the nation. Claims of presidential power to withhold the information that is indispensable for intelligent participation undermine this right and sap the foundations of democratic government. More than extravagant legend is required to sustain such claims, nothing less than demonstrable constitutional sanction, and, even then, proof that a presidential iron curtain is demanded by the highest wisdom.

James Knox Polk (1797–1849) was 11th U.S. president (1845–1849).

Berger finishes by saying that the president having secrets affects the credibility of the government.

Summary

These articles present two competing views about whether the president has the legitimate authority to refuse requests for information from Congress, the courts, or the people if he deems it necessary. Mark J Rozell bases the case for executive privilege on the need for national security, candid advice, historical necessity, the limits on congressional inquiry, and secrecy in other branches of government. He says that critics of executive privilege take too narrow a view of the Constitution; and while he concedes that the privilege is open to abuse, as history has shown, he argues that the doctrine is absolutely essential to the president fulfilling his constitutional duties.

On the opposite side of the fence Raoul Berger presents arguments against executive privilege. When the president keeps secrets from Congress or the people, Berger argues, he weakens Congress's powers of oversight and investigation, undermines democratic accountability, and diminishes respect for government. So, far from considering executive privilege to be a legitimate constitutional power, Berger regards it as a constitutional myth.

FURTHER INFORMATION:

Books:

Berger, Raoul, *Executive Privilege: A Constitutional Myth*. Cambridge, MA: Harvard University Press, 1974.

Henry, Alan P., and Schipps, David P. *Sell Out: The Inside Story of President Clinton's Impeachment*. Washington, D.C.: Regnery Publishing, Inc., 2000.

Rozell, Mark J. *Executive Privilege: The Dilemma of Secrecy and Democratic Accountability*. Baltimore and London: The John Hopkins University Press, 1994.

Woodward, Bob. *Shadow: Five Presidents and the Legacy of Watergate*. NY: Simon & Schuster, 1999.

Articles:

Dorsen, Norman, and Shattuck, John, "Executive Privilege: The President Won't Tell," in *None of Your Business: Government Secrecy in America,* edited by Norman Dorsen and Stephen Gillers. NY: Penguin Books, 1975.

Schmitt, Gary, "Executive Privilege," in *The Presidency in the Constitutional Order*, edited by Joseph Bessette and Jeffrey Tulis. Baton Rouge: Louisiana State University Press, 1981.

Useful websites:

www.ipl.org/POTUS
Internet Public Library site on U.S. presidents.
www.britannica.com/magazine/ebsco-id=236775
1997 article by Daniel Patrick Moynihan on "The Culture of Secrecy" in *Public Interest*.
www.britannica.com/magazine/ebsco-id=61933
1998 *National Review* article "Abusive Power" on President Clinton's invocation of executive privilege.

The following debates in the Pro/Con series may also be of interest:

In this volume:

Topic 9 Is the president too powerful?
Topic 16 Should a sitting president be criminally indicted?
The Watergate Affair, pages 172–173.
The Case of President Clinton, pages 200–201.

SHOULD THE PRESIDENT BE ABLE
TO KEEP SECRETS?

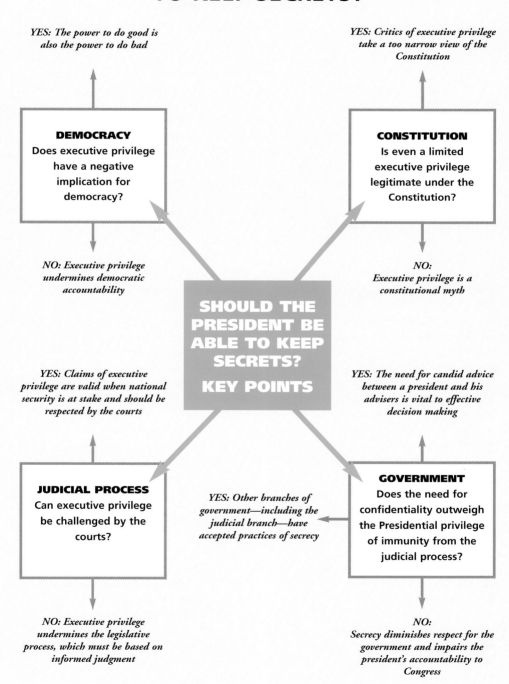

YES: The power to do good is also the power to do bad

DEMOCRACY
Does executive privilege have a negative implication for democracy?

NO: Executive privilege undermines democratic accountability

YES: Critics of executive privilege take a too narrow view of the Constitution

CONSTITUTION
Is even a limited executive privilege legitimate under the Constitution?

NO: Executive privilege is a constitutional myth

SHOULD THE PRESIDENT BE ABLE TO KEEP SECRETS?

KEY POINTS

YES: Claims of executive privilege are valid when national security is at stake and should be respected by the courts

YES: The need for candid advice between a president and his advisers is vital to effective decision making

JUDICIAL PROCESS
Can executive privilege be challenged by the courts?

YES: Other branches of government—including the judicial branch—have accepted practices of secrecy

GOVERNMENT
Does the need for confidentiality outweigh the Presidential privilege of immunity from the judicial process?

NO: Executive privilege undermines the legislative process, which must be based on informed judgment

NO: Secrecy diminishes respect for the government and impairs the president's accountability to Congress

THE CASE OF PRESIDENT CLINTON

Politics and Morality

"I am often troubled ... that sometimes we forget that we are all in this because we are seeking a good that helps all Americans."

—PRESIDENT BILL CLINTON

Independent counsel Kenneth Starr began to investigate President Clinton's involvement in the Whitewater land affair. This led to further probing into the president's possible sexual misconduct with former White House intern Monica Lewinsky. What follows is a timeline of the key events leading to President Clinton's impeachment trial.

1978–1979 Arkansas Attorney General Bill Clinton, his wife Hillary, James B. McDougal, and his wife Susan borrow $203,000 to buy 220 acres of land. In 1979 they form the Whitewater Development Company. They intend to build vacation homes.

1980 McDougal loans Hillary Clinton $30,000 to build a house at Whitewater.

1984 McDougal's savings and loan company falls under the scrutiny of federal regulators.

1989 McDougal is indicted on federal fraud charges. He is later acquitted.

1992 A Clinton presidential campaign aid alleges that the Clintons lost $68,000 on Whitewater. This figure is later changed to $40,000. Bill Clinton is elected President of the United States.

May to July 1993 Seven employees of the White House travel office are dismissed, allegedly to make way for friends of the new president. White House deputy counsel Vincent Foster begins to file three years worth of missing Whitewater tax returns

July Foster is found dead in a Washington park. The police rule his death a suicide.

November/December 1993 Kathleen E. Willey, Foster's secretary, allegedly tells Linda Tripp, a career government worker, that President Clinton made unwanted sexual advances toward her. She also suggests to Kenneth Starr that Foster's death may not have been a suicide.

1994 January: New York lawyer Robert B. Fiske, acting as Independent Counsel, starts an investigation into Whitewater. During the summer the House and Senate Banking committees begin the Whitewater hearings. Paula Jones files a lawsuit against Clinton alleging sexual harassment. Republican lawyer Kenneth W. Starr replaces Fiske after claims that there is a conflict of interest. Linda Tripp meets Monica Lewinsky, a former White House intern, at the Pentagon.

January to April 1995 The Senate Banking Committee reports that no laws were broken during the Whitewater deals. In April Starr interviews the Clintons.

July to August 1995 The Senate Special Whitewater Committee begins hearings. In August the House Banking Committee also finds that no laws were broken during the Whitewater deals. The McDougals along with Arkansas Governor Jim Guy Tucker are charged with bank fraud relating to questionable loans.

January 22 1996 Starr subpoenas Hillary Clinton in order to discover if Whitewater records were intentionally withheld. This is the first time that a First Lady has ever been subpoenaed.

April 1996 On the 22nd David Hale testifies at the Whitewater trial that in early 1985 Bill Clinton pressured him to make a fraudulent $300,000 loan to Susan McDougal. On the 28th Clinton denies Hale's allegations in a videotaped testimony.

May 26 1996 The McDougals and Tucker are convicted of fraud and conspiracy. Tucker is fined $319,000. James B. and Susan McDougal are sentenced to three and two years in prison respectively.

June to July 1996 A new Whitewater trial opens. Bankers Herby Branscum Jr. and Robert Hill are accused of illegally using bank funds to reimburse themselves for political contributions. Clinton denies offering them jobs in exchange for funding. Both men are later cleared. Starr concludes that Vincent Foster's death was suicide.

October to November 1997 Lewinsky tells Tripp of her affair with Clinton. In November Tripp records 17 hours of conversation with Lewinsky.

December 1997 An anonymous call leads to Lewinsky's subpoena in Paula Jones' trial. The judge disallows her deposition. Clinton allegedly urges Lewinsky to be evasive after a private meeting. Jones' lawyers now also subpoena Kathleen E. Willey.

January 1998 Tripp contacts Starr regarding the Lewinsky tapes. Lewinsky denies having an affair with Clinton in her affidavit. On the 26th Clinton declares he didn't have sexual relations with Lewinsky. The next day Starr opens a grand jury probe into Lewinsky's allegations.

March 1998 On the 8th James B. McDougal dies in prison. On the 28th Clinton invokes executive privilege to limit questions to his top aides regarding Lewinsky.

April 1998 The Paula Jones case is thrown out of court on the 1st. On the 25th Starr videotapes Hillary Clinton's testimony regarding Whitewater.

November 1998 Starr clears Clinton of firing the White House travel office workers and the improper collection of FBI files.

December 1998 Between the 13th and 19th the House Judiciary Committee approves six impeachment articles. Clinton settles the Paula Jones case for $850,000 and no apology.

July 1999 President Clinton's impeachment trial begins.

Clinton was cleared of the charges brought against him in the impeachment trial. However, further scandal arose when Clinton bypassed normal procedures in January 2001 to pardon the biggest tax defrauder in U.S. history—billionaire Mark Rich. Mr. Rich's wife had donated large sums of money to Clinton's election campaign.

Topic 16
SHOULD A SITTING PRESIDENT BE CRIMINALLY INDICTED?

YES
"YES, YOU CAN INDICT THE PRESIDENT"
THE WALL STREET JOURNAL, MARCH 9, 1998
GARY L. MCDOWELL

NO
"INDICT CLINTON? HOW I WISH IT WERE POSSIBLE"
THE WALL STREET JOURNAL, MARCH 18, 1998
ROBERT H. BORK

INTRODUCTION

What should be done in the event of allegations of serious misconduct by the president of the United States? Article II, section 4 of the Constitution states that a president cannot be taken to court, or indicted, until he has been impeached.

An impeachment is a set of charges not unlike an indictment in a criminal trial. Under the Constitution the House of Representatives has the sole power, by majority vote, to impeach the president; the Senate, with the chief justice of the Supreme Court presiding, has the sole power to try the president and decide whether the charges brought against him by the House of Representatives warrant conviction and removal from office. A two-thirds majority "of the Members present" is required to do so.

Scholars disagree about what constitutes an impeachable offense. Although there is little dispute over the meaning of treason and bribery, there

has been considerable disagreement over the meaning of "high crimes and misdemeanors." However this clause may be interpreted, scholars do tend to agree that an impeachable offense must involve something illegal or unconstitutional, not just unpopular. A related but separate issue about which there is even less agreement is whether a sitting president can be subject to criminal indictment and prosecution before impeachment.

This issue has arisen in regard to two modern presidencies in the United States—the administrations of President Nixon and President Clinton.

In the midst of his investigation into Nixon's involvement in the Watergate coverup (1973–1975) special prosecutor Leon Jaworski acquired compelling evidence of the president's criminal culpability. He then faced the question of whether to pursue a criminal indictment of the president. Instead, he advised the Watergate grand jury to name Nixon an unindicted coconspirator.

In the subsequent case of *United States v. Nixon* (1974) the Supreme Court accepted briefs and heard arguments on whether impeachment was the only means of pursuing charges against the president. It did not decide and the issue was left unexamined by any court after that. It did arise again, however, during the Clinton administration (1993–2001).

"I don't suppose there's any public figure that's ever been subject to any more violent personal attacks than I have."

—BILL CLINTON

In the course of his investigation into President Clinton's testimony in a sexual harassment lawsuit brought by former Arkansas state employee Paula Jones, independent counsel Kenneth Starr concluded that the president had possibly committed perjury and persuaded former presidential intern Monica Lewinsky to perjure herself in her own deposition in the Jones case.

A federal court ruling that authorized Starr to subpoena Clinton to testify before the grand jury investigating these possible crimes raised once again the issue of whether a sitting president can be subject to criminal indictment and prosecution. Clinton eventually backed down from putting this issue to the test by agreeing to appear before the grand jury voluntarily. In doing so, he avoided possible arrest, and

what is more, the Supreme Court avoided having to address the issue.

The following two articles present strongly opposed positions on the issue of whether a sitting president may be indicted for a criminal offense.

In "Yes, You Can Indict a Sitting President" Gary McDowell argues that the Constitution confers no presidential immunity from indictment. He derives principal support for his argument from the fact that there is no specific provision in the Constitution that affords such immunity.

Indeed, the Constitution's only provision for immunity from indictment, he points out, is that which is granted Congress, and even that does not cover more serious offenses like treason. McDowell thus concludes that: "Had the intention been to demand impeachment before indictment, the Framers would have spelled that out."

Former solicitor-general Robert Bork, in "Indict Clinton? How I Wish It Were Possible," concedes that "the constitutional text provides no express immunity for the president and, by contrast, does explicitly shield members of Congress from arrest during their attendance at their respective houses and in going to and from those sessions."

Unlike Gary McDowell, however, Bork does not think that this fact alone provides conclusive evidence that the president may be indicted for a criminal offense while still in office. Bork argues, in opposition to McDowell, that there is a presidential immunity from criminal prosecution that derives not from the Constitution's language but from "its history, its structure, and the requirements of constitutional functions."

YES, YOU CAN INDICT THE PRESIDENT
Gary L. McDowell

In the next few weeks [this article appeared in *The Wall Street Journal*, March 9,1998] Kenneth Starr is likely to find himself at a particularly vexatious fork in the legal road he has been traveling these past four years.

From the earliest Whitewater fraud investigations, through Travelgate and Filegate, to the allegations of possible perjury and witness tampering emanating from the Monica Lewinsky matter, Mr. Starr [see box opposite] will have to decide where to go with whatever evidence of presidential wrongdoing he has uncovered. One path, undoubtedly the smoother one, would lead him to the House of Representatives under the independent counsel statute, which obligates him to inform that House of any impeachable offenses.

Law

The other more treacherous way would take the independent counsel directly to a criminal indictment against President Clinton. Unfortunately, he is not likely to find much guidance in most of the recent discussions of these weighty matters.

The past few weeks have focused public attention on impeachment for the first time since Watergate, but this most basic and straightforward constitutional provision has been the subject of great confusion at nearly every level of public discourse. From the commonplace assumption that the constitutional standard of "high crimes and misdemeanors" means whatever Congress says it does (it does not; the phrase was a common law term of art to the Founders with a reasonably precise meaning) to the idea that a president cannot be indicted before he is impeached, history has been the victim of political calculations. This is especially troubling on the issue of whether indictment may precede impeachment.

The argument that a sitting president may not be indicted prior to impeachment derives not from the Constitution or even from a judicial decision as a matter of constitutional law. Rather, it originated in a memorandum prepared in 1973 by then-Solicitor General Robert Bork in the matter of Spiro Agnew. In that report, Mr. Bork drew a distinction between indictment of the president and indictment of the vice

See The Case of President Clinton, pages 200–201, for background on the Whitewater and Lewinsky affairs.

See The Watergate Affair, pages 172–173, for a timeline of events.

"Impeachment" is a formal accusation issued by a legislature against a public official charged with a crime or other serious misconduct.

COMMENTARY: Independent Counsel

The Ethics in Government Act was passed in 1978 and was a direct result of the Watergate affair (see pages 172–173). It was brought in to check governmental abuses of power. Among other things, it created the position of Special Prosecutor (or Independent Counsel) to investigate misdeeds by high government officials. Once appointed, counsel could investigate any allegations of misconduct, and he or she could only be dismissed by three federal judges and the attorney general. Since the president thus had no power over the counsel, Congress thought it had protected the democratic system from further abuse. Since then the majority of special investigations undertaken have not ended in indictments. An independent counsel was used in the Iran-contra affair, Whitewater, and the Lewinsky scandals (see pages 200–201, *The Case of President Clinton*). Critics have argued that in practice independent counsel investigations were little more than witch-hunts. Following the Starr investigation into President Clinton's conduct, the act, which was renewed every five years after its enactment, was allowed to expire on June 30, 1999. The attorney general now has sole responsibility for appointing outside prosecutors.

Kenneth W. Starr

"Starr lacks the two main qualifications of an independent prosecutor—he is not independent and he has never prosecuted a case."

—EDITORIAL, *NEWSDAY*

Republican attorney Kenneth W. Starr achieved fame in 1994 after he took over from Robert Fiske as independent counsel in the Whitewater investigation. He uncovered a seemingly inappropriate relationship between former White House intern Monica Lewinsky and President Clinton. Starr's evidence eventually led to impeachment proceedings against the president. Starr was born on July 21, 1946 in Vernon, Texas. He graduated from George Washington University and studied law at Duke University Law School. Starr later clerked under former Supreme Court Chief Justice Warren Burger (see *The Watergate Affair*, pages 172–173). He helped draft the Reagan opposition to the independent counsel statute (see above), a point that was later picked up on by his critics given his appointment as independent counsel in the investigation into President Clinton's affairs. Starr was also solicitor general under President George Bush. Since 1993 he has been a partner in the American law firm Kirkland & Ellis.

Spiro Agnew,
(1918–1996) was the
39th vice president
of the United States.
Agnew was forced
to resign in 1973
when the Justice
Department found
evidence of
corruption during
his years in
Maryland politics.

president and all other civil officers. In the case of Agnew, Mr. Bork concluded, there was no reason he could not be indicted prior to impeachment; such was not the case for the president, however, who would have to be impeached first. The basis of this distinction was certain institutional attributes peculiar to the presidency that Mr. Bork found "embedded" in the structure of the Constitution.

The Constitution

The problem with this interpretation is that it elevates an argument that might be reasonably inferred from the Constitution's overall design and structure over the clear language of the document itself. When the provisions of the Constitution dealing with impeachment are viewed in light of the history that inspired them, it is clear that there is no immunity from indictment conferred on the president or any other officer of the government. Nor is there any demand that impeachment must precede such an indictment.

The Constitution lays out the mechanics of impeachment, including the limits of the sanction, in Article I, 3: "Judgment ... shall not extend further than to removal from office and disqualification to hold and enjoy any office of honor, trust or profit under the United States: but the party convicted shall nevertheless be liable and subject to indictment, trial, judgment and punishment according to law."

See the
Constitution on
www.house.gov

Later, in Article II, 4, the Constitution provides that the president, vice president, and all civil officers "shall be removed from office on the impeachment for, and conviction of, treason, bribery, or other high crimes and misdemeanors." To make clear that impeachment is a political rather than a legal process, the Constitution specifically precludes the right to a trial by jury or the possibility of a presidential pardon or reprieve in cases of impeachment.

Impeachment

Alexander
Hamilton
(1757–1804) was
a U.S. statesman
and writer on
government. See
box page 81.

As Alexander Hamilton put it in *The Federalist*, echoing British constitutional history, impeachable offenses are those that "proceed from the misconduct of public men, or in other words from the abuse and violation of some public trust," what Sir William Blackstone had termed "mal-administration." Such political sins would include neglect of duty, abuse of power, or subversion of the Constitution. Although indictable offenses are not necessary for an impeachment, they may surely be deemed sufficient grounds to proceed. This is especially so in the case of the president, in whom any criminal behavior would likely be seen as a clear failure to "take care that the laws be faithfully executed." Indeed the language of the Constitution ..."the party convicted shall nevertheless be liable and subject to indictment, trial, judgment and punishment according to law"—was designed for just such a possibility.

Should there be evidence of criminal acts, and should that give rise to a successful impeachment and removal from office, the Founders did not wish to shield the person impeached from further legal proceedings under any notion of double jeopardy. High office offers no immunity from the ordinary rigors of the criminal law.

This is the crux of the argument.

Immunity

But neither does that constitutional language demand that impeachment must precede indictment. As legal historian Raoul Berger showed long ago, there is only one place in the Constitution where immunity is conferred on public officials, and that involves not holding members of the Senate and House liable to arrest for anything they may say or do in their respective chambers or "in going to and returning from the same." Even then the Founders did not include the more serious offenses, making clear that such immunity extended to "all cases, except treason, felony or breach of the peace."

See Topic 15 Should the President be able to keep secrets? "No" article by Raoul Berger.

As Mr. Bork pointed out in his memorandum denying immunity to the vice president, "[because] the Framers of the Constitution knew how to, and did, spell out immunity, the natural inference is that no immunity exists where none is mentioned."

See pages 208–211 for Bork's attitude to the indictment issue.

This logic applies equally to the role of the president. Had the intention been to demand impeachment before indictment, the Framers would have spelled that out.

Political choices

When Mr. Starr comes to that fork in the road he may well decide, on the basis of what would be best for the country, to turn it all over to the House Judiciary Committee and leave them to it. But that would be a political choice, not a constitutional one. There is no constitutional roadblock keeping him from taking the road directly to criminal indictment. Given the Republican majorities in both houses and the high poll ratings he now enjoys, Mr. Clinton might even thank him for it, preferring a jury of his peers to facing what Hamilton described in *The Federalist* as that "awful discretion" the Constitution gives to the political court of impeachments."

INDICT CLINTON?
HOW I WISH IT WERE POSSIBLE
Robert H. Bork

Bork starts with the premise that President Clinton is perceived as bad.

Robert Heron Bork (1927–) was Solicitor General during the Watergate investigation. He fired Special Prosecutor Archibald Cox (Oct. 20, 1973) in what became known as the Saturday Night Massacre. He is now a scholar at the American Enterprise Institute.

This makes Bork's argument different from McDowell's literal writeup of the case. It is a central debate in U.S. politics and law.

NO

Bad presidents inspire fresh constitutional thinking. The question our current chief executive has placed before the nation is whether he may be indicted for a criminal offense while still in office.

That question was raised only tangentially in Richard Nixon's case. When Vice President Spiro Agnew was found to have taken bribes, we in the Justice Department agreed that he could be indicted before he was removed from office by impeachment. Since Agnew claimed to be in the same situation as the president, we found it necessary in our brief to address that issue as well. In these matters little is certain, but I still think I was correct in contending, as solicitor general, that an incumbent president, alone among government officials, is immune from criminal liability. This subject is hotly controverted and has become so confused that it is worth rehearsing the arguments that lead to that conclusion.

It is true that the constitutional text provides no express immunity for the president and, by contrast, does explicitly shield members of Congress from arrest during their attendance at their respective houses and in going to and from those sessions. If text were all, that contrast would conclude the matter against the president. But text is not all. The Constitution has always been interpreted in light of its history, its structure and the requirements of constitutional functions.

Executive privilege
The clearest example of this is what has, somewhat misleadingly, been called "executive privilege." The constitutional text nowhere gives the president the right to withhold from litigants or Congress documents or the testimony of his aides concerning executive branch deliberations. Yet the courts have routinely recognized that privilege. The president must have the confidentiality necessary to the efficient performance of his duties. When the subpoena of Nixon's papers and audiotapes was upheld by a unanimous Supreme Court, Chief

Justice Warren Burger's opinion claimed the "authority to interpret claims with respect to powers alleged to derive from enumerated powers." Thus, the claim of an absolute privilege was said to be valid to "protect military, diplomatic, or sensitive national security secrets"—immunities important to the president's duties but nowhere mentioned in the Constitution. Even a generalized interest in confidentiality was recognized: "Nowhere in the Constitution [is] there any explicit reference to a privilege of confidentiality, yet to the extent this interest relates to the effective discharge of a President's powers, it is constitutionally based."

What sort of secrets might a president want to keep?

Nixon's claim, being based only on a generalized interest in confidentiality, was overcome by the need of the courts and parties in a criminal case for relevant evidence. Even then, however, the trial court was instructed to examine documents in private and to excise all statements that did not meet the test of admissibility and relevance.

Nor is the president's privilege unique. Legislative bodies and courts also demand and receive confidentiality for materials necessary to their functioning. That is why "executive privilege" would more accurately be called "governmental privilege." Yet these vast areas of confidentiality, necessary to the effective workings of government, escape mention in the text of the Constitution.

Is the president too powerful?

The debates in the Constitutional Convention, moreover, strongly suggest an understanding that the president, as chief executive, would not be subject to the ordinary criminal process. For example, Gouverneur Morris observed that the Supreme Court would "try the President after the trial of impeachment."

U.S. diarist and politician Gouverneur Morris (1752–1816) was one of the Framers of the Constitution.

The practical reason for this conclusion is that the president, who is responsible as no other single officer is for the affairs of the United States, should not be taken from duties that only he can perform unless and until the House and the Senate decide that he should be shorn of those duties. The scope of the power lodged in the president is unique. He is given the entire "executive power," including the powers of the commander in chief of the armed forces, the power to enforce the laws, the power to command the executive departments, the power to grant reprieves and pardons, and the powers shared with the Senate to make treaties and to appoint federal judges and other civil officers.

Bork argues that the president's role makes this a unique case.

Modern recognition of the uniqueness of the presidency in comparison with all other offices is found in the 25th

President Bill Clinton and First Lady Hillary Clinton during a fund-raising event for her New York Senate run in 2000.

Amendment, ratified in 1967, which provides for the replacement of the president during a period of temporary disability. The Constitution makes no provision, because none is needed, for a replacement during the temporary disability of a judge, a legislator, a vice president or any other subordinate executive branch officer.

Is impeachment the only solution?

I grant that the matter is not entirely free from doubt. Few important constitutional issues are. But the weight of constitutional argument is heavily on the side of the conclusion that a president may not be indicted until his term has ended or he has been removed from office by resignation or for conviction on impeachment. This president, it appears, will never resign; to wait for the end of his term would be to ratify his behavior. That leaves only impeachment. Indictment, if there is to be any, must await the outcome in the Senate.

Look at Kenneth Starr's report and President Clinton's rebuttals on www.all-links.com/icreport

One might easily wish it were otherwise. But that would contravene both the Constitution and sound policy. It is frequently said that constitutional conclusions accord with one's own predilections. You have, however, just read a contrary example.

Summary

The question of whether the Constitution allows an incumbent president to be criminally indicted is difficult to answer with certainty. Robert Bork concedes, for example, "the matter is not entirely free from doubt." These articles lay out alternative answers. Gary McDowell rests his argument in favor of the indictability of a sitting president on a strict interpretation of the Constitution. Since the Constitution does not expressly grant presidential immunity from criminal indictment, he concludes that the criminal indictment of a sitting president is permissible. The Framers would otherwise have made a point of stating otherwise. In sharp contrast to McDowell, Bork interprets the Constitution broadly to conclude that the president should not be subject to the ordinary criminal process. "The scope of the power lodged in the president is unique," Bork argues. Indeed, the president is, as Bork puts it, "responsible as no other single officer is for the affairs of the United States." As a consequence, it is hardly reasonable to subject the president to ordinary criminal prosecution. Bork therefore concludes that the president "should not be taken from duties that only he can perform unless and until the House and the Senate decide that he should be shorn of those duties."

FURTHER INFORMATION

Books:

Berger, Raoul, *Impeachment: The Constitutional Problems*. Cambridge, MA: Harvard University Press, 1973.

Kurland, Philip B., *Watergate and the Constitution*. Chicago: University of Chicago Press, 1978.

Westin, Alan, and Leon Friedman (editors), *United States vs. Nixon: The President before the Supreme Court*. New York: Chelsea House Publishers, 1974.

Article:

Greenhouse, Linda, "Can the President Be Prosecuted? No One Knows for Sure." *The New York Times*, July 28, 1998.

Useful websites:

www.americanpresidents.org
Gives key information on U.S. presidents.

www.cnn.com/SPECIALS/2001/Clinton
CNN special feature on Bill Clinton.

www.memory.loc.gov/ammen/pihtml/ppihome.html
"I do solemnly swear," American Memory, Library of Congress site. Features presidential inaugural speeches.

www.whitehouse.gov
White House official site. Features biography, speeches, links for all U.S. presidents.

The following debates in the Pro/Con series may also be of interest:

In this volume:

Topic 9 Is the president too powerful?

The Watergate Affair, pages 172–173.
The Case of President Clinton, pages 200–201.

SHOULD A SITTING PRESIDENT BE CRIMINALLY INDICTED?

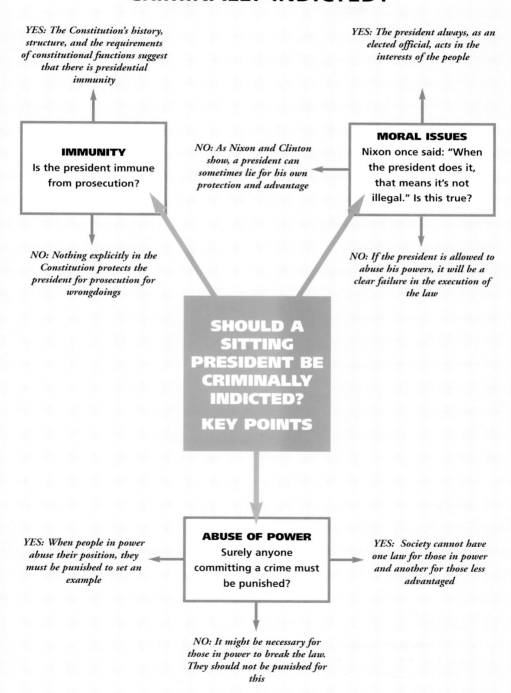

YES: The Constitution's history, structure, and the requirements of constitutional functions suggest that there is presidential immunity

YES: The president always, as an elected official, acts in the interests of the people

IMMUNITY
Is the president immune from prosecution?

NO: As Nixon and Clinton show, a president can sometimes lie for his own protection and advantage

MORAL ISSUES
Nixon once said: "When the president does it, that means it's not illegal." Is this true?

NO: Nothing explicitly in the Constitution protects the president for prosecution for wrongdoings

NO: If the president is allowed to abuse his powers, it will be a clear failure in the execution of the law

SHOULD A SITTING PRESIDENT BE CRIMINALLY INDICTED?

KEY POINTS

YES: When people in power abuse their position, they must be punished to set an example

ABUSE OF POWER
Surely anyone committing a crime must be punished?

YES: Society cannot have one law for those in power and another for those less advantaged

NO: It might be necessary for those in power to break the law. They should not be punished for this

GLOSSARY

absolutism a system of government based on a ruler who is responsible to no one, and so has unrestricted power.

ballot initiative a political proposition that originates with individuals or organizations that can have the proposition considered by voters either at local or state elections.

Bill of Rights the first 10 amendments to the U.S. Constitution. They were adopted as a single unit in 1791 to guarantee individual rights and limitations on state and federal government.

bureaucracy a form of government characterized by administrators and carefully defined hierarchies of officials.

capitalism an economic system in which private individuals and firms control the production and distribution of goods and services and make profits in return for the investment of capital, or money.

citizenship legal membership in a nation. Citizenship in the U.S. confers certain rights and privileges, but also certain duties.

communism a political doctrine based on the writings of Karl Marx (1818–1883) that aims to create a classless society through the violent overthrow of capitalism and the establishment of rule by the working class. *See also* socialism.

Congress the legislative branch of the U.S. government, composed of the Senate and the House of Representatives. *See also* House of Representatives, Senate.

conservative a word used to describe an instinct to support rather than change existing laws, institutions, and social structures.

constitution a written codification of the basic principles and laws under which a government operates. *See also* Founders.

corruption a decline in moral principles, especially in politicians, which leads to abusing power, lying, or taking bribes.

democracy a system of government based on the rule of the majority of the population. Citizens elect representatives to represent their wishes in government.

Democratic Party one of the two major parties in the United States. Historically the party has represented organized labor, minorities, and progressive reformers. The origins of the party date from 1792.

direct rule a system of government based on the direct expression of the people's will by such mechanisms as plebiscites and referenda.

electoral college the group of people who elect the president and vice president of the U.S. after a presidential election. Each state's representatives on the electoral college usually vote for the candidate who wins their state. Sometimes, as in 2000, the electoral college elects a president who did not win the popular vote.

election a way of choosing candidates for political office by voting for one of a number of choices.

federalism a system of government in which power is divided between a central authority and regional bodies, as in the relationship between the federal government in the U.S. and the states.

founders the men who signed the Declaration of Independence and drafted the Constitution, thus founding the United States. *See also* constitution.

great society a term used by President Lyndon B. Johnson to describe the goal of his social legislation after 1964.

House of Representatives the lower house of Congress, which tends to concentrate on local issues. There are 435 Representatives, allocated according to the population of the states, elected every two years. *See also* Congress, Senate.

impeachment the formal charging of a government official, including the president, with a crime or misdemeanor and his or her removal from office.

liberalism a political philosophy that values individual and economic equality and freedom.

meritocracy a system that is based on rewarding individuals of great talent and ability.

New Deal the domestic program of President Franklin D. Roosevelt between 1933 and 1939. It intended to bring economic relief and reforms in industry, agriculture, finance, labor, and housing, thus increasing federal government's activities.

president the head of state. The American president is also head of the government and commander-in-chief of the nation's armed forces.

primary system an electoral system in which party members vote to select their party's candidates for a final general election.

Reaganomics an economic approach followed by the administration of Ronald Reagan in the 1980s that emphasized private ownership, reduced government intervention in economic affairs, and tax breaks for the rich, whose benefits would "trickle down" to all Americans.

representative government a system in which voters elect representatives to carry on government on their behalf.

Republican Party one of the two major parties in the United States. Also known as the Grand Old Party. Traditionally the party stands for limited government and low taxes. The earliest meetings of those who can be identified as Republicans were held in 1853 and 1854.

Senate the upper house of the U.S. Congress, which tends to concentrate on national issues. The Senate comprises 100 senators, two from each state, elected for six-year terms. See also Congress, House of Representatives.

separation of powers the division of the United States government into three branches—the legislative (Congress and state legislatures), executive (the president, cabinet, federal departments, and state governors), and judicial (the Supreme Court and the system of courts and judges)—each of which balances the power of the others.

socialism a political doctrine that aims to create a classless society by removing businesses and commercial activity from private ownership and placing it in the hands of the state or various associations of workers. See also communism.

states' rights rights protected by the Tenth Amendment for U.S. states to pass and enforce certain of their own laws and to have their own political policies, regardless of federal attitudes.

suffragists a group of women who campaigned for women's right to vote in the early 20th century.

taxation the method by which federal, state, or local government collects money from individuals and businesses to fund the costs of government.

two-party system a system of democratic government dominated by two political parties, usually representing leftist and rightist views respectively, who may alternate power over time. The United States is largely a two-party system, despite the appearance of some popular third parties during electoral campaigns.

Universal Declaration of Human Rights a codification of basic human rights and freedoms drafted by an international committee after World War II and adopted by the United Nations in 1948.

Watergate the name given to a political scandal between 1972 and 1975, when Richard Nixon's Republican Party was found to have criminally interfered with the workings of the Democratic Party. The Watergate Hotel in Washington, D.C., was the scene of the first detected break-in by Republican sympathizers.

Acknowledgments

Topic 1 Is Direct Rule by the People Better than Representative Democracy?
Yes: From "On Deputies or Representatives" in *Rousseau's Political Writings: A Norton Critical Edition,* edited by Alan Ritter and Julia Conaway Bondanella, translated by Julia Conaway Bondanella. Copyright © 1988 by W. W. Norton & Company, Inc. Used by permission.
No: From "Of the Republican Government and the Laws in Relation to Democracy" in *The Spirit of the Laws,* Vol. 1, Book II, Chapter 2 by Baron de Montesquieu, translated by Thomas Nugent. Reproduced from the public domain edition published by G. Bell & Sons (London), 1914.

Topic 2 Are All Human Beings Created Equal?
Yes: From "Is Equality Possible?" in *Arguing for Equality* by John Baker. Copyright © 1987 by Verso, London, England. Used by permission.
No: From "The Vital Lie" and "Nature and Nurture" in *In Defense of Elitism* by William A. Henry III. Copyright © 1994 by William A. Henry III. Used by permission of Doubleday, a division of Random House, Inc., New York.

Topic 3 Are Democracy and Capitalism at Odds with Each Other?
Yes: From "Capitalism or Democracy?" by Robert Lekachman in *How Capitalistic is the Constitution?*, edited by Robert A. Goldwin and William A. Schambra, 1982. Reprinted by permission of The American Enterprise Institute for Public Policy Research, Washington, D.C.
No: From "The Relation between Economic Freedom and Political Freedom" in *Capitalism and Freedom* by Milton Friedman. Copyright © 1982 by The University of Chicago Press, Chicago, Illinois. Used by permission.

Topic 4 Is the United States Truly Democratic?
No: From "On Removing Certain Impediments to Democracy in the United States" by Robert A. Dahl in *The Moral Foundations of the American Republic*, 3rd edition, edited by Robert Horowitz. Copyright © 1986 by the University Press of Virginia, Charlottesville, VA. Reprinted with permission.
Yes: From "In Defense of Republican Constitutionalism: A Reply to Dahl" by James W. Ceaser in *The Moral Foundations of the American Republic*, 3rd edition, edited by Robert Horowitz. Copyright © 1986 by the University Press of Virginia, Charlottesville, VA. Reprinted with permission.

Topic 5 Is the Federal Bureaucracy Too Big?
Yes: From "America by the Throat" in *America by the Throat: The Stranglehold of Federal Bureaucracy* by George Roche, 1983. Copyright © 1983 by Devin-Adair Publishers, Old Greenwich, CT . Used by permission. All rights reserved.
No: From "Stop Bashing the Bureaucracy" by Dean Yarwood in *Public Administration Review*, Nov./Dec. 1996, Vol. 56, No. 6, pages 611–613. Copyright © 1996 by the American Society for Public Administration, Washington, D.C. Used by permission.

Topic 6 Should More Power Be Given to State Governments?
Yes: From "Madison and Modern Federalism" by Jean Yarbrough, in *How Federal is the Constitution?*, edited by Robert A. Goldwin and William A. Schambra,1987. Reprinted by permission of The American Enterprise Institute for Public Policy Research, Washington, D.C.
No: From "The Idea of the Nation" by Samuel H. Beer, in *How Federal is the Constitution?*, edited by Robert A. Goldwin and William A. Schambra, 1987. Reprinted by permission of The American Enterprise Institute for Public Policy Research, Washington, D.C.

Topic 7 Does the Two-Party System Adequately Represent the People?
Yes: From "In Defense of the American Party System" by Edward C. Banfield in *Political Parties in the Eighties*, edited by Robert A. Goldwin, 1980. Reprinted by permission of The American Enterprise Institute for Public Policy Research, Washington D.C.
No: From *The Politics of American Discontent: How a New Party Can Make Democracy Work Again* by Gordon S. Black. Copyright © 1994 by John Wiley & Sons, Inc., New York. Us ed by permission.

Topic 8 Does the Separation of Powers Produce Ineffective Government?
Yes: From "To Form a Government" by Lloyd Cutler in *Separation of Powers—Does It Still Work?*, edited by Robert Goldwin and Art Kaufman. Copyright © 1980 by *Foreign Affairs*, Fall 1980. Used by permission.
No: From "In Defense of Separation of Powers" by James W. Ceaser in *Separation of Powers—Does It Still Work?*, edited by Robert Goldwin and Art Kaufman, 1986. Reprinted by permission of The American Enterprise Institute for Public Policy Research, Washington, D.C.

Topic 9 Is the President Too Powerful?
Yes: From "The Runaway Presidency" by Arthur M. Schlesinger, Jr., in *The Atlantic Monthly*, November 1973, Vol. 232, No. 5, pages 43–55. Copyright © 1973 by Arthur M. Schlesinger, Jr. Used by permission.
No: From "Talking about the President: The Legacy of Watergate" by Suzanne Garment in *The Fettered Presidency: Legal Constraints on the Executive Branch*, edited by L. Gordon Crovitz and Jeremy A. Rabkin, 1989. Reprinted by permission of The American Enterprise Institute for Public Policy Research, Washington, D.C.

Topic 10 Should People Be Able to Legislate Directly through Ballot Initiatives?

Acknowledgments

Yes: From *Strong Democracy: Participatory Politics for a New Age* by Benjamin R. Barber. Copyright © 1984 by The Regents of the University of California. Used by permission of the University of California Press, Berkeley and Los Angeles, CA.
No: From *Democracy Derailed: Initiative Campaigns and the Power of Money* by David S. Broder. Copyright © 2000 by Harcourt, Inc., Orlando, FL. Used by permission.

Topic 11 Can the Wealthy Buy Their Way into Political Office?
Yes: From "Democracy and Dollars" in *Political Money* by David W. Adamany. Copyright © 1975 by The Century Foundation, Inc., New York. Reprinted by permission.
No: From "Does Money Win Elections?" in *The Costs of Democracy* by Alexander Heard. Copyright © 1960 by the University of North Carolina Press, renewed 1988 by Alexander Heard. Used by permission.

Topic 12 Does the Primary System Produce the Best President?
Yes: From "In Defense of the Presidential Nominating Process" by Robert E. DiClerico in *Choosing Our Choices: Debating the Presidential Nominating Process*, edited by Robert E. DiClerico and James W. Davis. Copyright © 2000 by Rowman and Littlefield Publishers, Inc., Lanham, MD. Used by permission.
No: From "Party 'Reform' in Retrospect" by Edward C. Banfield in *Political Parties in the Eighties*, American Enterprise Institute and Kenyon College, Gambier, OH, 1980. Reprinted by permission of The American Enterprise Institute for Public Policy Research, Washington, D.C.

Topic 13 Should the Electoral College Be Abolished?
Yes: From "The Electoral College and Direct Election of the President and Vice President" by Senator Birch Bayh in the U.S. Senate Committee of the Judiciary, 95th Congress, 1st session, January 27, published by the U.S. Government Printing Office, Washington, D.C., 1977.

No: From "The Electoral College and Direct Election of the President and Vice President" by Herbert J. Storing in the U.S. Senate Committee of the Judiciary, July 22, published by the U.S. Government Printing Office, Washington, D.C., 1977. Both articles courtesy of U.S. Government Printing Office.

Topic 14 Should Moral Principle Matter in Politics?
No: From *The Prince* by Niccolò Machiavelli, translated by Harvey C. Mansfield. Copyright © 1984 by the University of Chicago Press, Chicago, IL. Used by permission.
Yes: From "Competent or Ethical?" in *Honest Government: An Ethics Guide for Public Service* by W. J. Michael Cody and Richardson R. Lynn. Copyright © 1992 by W. J. Michael Cody and Richardson R. Lynn. Reproduced with permission of Greenwood Publishing Group, Inc., Westport, CT.

Topic 15 Should the President Be Able to Keep Secrets?
Yes: From "Arguments in Favor of Executive Privilege" in *Executive Privilege: The Dilemmas of Secrecy and Democratic Accountability* by Mark J. Rozell. Copyright © 1994 by The Century Foundation, New York. Used by permission.
No: From *Executive Privilege: A Constitutional Myth* by Raoul Berger. Copyright © 1974 by the President and Fellows of Harvard College. Used by permission of Harvard University Press, Cambridge, MA.

Topic 16 Can a Sitting President Be Criminally Indicted?
Yes: From "Yes, You Can Indict the President" by Gary L. McDowell, *The Wall Street Journal*, March 9, 1998. Reprinted from *The Wall Street Journal*, copyright © 1998 by Dow Jones & Company, Inc. All rights reserved. Used by permission.
No: From "Indict Clinton? How I Wish It Were Possible" by Robert H. Bork, *The Wall Street Journal*, March 18, 1998. Reprinted from *The Wall Street Journal*, copyright © 1998 by Dow Jones & Company, Inc. All rights reserved. Used by permission.

Brown Partworks Limited has made every effort to contact and acknowledge the creators and copyright holders of all extracts reproduced in this volume. We apologize for any omissions. Any person who wishes to be credited in further volumes should contact Brown Partworks Limited in writing: Brown Partworks Limited, 8 Chapel Place, Rivington Street, London EC2A 3DQ, U.K.

Picture credits

Cover: Brown Partworks Ltd.; **Corbis:** Bettman Archive 78, 128, 172 m/r. 180; Zen Icknow 6–7. 156 Richard T. Nowitz 58; Roger Ressmeyer 43; **Hulton Archive:** 14, 18: Archive Photos 94; Central Press 66; Keystone 70, 115, 200/01; Observer 172 m/l, Topical Press Agency 31; **PA Photos:** European Press Agency 210

217

SET INDEX

Page numbers in **bold** refer to volume numbers; those in *italics* refer to picture captions.